658.47
A79 5P

P9-EEM-213

# Fighting Corruption in East Asia: Solutions from the Private Sector

*Jean-François Arvis, Ronald E. Berenbeim*

**THE WORLD BANK**
Washington, D.C.

POINT LOMA NAZARENE UNIVERSITY
RYAN LIBRARY
3900 LOMALAND DRIVE
SAN DIEGO, CALIFORNIA 92106-2899

© 2003 The International Bank for Reconstruction and Development/The World Bank
1818 H Street, N.W.
Washington, D.C. 20433
Telephone: 202-473-1000
Internet: www.worldbank.org
E-mail: feedback@worldbank.org

All rights reserved.

1 2 3 4 05 04 03

The findings, interpretations, and conclusions expressed herein are those of the author(s) and do not necessarily reflect the views of the Board of Executive Directors of the World Bank or the governments they represent.

The World Bank does not guarantee the accuracy of the data included in this work. The boundaries, colors, denominations, and other information shown on any map in this work do not imply any judgment on the part of the World Bank concerning the legal status of any territory or the endorsement or acceptance of such boundaries.

**Rights and Permissions**

The material in this work is copyrighted. Copying and/or transmitting portions or all of this work without permission may be a violation of applicable law. The World Bank encourages dissemination of its work and will normally grant permission promptly.

For permission to photocopy or reprint any part of this work, please send a request with complete information to the Copyright Clearance Center, Inc., 222 Rosewood Drive, Danvers, MA 01923, USA, telephone 978-750-8400, fax 978-750-4470, www.copyright.com.

All other queries on rights and licenses, including subsidiary rights, should be addressed to the Office of the Publisher, World Bank, 1818 H Street NW, Washington, DC 20433, USA, fax 202-522-2422, e-mail pubrights@worldbank.org.

Cover photograph: courtesy of the Independent Commission Against Corruption (ICAC) of Hong Kong, China; copyright ICAC.

ISBN 0-8213-5535-X

**Library of Congress cataloging-in-publication data has been applied for.**

# Contents

**Figures**

# Acknowledgments

This research has been supported by grants from the government of Denmark, the government of France, the government of Japan, and the government of Singapore.

Our gratitude goes first to the companies that agreed to be interviewed.

Major contributions to the case studies were made by Mr. Jacques Carbou, Ms. Kris Day, Mr. Takaji Hishiyama, Professor Iwao Taka, Dr. Eric Teo, Professor Toru Umeda, and the International Business Ethics Institute.

We are also especially grateful to many colleagues from the World Bank Group, including Loup Brefort, Jamil Kassum, Homi Kharas, Olivier Fremond, Cheryl Gray, Joel Hellman, Mike Lubrano, Behdad Nowroozi, Djordjija Petkoski, Jean-Jacques Raoul, Andrew Stone, Anne Simpson, Stoyan Tenev, and Nigel Twose; we also thank Vinay Bhargava, Gary Fine, Arvind Gupta, Cally Jordan, Christian Kammer, Michael Kramer, Sawar Lateef, Maiko Miyake, Guy Pfeffermann, William Rex, Stefanie Teggerman, and Chunlin Zhang.

Major help was extended by a number of organizations, such as the anti-corruption division in the OECD, Transparency International, the Independent Commission against Corruption (Hong Kong), the Federation of Korean Industry, the Asian Institute of Management, the FIDIC, the Institute for Policy Studies (Singapore) and Reitaku University (Japan).

Many individuals provided encouragement and valuable insights. They include Roderick Hills, Stanley Sporkin, Irène Hors, Kathryn Gordon, Jane Hansel, Jean-Pierre Méan, Michel Béguery, Philippe d'Iribarne, Professor Stephen Cheung, Professor Shang Jin Wei, Emil Balaigonta, Jean-Michel Severino, and Alexandra Wrage.

Thanks also to Doris Chung and Katie Shaw for their patient assistance in the research and Rachel Weaving for her editorial contributions to the manuscript.

Book design, editing, production, and dissemination were coordinated by the World Bank's Office of the Publisher.

# Foreword

The critical need for private sector involvement in the fight against corruption is now an accepted fact, particularly in East Asia, where there is a buoyant private sector and where corruption has often been equated with cronyism. Cutting off corruption's supply side is a vital step in limiting the economic damage inflicted by corrupt practices. Despite the importance of private sector efforts in this regard, little attention has been paid to company anticorruption programs and to trying to learn from company experience.

This book, which is based on research cosponsored by the World Bank and the Conference Board, provides detailed documentation of the efforts of Western and Asian companies to develop good standards of business conduct in their East Asian operations. It provides evidence that a common set of principles for resisting corruption can be established notwithstanding the rich cultural diversity and ownership structure of firms based in that region.

This research brings a number of important results and messages:

Recent corporate scandals in the United States and elsewhere serve as a reminder that fraudulent behavior cannot be tamed solely with new laws, new regulations or reliance on market pressures. There is no substitute for ethical commitment to certain standards of business conduct and their instrumentalization into the type of compliance systems investigated here.

The complexity of global business practices in this increasingly globalized world cannot, realistically, be monitored or controlled by law enforcement agencies alone. Determined prosecution has and will detect and punish some offenders but a satisfactory global economic environment will not exist unless we are able to establish and implement commonly accepted standards of business conduct.

In significant part the efforts of these companies were stimulated by U.S. companies that have, over the past 25 years, developed procedures to deal with the U.S. Foreign Corrupt Practices Act [1977] and the U.S. Organizational Sentencing Guidelines [1991]. The book provides convincing evidence that Asian and European companies have moved recently in much the same way as their U.S. counterparts did more than a decade ago, partly in response to the adoption of the 1997 OECD convention against bribery. They have formulated and developed their own compliance systems—ones that take into account the distinctive requirements of their own national and business cultures.

Nevertheless, the book is not promoting specific guidelines or a "one size fits all" solution. The authors have paid particular attention to dissemination mechanisms and initiative, especially when it comes to helping suppliers and smaller local firms to develop their own response to corrupt practices. This may involve various forms of partnerships that include business groups, academic organizations, nongovernmental organizations and also government agencies or international organizations. Many examples are provided here; these not only add to the credibility of the private sector response to corruption in East Asia, but also show that there is potential for major developments in the near future.

The authors have created an invaluable document. It should be the guidebook to companies, policymakers, academics and nongovernmental organizations that seek a more ethical governance system for the developing world.

*Roderick Hills*
*Partner, Hills & Stern*
*Former Chairman of the Securities*
  *and Exchange Commission*
*Founding member and Former Chairman*
  *of the US-ASEAN Business Council*

*Jemal-U-Din Kassum*
*Vice President*
*East Asia and Pacific Region*
*The World Bank*

# Abbreviations

| | |
|---|---|
| ADB | Asian Development Bank |
| APEC | Asia-Pacific Economic Cooperation |
| BERC | Business Ethics Research Center (Japan) |
| BPI | Bribe Payers Index (Transparency International) |
| CEO | chief executive officer |
| CFO | chief financial officer |
| CPI | Corruption Perceptions Index (Transparency International) |
| CPIB | Corrupt Practices Investigation Bureau (Singapore) |
| EAP | East Asia and Pacific region |
| EOA | Ethics Officer Association |
| FCPA | Foreign Corrupt Practices Act (United States) |
| FDI | foreign direct investment |
| FIDIC | International Federation of Consulting Engineers (Fédération Internationale des Ingénieurs Conseils) |
| FKI | Federation of Korean Industries |
| GCGF | Global Corporate Governance Forum |
| HKEDC | Hong Kong Ethics Development Centre |
| ICAC | Independent Commission Against Corruption (Hong Kong, China) |
| ICC | International Chamber of Commerce |
| IFC | International Finance Corporation |
| IMF | International Monetary Fund |
| IPS | Institute for Policy Studies (Singapore) |
| ISO | International Organization for Standardization |
| JFTC | Fair Trade Commission of Japan |
| NGO | nongovernmental organization |
| OECD | Organisation for Economic Co-operation and Development |
| OECD Anti-Bribery Convention | OECD Convention on Combating Bribery of Foreign Public Officials in International Business Transactions |

| PECC | Pacific Economic Cooperation Council |
|------|--------------------------------------|
| PERC | Political and Economic Risk Consulting |
| R-BEC | Business Ethics and Compliance Research Center, Reitaku University (Japan) |
| ROSC | Reports on the Observance of Standards and Codes |
| SEC | Securities and Exchange Commission (United States) |
| SME | small and medium-size enterprise |
| SOE | state-owned enterprise |
| SRI | socially responsible investing |
| TRACE | Transparent Agents and Contracting Entities |
| UCPL | Unfair Competition Prevention Law (Japan) |
| WBES | World Business Environment Survey |
| WBI | World Bank Institute |
| WTO | World Trade Organization |

# Executive Summary

Initiatives by the public sector to fight corruption on the "demand side" have generally drawn more attention than "supply-side" efforts by private companies. Yet policymakers, international organizations, and advocacy groups such as Transparency International regard such preventive efforts, now under way in all regions, as a critical component of the anticorruption toolkit.

All types of firms—large and small, multinational and local—recognize that corruption raises the cost of doing business. Recent studies such as the World Business Environment Survey provide a wealth of evidence on firm perceptions and behaviors regarding corruption. Managers of medium-size firms perceive the intensity of the problem in much the same way as do representatives of international companies in the same country. Not surprisingly, smaller firms tend to be more vulnerable to corrupt practices.

Most company-based programs for fighting fraud and corruption rely on ethics and the implementation of compliance systems. These systems typically consist of statements of values, company codes of conduct, training programs, and decisionmaking and reporting mechanisms. This approach was pioneered in the 1970s by U.S. multinational corporations after revelations of unethical practices and in response to the 1977 U.S. Foreign Corrupt Practices Act. Until recently, the compliance approach was greeted with skepticism outside the United States. Critics argued that efforts to implement those techniques would fail in other business cultures. Skeptics also questioned the effectiveness of company anticorruption programs—a view reflected in the poor ratings of U.S. exporters in the Bribe Payers Index, prepared by Transparency International.

But such views have changed considerably since the late 1990s. Compliance systems are now being implemented, with various degrees of sophistication, by companies in high-income countries in Europe and Asia, and in emerging markets. Meanwhile, many existing programs in North America have been redesigned. Recently, the importance of internal mechanisms has received worldwide attention in the wake of major corporate governance scandals in which poor ethics and compliance played no small part.

In 2000 the Conference Board, an independent global business membership organization, asked major companies worldwide for information on their anticorruption programs. The survey found compliance-style anticorruption programs in 42 countries. Of the respondents, 40 percent were based outside North America and Western Europe—a sharp difference from earlier surveys, which found that the approach had not spread beyond North America and the United Kingdom.

To better understand how compliance programs work, the Conference Board and the World Bank's East Asia and Pacific Region investigated the programs of East Asian companies, as well as subsidiaries of North American and European firms operating in East Asia. The research focused on:

- Identifying the state of the art in corporate compliance programs
- Understanding mechanisms and incentives driving program implementation
- Identifying the existing vehicles for knowledge building and dissemination of good practices
- Creating case studies of companies as a knowledge base of best practices.

East Asia proved a unique area on which to focus. The diversity of origin of private sector operators makes it a melting pot of business cultures. In the Chinese world, the traditional network-based business practice of *guanxi* has often been considered an obstacle to the adoption of rule-based systems. Yet at the same time, the emergence of large East Asian corporations engaged in regional and global activities is providing an impetus toward the adoption of global standards in management.

## External and Internal Incentives

Prohibition of bribery is universal, but the most far-reaching measures are those that address firm behavior outside the home country. Under the U.S. Foreign Corrupt Practices Act (FCPA), U.S. companies can be prosecuted for engaging in corrupt practices outside the United States. The Convention on Combating Bribery of Foreign Public Officials in International Business Transactions, adopted in 1997 by the Organisation for Economic Co-operation and Development (OECD), has so far been ratified by 35 countries, including five non-OECD members in emerging economies (but none in Asia). The Anti-Bribery Convention embraces and codifies the FCPA's extraterritoriality principle, essentially putting transnational and national bribery on the same footing. The convention also contains provisions that will ultimately drive a convergence of national anticorruption regimes worldwide.

The OECD Convention targets not only direct payments but also third-party payments—a main channel of corruption. Because the convention makes companies liable for the behavior of their branches and affiliates and, to a significant degree, for the conduct of their business partners, it encourages companies to put in place thorough and global compliance mechanisms and to implement local ethics programs that include intermediaries and suppliers. Another important feature of the convention that is reflected in corporate codes is a focus on grand corruption. Taking a pragmatic approach, the FCPA and the OECD Convention tolerate petty corruption such as facilitation payments (small amounts paid to "get things done").

Although a legal instrument such as the FCPA prohibits certain conduct, at home or abroad, it does not offer companies incentives for developing compliance systems, and the probability of getting caught is rather low. In 1991 the U.S. government issued Organizational Sentencing Guidelines, thus giving companies the carrot needed to encourage development of sophisticated compliance systems. The guidelines allow for much lower fines and penalties if it can be established that a company had an effective compliance system and that any unlawful activity was the work of a rogue employee rather than an established company practice. This approach resulted in a fruitful dialogue between enforcement agencies such as the Securities and Exchange Commission (SEC) and private firms. In recent years such a partnership approach to enforcement, extending help and incentives to firms, has gained wide acceptance. Among the good examples to be found in East Asia is Hong Kong's Independent Commission Against Corruption.

Increasing legal pressure does not fully account for companies' motivation to establish anticorruption programs. Anticorruption programs are also driven by forces within firms. A growing number of companies do business in complex political and cultural environments, subjecting them to greater scrutiny from civil society and nongovernmental organizations (NGOs). Indeed, ethics is a core component of the broader agenda of corporate social responsibility that is gaining wide support at the global level from large multinational corporations, NGOs, and international organizations such as the OECD and the United Nations.

In addition, companies now realize that turning a blind eye to corruption outside the company breeds poor ethics within the company and increases the risk of internal fraud. Thus, a compliance system is often part of comprehensive risk management efforts that encompass internal and external corruption. Companies in emerging markets that desire a global reach are beginning to adopt a similar approach. (There is quantitative evidence that more transparent companies have better access to capital markets.) For smaller firms and intermediaries, awareness of business ethics and minimum standards of compliance will prove a condition for engaging in business with larger corporations.

## Components of an Effective Program

Basic compliance systems often require significant adaptation, but they are much the same in companies around the world. Anticorruption programs in companies from all sectors and regions share three components: a clear statement of values strongly supported by top management; training and dissemination grounded in the experience of company staff; and effective information and support systems.

Although research does not support claims that compliance systems encounter serious cultural resistance, culture does raise a major implementation issue. The challenge for companies is to formulate core principles and implement credible procedures adapted to local business cultures. In particular, for companies operating in industries with substantial local ownership (as is common in China), the need to adapt training, dissemination, and information processes to local customs is more than an intellectual exercise.

### Values

Ethics programs that respond to risk management needs are part of an inclusive process that draws on a company's collective intelligence and experience. Employees from all regions, businesses, and job categories participate in surveys, discussions, and focus groups to formulate values statements and warning systems. For example, in carrying out its most recent code-drafting process, Merck surveyed 22 percent of its workforce. As part of this dynamic process, each component is periodically reviewed for relevance and assessed for effectiveness. Societé Générale de Surveillance mobilized its workforce to develop a program and conducted training sessions in more than 20 languages.

Company leaders should be actively involved in values formulation. Board members and managers must participate visibly in code drafting and program design.

### Training and Dissemination

Consistent with the view that every employee's conduct exposes a company to risk, most compliance programs now require that all employees—not just managers—have some familiarity with company codes and practices and discuss their practical application. Senior executives and employees involved in critical functions such as sales or procurement typically receive more extensive training.

Case studies, often drawing on a company's experience, are invariably part of ethics program discussions. Not surprisingly, the most debated issue is the fine line between bribes and facilitation payments. Sometimes at a company's insistence, and increasingly at their own request, suppliers and joint-venture partners engage in these discussions. Companies strongly prefer to use their own senior executives as trainers. Where consultants are involved, it is often to train the trainers.

## Information and Support Systems

Of the three components of ethics systems, warning systems encounter the most cultural resistance. But research and company experience have found successful warning systems in most regions and industries, indicating that generalizations about the unwillingness of people in certain cultures to use these systems, for fear of being be seen as "informers," are vastly overstated. A country manager based in China confirmed this finding: "We have a reasonable utilization of whistle-blowing in China. The volume of complaints may not be as high as in the United States, but we do get them. And roughly 40 percent of the informants identify themselves." Resistance to whistle-blowing may be more rooted in the culture of the company than in that of the country in which the firm is doing business. Most warning-system hotlines evolve from an initial stage in which employees call in with every kind of complaint, to a phase in which legitimate irregularities are discovered, to a final stage in which callers seek advice and in obtaining it are counseled on how to avoid bad decisions.

## Are Ethics Programs Effective?

Company spokespeople say that their ethics programs work. They cite records of participation in training programs, as well as surveys confirming employee interest and involvement in these discussions. An even more important measure may be the use of hotlines. A large volume of relevant, serious complaints is a positive sign. But company spokespeople say that the ultimate indicator of success is heavy user reliance on the complaint process for advice rather than to report infractions requiring remedial action.

Whether these programs are successful or not, companies are under growing pressure to assume more responsibility for compliance. Using incentives to encourage self-monitoring is potentially more cost-effective and cost-efficient than sanctions-based public enforcement. Self-monitoring is especially useful in the many countries with limited resources for law enforcement.

More difficult to assess is the impact of self-monitoring on anticorruption policies in host countries. There is evidence of companies losing business as a result of a strict stand on corruption. But there are also cases in which adherence to principles delivers rewards: for example, a telecom company regained lost business when political upheaval in an East Asia country voided corrupt deals entered into by a previous administration.

## Internal Control and Governance

Practitioners recognize the link between good corporate governance and effective anticorruption programs. The East Asian financial crisis of 1997 showed that weak corporate governance could result in widespread, damaging corruption. The increase in anticorruption programs in the private sector coincides with the recent global focus on proper accounting and auditing practices and on corporate governance. Increasingly, corporate governance guidelines refer to compliance systems.

At the operational level, this link is straightforward. Because bribery is universally prohibited, it requires "creative" accounting and dissimulation that are incompatible with modern accounting and disclosure standards applicable to both listed and nonlisted corporations. The core principle of transparency is explicitly recognized in the OECD Anti-Bribery Convention.

Surveys conducted by the Conference Board since the mid-1980s have shown, in every region, steadily increasing involvement by boards of directors and audit committees in the formulation and delivery of ethics programs. For example, a 1987 survey found that 21 percent of company boards played a role in ethics programs; by 1999, the figure was 78 percent. Almost one-third of the companies responding to the most recent survey cited "heavy" board participation. Not surprisingly, case studies show that good corporate governance of affiliates is crucial for effective anticorruption programs in large corporations—particularly, those operating through joint ventures.

## Building and Disseminating Knowledge of Good Practices

Benchmarking and experience sharing are primary mechanisms for disseminating best practices. This kind of information sharing is also used to establish commitment among industries, countries, and regions. Associations of motivated executives with international exposure have been key factors in the recent proliferation of ethics programs in Japan through the

Business Ethics Research Center (BERC). Similarly, the Federation of Korean Industries designed its program model by benchmarking other experiences. The development of guidelines and standards, such as the Transparency International/Social Accountability International principles for countering bribery, might play a useful role in the future, as could the emerging commercial services that assess or score the transparency and compliance of corporations.

Large multinational and regional corporations also play a direct role. Jardine Matheson in Hong Kong (China) is imposing strict ethical requirements on its suppliers. Merck's Korean branch has been instrumental in promoting a code for that country's pharmaceutical industry. Transparent Agents and Contracting Entities (TRACE), a recently created network of large corporations that includes a huge Asian participation, targets intermediaries and suppliers to raise their awareness and help them develop appropriate procedures.

Anticorruption dissemination efforts can also build on existing networks, such as those of the institutes of corporate directors and institutes of accountants in many East Asian countries, that are dedicated to promoting good corporate governance in emerging markets. Capacity building is needed, through knowledge building at the local level (a function carried out in Japan by BERC) and at the global level by organizations such as the Conference Board, and by way of education of future leaders (through business schools).

Public policies increasingly catalyze best practices in the private sector. Regulators such as the U.S. Securities and Exchange Commission and the Independent Commission Against Corruption in Hong Kong already play this role. Combining legislation or regulations with incentives for internal systems is a pragmatic way of reducing the supply side of corruption by leveraging the public sector's often scarce enforcement resources.

# Part I

# Chapter 1
# Introduction

Worldwide, private firms—large and small, multinational and local—agree that corruption increases the cost of doing business. Analysis of corruption issues has typically focused on public sector initiatives to reduce corruption from the demand side.[1] At the same time, however, individual private companies in all regions have been developing their own responses in the form of internal anticorruption programs, and both policymakers and advocacy groups such as Transparency International have come to recognize these supply-side efforts as a critical component of the anticorruption toolkit. This book explores how firms in East Asia are fighting corruption by adopting business ethics codes and compliance systems.

The East Asian financial crisis of 1997 was a stark reminder that high levels of corruption, poor corporate governance, and dubious business practices can be a lethal combination, especially for the poor. The nexus between corrupt political leaders and unscrupulous conglomerates contributed to the collapse of financial markets that plunged millions into poverty. Given the destructive power of such links, anticorruption policy has as its core goal the establishment (or reestablishment) of transparency and the rule of law in both the public and private sectors.

Company compliance programs could seem a rather narrow focus, and indeed the subject is only one aspect of the relationship between the private sector and corruption. But its importance has been acknowledged by legislators who refer to company programs in anticorruption laws (notably, those addressing transnational prohibitions) and within the private sector itself. In 2000 a survey by the Conference Board—a global non-profit organization that, among other activities, studies business management issues—found compliance-style anticorruption programs in 42 countries. Forty percent of the respondents were headquartered outside North America and Western Europe. Company compliance programs are also attracting attention from groups and organizations in emerging economies, notably in East Asia—as witness the increased emphasis on the subject in conferences dealing with corruption and corporate governance.

Integrity in business matters has come to be seen by shareholders and the public as an essential component of corporate social responsibility, especially for multinational corporations operating in developing countries. It is recognized as such by the guidelines and standards recently issued by the United Nations, the Organisation for Economic Co-operation and Development (see OECD 2001), and other groups.

The large corporations in which compliance programs tend to be concentrated can play a key role in disseminating ethical business standards to other firms. These companies face issues of ethics and compliance not only within their own operations but also with their suppliers, local business partners, and intermediaries. They therefore have strong incentives for disseminating best practices, either directly or by supporting organizations that are dedicated to providing relevant resources to firms. Evidence suggests that these beneficial processes are becoming more common. Legal and regulatory measures can strengthen firms' incentives to promote ethical standards.

Internal controls and compliance are the nuts and bolts of good corporate governance; to use the familiar comparison between the corporate structure and a country's institutions, compliance is the firm-level equivalent of the legal framework. But for a firm as for a state, adherence to ethical values and compliance with the law rely heavily on the internal culture, which affects the attitudes of the people within the organization. Recent corporate scandals in the United States and other countries have highlighted the importance of developing a culture of compliance and of visibly maintaining strong ethical values and a strong ethical commitment at the managerial level, backed by good internal controls.

To gain a better understanding of how corporate compliance programs work in practice, the Conference Board and the East Asia and Pacific (EAP) Region of the World Bank investigated programs in East Asian companies, as well as in subsidiaries of North American and European firms in the region. The aims of the research were to:

- Identify the state of the art in corporate compliance programs
- Understand the mechanisms and incentives in use for implementing programs
- Undertake company-specific case studies with a view to developing a knowledge base of good practices for training and dissemination.

East Asia is a fertile area for this type of study. First, it is a region in which several different business cultures meet—among them, *guanxi* ("connections"), a tradition long followed by Chinese businesses worldwide; the Japanese and Korean models; and the Western-style approach to business ethics. Second, cross-cultural issues in business ethics are becoming increasingly salient in the region, even for local corporations, as firms expand across national boundaries and increase their involvement in regional and extraregional trade. And, third, according to expert opinions and surveys, East Asia offers a unique microcosm of diverse ethical practices within countries and very different country situations as regards corruption. For example, Singapore consistently tops global governance ratings, while neighboring Indonesia usually fares poorly in the same surveys.

In all, 22 firms were interviewed in depth for this study, often with the help of local experts, who played an important role in eliciting information in this sensitive area.[2] Companies with head offices outside East Asia and Pacific (in North America and Europe) were surveyed with an explicit focus on their operations in East Asia, and their local managers were interviewed whenever possible.

Part I of this book provides an analytical framework for understanding, planning, and evaluating company compliance programs. Chapter 2 looks at the characteristics, causes, and effects of corruption and discusses a number of issues in the political economy of the supply side of corruption. It also examines which types of firm are more vulnerable to corruption, drawing on evidence from a range of sources, including recent surveys carried out under World Bank supervision. Chapter 3 reviews the pressures and incentives that have led companies to adopt compliance programs. Chapter 4 describes the design of these programs, with preliminary comments on how they are working in practice, and outlines the elements that most companies consider essential to an effective program.

Both the design of programs and expectations for their success need to take account of the environment in which companies operate. Chapter 5 accordingly looks at prevailing standards of corporate governance and the link between norms and reforms in the public and private sectors. The chapter also explores the powerful tradition of guanxi in Chinese business communities and its interface with more recently introduced concepts of business ethics. Chapter 6 describes the resources and the actual initiatives, both private and public, that companies can draw on to formulate and implement corporate ethics programs. Chapter 7 summarizes the conclusions from the study.

The case studies in part II report on real experiences of countries and firms with compliance programs, making this report probably the first document of its kind. The appendixes discuss methodological issues and present a list of useful resources.

This book was written with, first of all, a corporate readership in mind. The analysis of the incentives that firms face and of the mechanisms available for disseminating techniques to combat corruption may also be of interest to business or advocacy groups working on ethics and corporate governance, to policymakers, and to academic researchers.

# Notes

1. A companion volume, edited by Vinay Bhargava and Emil Bolongaita, will describe public sector initiatives in East Asia.

2. The geographic distribution of the headquarters of the firms included in the survey is as follows: Japan, six firms; Hong Kong (China), three; the Republic of Korea, two; the Philippines, two; Singapore, two; Europe, four; and North America, three. This sample does not exhaust the list of firms with interesting experiences in implementing such programs. Firms were chosen purely for practical and opportunistic reasons—for example, because they had existing working relationships with the collaborators in this research.

# Chapter 2
# Corruption: The Firm's Perspective

The choice that corruption poses for the individual firm often parallels the famous prisoner's dilemma.[1] In a situation of competition in a corrupt environment, the firm will fear that if it does not pay bribes, it might lose business to competitors willing to pay, and so everyone pays bribes. Yet all competitors are better off if cooperative behavior emerges whereby everybody trusts that the others will not engage in bribery.

The development of ethics and compliance promotes higher standards of business conduct that could be implemented at least within a homogeneous business community. In principle, it provides a cooperative solution to the prisoner's dilemma. This may appear a naive or overoptimistic statement, despite the fast-growing popularity of compliance systems not only in large multinational companies but also in the regional and local private sector. Indeed, there are a number of objections to or questions concerning the cooperative solution. The most trivial is that private sector restraint can address symptoms and, at best, mechanisms but cannot deal directly with the roots of corruption. There is no full private sector substitute for public sector reforms in key areas such as civil service reform, finance, and regulation aimed at reducing incentives and opportunities for corruption (see box 2.1).

But firms are not passive onlookers; the very way in which they react to business constraints, including corruption, in their environment affects that environment. The private sector response to corrupt practices is especially important given that bribery and extortion take many forms, follow many channels, and mutate, like viruses, into new strains. As a consequence, enforcement and prosecution raise serious practical challenges in the absence of some form of private sector cooperation. This connection is discussed in subsequent chapters. The first part of this chapter examines the nature of corrupt practices and the critical issues that corporate programs have to deal with.

In recent years the interaction between the firm and its environment has been studied intensively on the basis of enterprise surveys pioneered by the World Bank. The second part of this chapter revisits the empirical

---

**Box 2.1.  The Roots of Corruption and the Reform Agenda**

| *Root* | *Key area of reform* |
|---|---|
| Absence of political rights and civil liberties; capture by a few vested interests; weak civil society | *Accountability of the political leadership*<br>• Political competition and transparency<br>• Rules addressing conflict of interest and state capture<br><br>*Civil society participation*<br>• Freedom of information<br>• Role of media and nongovernmental organizations |
| Absence of rule of law | *Rule of law*<br>• Independent and effective judiciary<br>• Independent prosecution and enforcement<br>• Legislative oversight |
| Public finance and regulation: monopolies, excessive regulation and taxes | *Financial reforms and competitiveness*<br>• Competition and cost of entry: deregulation and demonopolization<br>• Procurement reform<br>• Transparency in the private sector: ethics and corporate governance |
| Poor professionalism in the civil service | *Civil service and public sector management*<br>• Meritocracy and transparency<br>• Adequate pay and incentives<br>• Budget management and audit reform<br>• Institutional reforms of key agencies such as customs and tax<br>• Decentralization |

*Source:* Thomas and others (2000: ch. 6).

---

evidence, both worldwide and from East Asia. Beyond the bare fact that corruption is bad for business, the data point to a number of determinants of firm vulnerability and a (negative) link to performance. Ultimately, the evidence also supports the relevance of the cooperative solution to the dilemma.

# Types of Corruption

The first step in resisting corrupt practices is to define them (box 2.2). The commonly accepted taxonomy (see Rose-Ackerman 1996) distinguishes among the many forms of corruption by nature and by level.

*By nature*
- Paying for benefits—for example, to influence bidding results, buy an administrative decision, or shape a judicial decision
- Paying to avoid costs—for example, to ensure that something that is due is done on time.

*By level*
- Petty corruption, which in its mildest form is similar to tips
- Grand corruption in government business: public works, public procurement, licenses, or privatization.

---

**Box 2.2.  Some Definitions**

*Corruption (or graft).* The most comprehensive concept. It has three different manifestations:

- Active corruption or bribery (giving)
- Passive corruption (receiving), including extortion
- Misappropriation and fraud, which may or may not be associated with commercial transactions.

*Extortion.* Abuse of power to solicit illegal payments.

*Kickback.* An illegal payment made to the person who facilitated the transaction. Unlike an ordinary bribe, a kickback is paid after the transaction takes place. Kickbacks are often paid in installments. They are the most common practice in grand corruption schemes.

*Bribe.* The reward offered to a corrupt person to induce that person to act in the interest of the giver.

*State capture.* The situation in which government policies, laws, and regulations are shaped by the corrupt interests of a small corporate elite.

*Facilitation payments.* Also called "grease money"; small payments made to speed common administrative procedures.

---

## Petty Corruption and Facilitation Payments

Petty corruption is common in the ordinary business operations of local and international corporations in Asia. Most of it takes the form of small payments to low-level bureaucrats to help speed slow-moving public services and can thus be classified as facilitation payments. Areas in which such payments are common include customs, business licenses, work visas, and police protection. It was recently reported that without grease payments, the registration of a new company in Indonesia would take at least two years (*Financial Times*, April 4, 2002).

In the context of international transactions, most private firms adopt a practical stance and tolerate small facilitation payments. As one company spokesman explained,

> Unfortunately, if we don't make these payments, we don't get telephone lines when we need them. We don't get the visas we need to go from one country to another where we have operations. Legal matters aside, if making these truly nominal payments in emerging economy locations means that we can operate in them effectively, I think our local clients, employees, suppliers, and their communities benefit. Demonstrating that a five dollar facilitating payment has the same impact as a five million dollar bribe would be difficult.

Such tolerance is reflected in the laws of most developed countries against bribery abroad. It is recognized that petty corruption is practically impossible to eliminate without first tackling grand corruption, which has more devastating consequences. A 1988 amendment to the U.S. Foreign Corrupt Practices Act was the first to grant an exception for facilitation payments, and it influenced subsequent conventions, laws, and guidelines.[2] But beyond the practical concerns, facilitation payments are not uncontroversial.[3] Some businesspersons recognize that facilitation payments are not always inevitable and that creative solutions using technical or commercial innovation may override extortive demands. In the example of phone hookups quoted above, the wide availability of cellphone technology in East Asia gives companies a firm leverage on demands by the traditional phone company's employees.

Petty corruption cannot be considered innocuous. Facilitation payments that are readily "afforded" by large corporations can be a nightmare for a small local business (especially if harassed by local police officers) or, indeed, for the average citizen facing harassment from low-level government officials in the course of the ordinary business of life. The impact of corruption on the poor has been widely documented (Partnership for Governance Reform in Indonesia 2001). But even for a large

---

**Box 2.3. Too Many Facilitation Payments—A Lost Contract**

In Thailand the Customs and Excise Department asked the Société Générale de Surveillance (SGS) for a payment every time the department approved certificates. Approval simply consisted of affixing a stamp to the certificate to confirm that SGS personnel had performed the inspection work it was contracted to do.

Although each payment was less than US$100, this was not small when compared with the inspection fee. The practice became so common that the payments came to represent some 30 percent of the revenue of the particular business and well above US$100,000 a year. SGS felt that such an accumulation of modest sums could no longer qualify as facilitation payments and that the practice had to be discontinued.

Following the enactment of the company's Code of Ethics, SGS's national chief executive in Thailand submitted the payments matter to the chief compliance officer. The solution was agreed on by the chief compliance officer, the Executive Board member responsible for the sector, and the area controller and was reported to the Ethics Committee. It was decided to stop making the payments and consequently to lose contracts and revenues in this particular sector. The value of the lost business was estimated at around US$1 million a year.

---

corporation, the costs of facilitation payments can mount to damaging levels amounting to grand corruption (see box 2.3).

Finally, systemic petty corruption provides fertile ground for private corruption and fraud at the expense of companies. Low-level commercial espionage can be an outcome. Indeed, in many countries it is virtually impossible to keep company information confidential. Since this strongly affects the conditions for competition, preventing fraud and commercial espionage is a major concern that is reflected in the internal codes of ethics of multinational companies.

## Grand Corruption

The classic environment for grand corruption is government procurement through competitive bidding, whether international or not. Fraud and corruption mechanisms have been widely documented in this context.[4] Frequent cases of extortion involving local and international firms alike are found in a variety of public services. Tax collection, customs, and police are commonly problematic areas that, along with public procurement procedures, are priority targets of governance reform in the public sector (see figure 2.1).

## Figure 2.1. Degree of Corruption in Selected Public Services in Indonesia as Assessed by Private Sector Executives

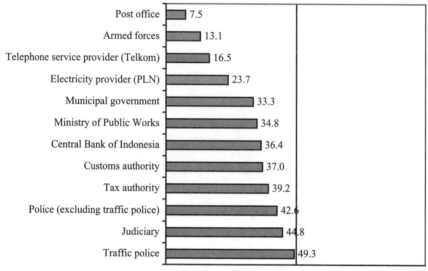

Post office — 7.5
Armed forces — 13.1
Telephone service provider (Telkom) — 16.5
Electricity provider (PLN) — 23.7
Municipal government — 33.3
Ministry of Public Works — 34.8
Central Bank of Indonesia — 36.4
Customs authority — 37.0
Tax authority — 39.2
Police (excluding traffic police) — 42.6
Judiciary — 44.8
Traffic police — 49.3

Percentage of respondents viewing the service as corrupt

*Note:* Number of respondents: 400.
*Source:* Partnership for Governance Reform in Indonesia 2001.

As the private sector's role has expanded in recent years, new types of bureaucratic interaction have created opportunities for corruption. Examples include the granting of licenses (for instance, in the pharmaceutical industry), privatization, and private provision of public services. Although the greater involvement of the private sector tends to increase transparency, privatization creates opportunities for corruption because it offers the potential for asset stripping and because it requires large and financially complex transactions, consultancy work, and regulatory interventions.

It is an open secret in the international business community that in the late 1990s rates of bribery on typical government services were very high. Payments of around 15 percent were common in many countries, and the rate could reach 30 percent. Some local corporations also have to pay very high rates, as shown by firm-level surveys in developing economies (figure 2.2).[5]

Because bribers need to recover the cost of the bribes, grand corruption leads to other abuses. Two broad categories are fraud and bid rigging.

- *Fraud.* This abuse can take many forms, including inflated rates, substandard goods and services, and false billings, all of which require the active or passive complicity of the bribe recipients.

**Figure 2.2.  Share of Firms Acknowledging Paying More Than 10 Percent of Sales Value in Bribes in Selected Countries**

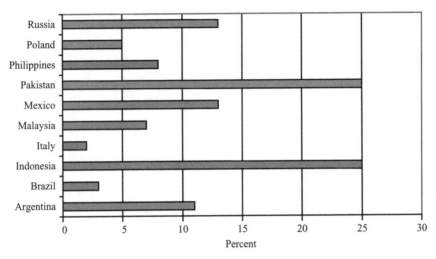

*Source:* World Business Environment Survey, 2000.

- *Bid rigging.* In essence, bid rigging reduces commercial and development costs, which can be huge in certain industries, such as public works and utilities. In some countries the designated winner of the bid compensates losers for their bidding costs. Systematic bid rigging requires a fairly high degree of organization, including cartelization of the industry at the country level at the expense of outsiders, and some form of capture of the government departments involved.

## State Capture versus Cronyism

State capture occurs when a few private interests effectively control the decisions of people in power and shape government policies according to their interests, primarily to maintain a legal or de facto monopoly. Hellman, Jones, and Kaufmann (2000) have underlined the importance of state capture in transition economies. It is an especially high risk in countries that depend heavily on exports of primary commodities—from bananas to petroleum and minerals. Historically, analysts have focused on state capture by foreign investors, but attention has recently shifted to cases of capture by local interests.

In East Asia and the Pacific the economic crisis of 1997 revealed a high degree of collusion between governments and private interests. The traditional Chinese business culture of guanxi puts the emphasis on the human network instead of on contractual relationships (see chapter 5 in

## Table 2.1. What Is Needed to Win a Government Contract in Indonesia? (percentage of responses by businesses)

| | Quality of product or services | Personal connections | Bribes |
|---|---|---|---|
| Important | 84 | 66 | 32 |
| Neutral | 16 | 24 | 34 |
| Unimportant | 0 | 10 | 34 |

Source: Partnership for Governance Reform in Indonesia (2001): enterprise survey.

this volume). Indeed, personal connections are widely considered a key to the award of business in the region (table 2.1) and constitute fertile ground for cronyism and corruption. Nevertheless, even in countries affected by systemic corruption, there is little evidence of state capture in East Asia—not a surprise, given the size, diversity, and relative openness of the region's economies.[6]

## Legitimate Social Purpose but Improper Transactions

Some interactions, although illegal (or not clearly legal), serve some legitimate public purpose from the recipient country's perspective rather than merely benefiting a few individuals. They typically take the form of extra demands by government agencies outside the scope of business contracts. For example:

- One of the companies interviewed for this study related that an Asian public agency that granted licenses had asked the company to pay tuition and expenses for government regulatory officials to enroll in a U.S. university program. The request was presented as an opportunity to enable promising young developing country bureaucrats, selected through a transparent process, to acquire expertise that neither the individual nor the country could afford. The stipend sought would improve the expertise of an agency whose support and approval was important to the company in doing business in the country.
- In Indonesia some public agencies requested additional payments according to rates that were quasi official and were used exclusively to endow a fund that paid salary supplements to all employees.

Other examples encountered by companies surveyed in this study include requests to fund a public hospital and to pay for a state funeral. These types of socially oriented request, which are far from uncommon, are not as shocking as grand corruption cases. Nevertheless, they are problematic. Lack of transparency is detrimental to fair competition, and there is potential for abuse. The underlying concerns are ultimately better addressed through appropriate institutional or administrative changes. Today, most international corporations consider this type of solicitation as incompatible with their codes of conduct.

## Channels of Corruption

Companies and governments need to know how corruption takes place if they are to reduce and guard against illicit activities. The channels for corruption can be divided into direct payments and indirect payments.

### Direct Payments

Direct payments for corrupt purposes, whether in money or in kind, are risky. They are now clearly banned under the 1997 OECD Convention on Combating Bribery of Foreign Public Officials in International Business Transactions (see box 2.6, below) and under national laws.

Direct payments related to grand corruption are seldom made in cash, since it is difficult for the briber to generate large amounts from banks and for the recipient to spend the money without raising suspicion. The preferred method has been to pay into special accounts, usually held by an offshore shell company linked to the recipient. This is now prohibited, and anti–money laundering initiatives make it more difficult than before, especially for international transactions.

For smaller sums, cash is often used, but payments in kind are also popular, especially in the least advanced countries. These take various forms, such as:

- Lavish business gifts and banqueting
- Delivery under the contract of goods such as vehicles that actually serve the personal use of the bribe recipient
- "Business" travel or "training"
- Advantages such as jobs or scholarships given to relatives of the bribe recipient.

### Indirect Payments and Intermediaries

The main channels of corruption are indirect payments through third parties. Use of the umbrella of a technically "clean" business deal with a third party is very convenient.[7] It is, to be sure, illegal—for instance, under the U.S. Foreign Corrupt Practices Act, a U.S. company is accountable for the misconduct of third parties that act on its behalf—but the likelihood of being caught is not very high. Complex circuitry can be set up, providing many opportunities to build firewalls. Experience shows that this is a difficult area for prosecutors to investigate; the necessary international cooperation is not always forthcoming.

Clearly, some third parties are legitimate business partners that provide real goods and services. For example, they may be advisers or lobbyists who are representatives but not employees or affiliates of the hiring company. But it is widely suspected that such agents can simultaneously play the role of intermediary, delivering bribes with or without the explicit consent of the company. To help avoid this, companies can employ agents with clean reputations and compensate them in line with the services they provide.

Commercial ventures (for example, through coinvestment or contracts) with local or regional corporations are a natural way of doing international business. In essence, goods, services, and technology are exchanged for market knowledge and lobbying influence in the host country. This may backfire, however, and some of the companies surveyed for this study said that their policy is to avoid investing in joint ventures. Another area of concern is the potential risk of fraud and misconduct by subcontractors.

Some third parties have a purely fraudulent purpose. They include:

- Offshore vehicles linked to the briber, such as shell companies. These are clearly unwelcome now under various anticorruption and anti–money laundering initiatives.
- Front companies, usually disguised as consulting companies, linked to the recipients of bribes.
- A professional corrupt middleman, often designated as a loan broker. The middleman, registered as a business consultant based in some accommodating jurisdiction, approaches international corporations on behalf of corrupt officials and organizes subcontracted deals to extract money from the main contract and to launder it for himself and the network of corrupt officials.

A company wishing to avoid corruption cannot ignore the corrupt practices of a partner. Not surprisingly, the behavior of business partners is becoming a central issue for the compliance systems of large corporations (see "Application to Business Partners" in chapter 4 and examples in the case studies in part II).

## Corruption Is Bad for Business

The fact that corruption hinders the development of the private sector is now widely accepted, to the point that many practitioners tend to rank it as one of the most serious obstacles to business (see box 2.4).

---

**Box 2.4. Expert Opinion: Corruption as the Number One Obstacle to Private Sector Development**

The International Finance Corporation (IFC) is the private sector arm of the World Bank Group. In 2001 the IFC surveyed its staff to tap their first-hand knowledge about the investment climate in the IFC's countries of operation. More than 400 staff members responded to the questionnaire for their countries of expertise. Results are available for 45 countries.

Among 21 features of the environment for private sector development, respondents pointed to the incidence of corruption in the private sector as the main issue in 29 of the 45 countries and as the second most important issue in another 8.

As is shown in the figure, the IFC findings agree very well with Transparency International's Corruption Perceptions Index, which relies on a broader statistical base and looks at the prevalence of corruption from a broader perspective than that of the investor alone.

**IFC and Transparency International Corruption Ratings Compared**

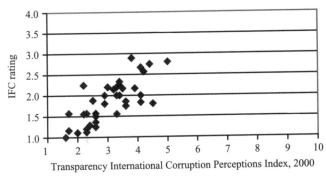

*Source:* IFC Economics Department and authors' calculations.

---

This recognition is comparatively recent, however. For decades, business communities accepted bribery as, at worst, a normal business practice (with official blessing) or, at best, an inescapable requirement to "do as the Romans do" in the most affected countries. Economists, for their part, tended to view corruption as a reasonable response to bureaucratic inefficiency (see Leff 2001). In this interpretation—the "grease hypothesis"—paying bribes softens the consequences of ill-designed or ill-implemented policies and regulations by allowing some reallocation of resources toward the most efficient firms. Thus, corruption is a (mitigating) consequence of underdevelopment.

In the 1980s and 1990s, however, economists and political scientists such as Rose-Ackerman (1996) and Klitgaard (1991) developed the opposite view: that corruption has adverse consequences for development. Their position is increasingly supported by evidence. The grease hypothesis does not recognize that grand corruption actually reduces bureaucratic efficiency rather than enhances it; the possibility of corrupt behavior distorts the incentives of bureaucrats, who act to create rewarding opportunities for themselves rather than to further the public good. From the perspective of the private sector, corruption amounts to an extraction that is much more detrimental to business development than are legal mechanisms such as taxes (Shleifer and Vishny 1993). Not only is corruption often unpredictable; even when it is "organized," its arbitrariness and lack of transparency make it harmful.

## Insights from Recent Research

Since the mid-1990s, empirical cross-country assessments based on survey data have confirmed the negative alchemy between corruption and development.[8] Among the most relevant findings for the present study are the following:

- Corruption depletes domestic investment (Mauro 1998).
- Corruption affects the composition of capital flows and substantially reduces flows of foreign direct investment (Wei 2000b).
- There is no Asian exception (see below).
- Corruption, like red tape, not only impedes macroeconomic performance but also holds back the performance of individual firms (whose vulnerability differs depending on their characteristics).
- Other things being equal, firms paying more bribes spend more time negotiating with bureaucrats and pay a higher cost for capital (Kaufmann and Wei 2000).

The acquisition of this knowledge about the macroeconomic consequences of corruption was made possible in part by the creation of instruments for measuring corruption consistently. Political risk agencies began developing indexes of corruption in the 1980s. Transparency International, a nongovernmental organization (NGO), introduced its widely used Corruption Perceptions Index in 1996. As implied by its name, this index, which is based on a series of surveys, does not measure corruption by its outcome; rather, it presents an average perception of how serious corruption is, on a scale from 1 (worst) to 10 (no corruption). Kaufmann, Kraay, and Zoido-Lobatón (2002) have shown that there is a high degree of consistency among the various perceptions indexes, even though they use different methods and survey different populations. The Political and Economic Risk Consultancy (PERC), based in Hong Kong (China), is producing a yearly in-depth analysis of corruption in Asian countries, with a rating similar to Transparency International's and broadly consistent with it.

## Is There an Asian Exception?

Debate persists on whether some form of organized corruption may be less harmful than disorderly corruption, as common sense and anecdotal evidence seem to suggest (Campos 2002). A popular idea before the Asian financial crisis was that in East Asia corruption is more orderly and less harmful to development than in other parts of the world. Some East Asian countries have consistently scored below average on the corruption scale (see table 2.2) but have nevertheless attracted considerable foreign direct investment (FDI) and have experienced significant growth.

Economists who have looked at this issue in the aftermath of the Asian crisis could not find support for the Asian exception, although the debate is not closed.[9] Wei (2000b) disproves the notion that corruption depletes FDI in the East less than elsewhere, once other factors that explain FDI flows are taken into account. And surveys of firms worldwide show that

**Table 2.2. Corruption Perception Indexes in Selected East Asian Economies, 2001 (from 1, most corrupt, to 10, no corruption)**

|  | Transparency International rating | Political and Economic Risk Consultancy rating[a] |
|---|---|---|
| Singapore | 9.2 | 9.3 |
| Australia | 8.5 | n.a. |
| Hong Kong (China) | 7.9 | 6.6 |
| Japan | 7.1 | 7.8 |
| Taiwan (China) | 5.9 | 4.6 |
| Malaysia | 5.0 | 4.6 |
| Korea, Rep. of | 4.2 | 3.7 |
| China | 3.5 | 2.9 |
| Thailand | 3.2 | 2.3 |
| Philippines | 2.9 | 1.9 |
| Vietnam | 2.6 | 1.2 |
| Indonesia | 1.9 | 1.3 |

n.a. Not applicable.
a. Rescaled according to Transparency International convention.
*Source:* Transparency International, "Annual Report 2001."

East Asian entrepreneurs rate corruption as a serious problem among business constraints just as much as do their counterparts elsewhere (see table 2.3).

# Determinants of Vulnerability

Recent years have seen a growing number of firm-level surveys based on country-specific surveys or on cross-country databases. From 1995 to 1997, the World Bank and the World Economic Forum surveyed several thousands of firms worldwide. The most comprehensive relevant database is probably the World Business Environment Survey (WBES) initiated by the World Bank (box 2.5). The surveys provide a fresh understanding of the interplay between enterprise growth and a number of business constraints such as corruption. In East Asia detailed surveys have been conducted in Thailand, as part of the WBES, and in Indonesia by the Partnership for Governance Reform in Indonesia, an advocacy organization supported by the World Bank and the United Nations Development Programme (see Partnership for Government Reform in Indonesia 2001). More limited coverage is available for Cambodia, China, Malaysia, the Philippines, and Singapore.

## A Universal Rejection

Bribery and corruption patterns are shaped by well-documented national or regional features that are rooted in particularities of history or culture (Heidenheimer and Johnston 2001). Even so, the surveys show that, worldwide, private firms perceive corruption as a major obstacle to their sustainable growth. Indexes based purely on insiders' perceptions are very much in line with those such as the Transparency International Corruption Perceptions Index that incorporate the opinions of international experts (figure 2.3). Furthermore, firms have a very consistent understanding of the major roots of corruption (see table 2.4).

## Size Matters

Firm-level assessments, including the WBES, show that vulnerability to corruption varies enormously by size of firm within a given country. This can be seen from statistics on the bribes actually paid by companies, calculated as a proportion of their sales. Interactions with the bureaucracy and opportunities for extortion depend on the line of business, but in general, large and foreign-owned firms pay substantially less in bribes, as is illustrated by figure 2.4, for Thailand. Although some form of bias in the

Table 2.3. Entrepreneurs' Opinions on Obstacles to Business Growth (average rating in the country, from 1, no obstacle, to 4, major obstacle)

| | China | Malaysia | Singapore | Indonesia | Philippines | Thailand | India | Argentina | Mexico | Poland | Russia |
|---|---|---|---|---|---|---|---|---|---|---|---|
| Availability of financing | 3.35 | 2.32 | 1.86 | 2.86 | 2.68 | 3.11 | 2.55 | 2.99 | 3.19 | 2.41 | 3.21 |
| Infrastructure | 1.96 | 1.79 | 1.35 | 2.36 | 2.84 | 2.81 | 2.77 | 1.92 | 2.31 | 1.63 | 2.09 |
| Policy instability | 2.27 | 1.95 | 1.47 | 3.10 | 2.91 | 3.48 | 2.84 | 3.10 | 3.29 | 2.65 | 3.43 |
| Inflation | 2.28 | 2.29 | 1.56 | 3.14 | 3.40 | 3.36 | 2.87 | 2.01 | 3.42 | 2.57 | 3.51 |
| Exchange rate | 1.79 | 1.93 | 1.82 | 3.36 | 3.45 | 3.63 | 2.48 | 1.81 | 3.19 | 2.21 | 3.12 |
| Street crime | 1.80 | 1.74 | 1.20 | 2.66 | 2.85 | 3.52 | 1.99 | 2.47 | 3.38 | 2.34 | 2.60 |
| Organized crime | 1.72 | 1.58 | 1.29 | 2.55 | 2.58 | 3.73 | 1.90 | 1.90 | 3.31 | 1.94 | 2.56 |
| Taxes and regulations | 2.08 | 1.86 | 1.50 | 2.54 | 3.08 | 3.22 | 2.28 | 3.32 | 3.20 | 3.04 | 3.53 |
| Corruption | 2.03 | 1.85 | 1.25 | 2.63 | 3.11 | 3.47 | 2.80 | 2.62 | 3.33 | 2.21 | 2.55 |
| Police | 1.56 | 1.69 | 1.32 | 2.20 | 2.28 | 2.13 | 2.01 | 2.33 | 2.84 | 2.21 | 2.13 |

Note: Entrepreneurs were asked to judge on a four-point scale how problematic each factor was for the operation and growth of their business.
Source: World Business Environment Survey, 2000.

---

**Box 2.5. The World Business Environment Survey**

The World Business Environment Survey (WBES) is a unique source of both quantitative and qualitative information on the impact of corruption at the firm level. It includes not only subjective information about perceived levels of corruption but also some quantitative data about the frequency and level of bribery and its prevalence within a number of public services.

The survey was carried out in 1999–2000 under World Bank supervision in 83 countries with the aim of improving understanding of the constraints on the development of private business. Targeting at least 100 medium-size corporations in each country, it focused on issues such as the quality of public services, rules and regulations, the legal system, corruption, predictability of policies, financial infrastructure, and competition. The full database covers more than 10,000 companies.

Several questions deal directly with corruption and bribery. One measures the perception—from 1 (best) to 4 (worst)—of corruption as an obstacle to business (one of 12 institutional, physical, and financial obstacles covered). Another measures the level of bribes paid as a percentage of the firm's sales, on an ascending scale of 1 to 7.

Information from the WBES has made possible new, in-depth research in the area (see Batra, Kaufmann, and Stone 2003).

---

## Figure 2.3. Perceptions of Corruption as an Obstacle to Business

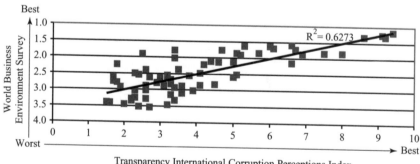

Transparency International Corruption Perceptions Index

*Note:* The WBES rating is for the perception of corruption as an obstacle to business on a scale of 1 (best) to 4 (worst).

*Source:* World Business Environment Survey, 2000, and authors' calculations.

## Table 2.4. Principal Causes of Corruption in Indonesia

| Top-ranked cause | Percentage of respondents |
|---|---|
| Low salaries of public officials | 37 |
| Lack of controls and lack of accountability of public officials | 21 |
| Lack of morals (ethics) | 17 |
| Poor law enforcement; inadequate punishment of corrupters | 10 |
| Cultural reasons | 5 |
| Lack of an independent and effective judiciary | 3 |
| Too many and too complex government regulations | 3 |
| Lack of an effective corruption-reporting system | 2 |
| Lack of democracy | 2 |
| Legacy of New Order regime | 1 |
| High cost of living | 1 |
| Lack of effective civil society | 0 |

Source: Partnership for Governance Reform in Indonesia 2001: enterprise survey.

surveys cannot be ruled out, the greater vulnerability of smaller firms seems to be quite general and has been documented by studies carried out at the country level around the world, including the Partnership for Governance Reform in Indonesia survey.

The econometric analysis reported in appendix A in this volume shows that the difference in vulnerability between smaller firms (with fewer than 50 employees) and larger firms (with more than 500 employees) is equivalent to the effect of a substantial reduction in the level of corruption in the country at large—that is, to a 2-point reduction in the Transparency International Corruption Perceptions Index for that country.

## Figure 2.4. Vulnerability to Extortion in Relation to Size of Firm, Thailand

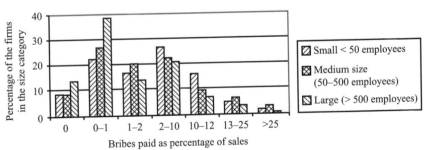

Source: World Business Environment Survey, 2000, and authors' calculations.

These observations are consistent with the fact that large and foreign-owned corporations are more likely than small local ones to rely success-fully on internal procedures to resist extortion. Regional or country managers of international firms who were interviewed for the present study tended to confirm this view and also mentioned that the ability to invoke a firm's anticorruption rules and procedures helped in resisting extortion in the field.

Not surprisingly, vulnerability to extortion is dependent on other attributes, such as the industry sector or whether the firm supplies the public sector. In the survey for Indonesia it appears that about two-thirds of the firms in construction and public works, the most vulnerable sector, acknowledge paying at least 5 percent of their sales in bribes. Only one-third of the firms in manufacturing and financial services gave this response.

## A Negative Alchemy

It is now well established in the literature that in most countries firms engaging in corrupt practices experience lower performance (see fig-ure 2.5). The causality is debatable. It could be that firms experiencing dif-ficult times are tempted to salvage business by bribing public officials. Or it could be that time and resources are expended in corrupt practices at the expense of firm competitiveness. Indeed, there is some correlation between the level of bribery and the time spent by managers with the bureaucracy (Gray and Kaufmann 1998).

Furthermore, bribery appears to have a rather low yield. Firms sur-veyed for the WBES were asked to gauge the degree of predictability of

## Figure 2.5. Vulnerability to Extortion in Relation to Firm Performance, Thailand

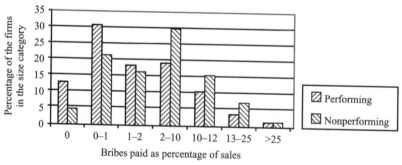

Source: World Business Environment Survey, 2000, and authors' calculations.

## Figure 2.6. Vulnerability to Extortion in Relation to Predictability of Bribery Demands or of Outcomes, Thailand

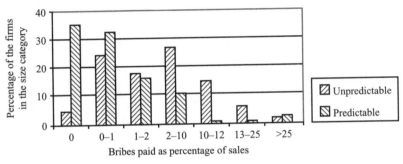

*Note:* Firms in the "predictable" group find that the amount to be paid is usually known in advance and that the bribee "delivers."
*Source:* World Business Environment Survey, 2000, and authors' calculations.

bribery, particularly regarding the amount to be paid or the expected outcome of additional payments. According to the survey, the more firms pay, the more unpredictable is the result (see figure 2.6).

The individual firm's response to bribery is not fully determined by its characteristics or its environment. Beyond averages, there are wide differences in vulnerability and in the acceptance of corruption in a corruption-prone country (see figures 2.4–2.6). Another illustration of the idiosyncratic nature of attitudes toward corruption is that in a given country the perception of corruption as a business constraint is only poorly correlated with actual vulnerability and other business constraints (see appendix B). In the end, there is room for better standards of behavior in which firms avoid being locked into the vicious circle of low growth and corruption.

## Bribery in International Transactions

Bribery by international firms has been singled out as one of the main channels of grand corruption. In the OECD countries it is the target of national regulations in accordance with the OECD Convention (see box 2.6), and multinational corporations based in these countries have developed compliance systems to prevent it. Among firms doing business internationally, factors that may encourage transnational bribery include the type of industry, the size of the firm, and the home country of the firm.

---

**Box 2.6. OECD Anti-Bribery Convention**

The Convention on Combating Bribery of Foreign Public Officials in International Business Transactions was signed in December 1997 by OECD member countries and five nonmembers: Argentina, Brazil, Bulgaria, Chile, and the Slovak Republic. Slovenia signed in 2001. Article 1 of the convention provides that:

Each (signatory) Party shall take measures as may be necessary to establish that it is a criminal offense under its law for any person intentionally to offer, promise, or give undue pecuniary or other advantage, whether directly or through intermediaries, to a foreign public official, for that official or for a third party, in order that the official act or refrain from acting in relation to the performance of official duties, in order to obtain or retain business or other improper advantage in the conduct of international business.

This definition explicitly bans third-party bribery mechanisms. It implicitly allows facilitation payments, as they do not create an improper competitive advantage for the firm that pays them.

---

## Type of Industry

It is no secret that levels of corruption vary widely among industries. By their nature, deals in certain sectors provide more opportunities for grand corruption, given their higher degree of government involvement, discretionary powers, secrecy, and contract size. The most notoriously vulnerable areas are defense and public works.

## Size of Firm

In large corporations, managers are themselves increasingly international or at least have international exposure, and the espoused values and business practices of large corporations are converging, partly as a result of increased sharing of experience in some areas. By contrast, managers of small and medium-size exporters from developed countries have limited awareness of policy and legal changes. Although these firms supply a small share of FDI flows to emerging economies and a minority share of exports, their practices are of growing concern to policymakers (Netherlands 2001). Beyond OECD countries, practices of small and medium-size exporters appear to be an issue of concern in Singapore (see the case studies in part II) and in Hong Kong (China).

## Nationality

The conventional wisdom is that business practices differ greatly according to the nationality of the firm. Until the adoption of the OECD Convention in 1997, bribery in international trade and investment was recognized as acceptable to differing degrees, depending on the home country. Differences in national laws can affect the fairness of competition, especially in export industries, and transnational bribery is therefore a politically sensitive issue. Indeed, the adoption of the OECD Convention was driven not only by moral considerations but also by the perceived need to reestablish a level playing field for international firms from OECD member countries and other countries.

Does a firm's home country influence its propensity to bribe? The Bribe Payers Index (BPI), issued by Transparency International since 1999 as a benchmark for assessing the implementation of the OECD Convention, strongly suggests that the answer is yes. The latest (2002) edition of the BPI is based on opinions gathered from 835 executives in 15 major emerging markets. The executives ranked 21 leading exporting countries in terms of their corporations' perceived propensity to pay bribes abroad (see appendix B).

The BPI differs widely by country (see table 2.5). Although the BPI provides a rather disturbing assessment of the business practices of major exporting countries such as Germany, Japan, and the United States, it shows that no exporting country is perceived as bribe-free. East Asian economies fare rather poorly in this ranking—even those such as Singapore and Hong Kong (China) that have a high reputation for ethics at home according to the Corruption Perceptions Index (CPI).

From a policy point of view, a significant finding from the BPI statistics is that local firms are much more prone to bribery than firms from other countries (see the last row in table 2.5). This observation, supported by firm-level surveys (such as the WBES), is consistent with the idea that international corporations have a key role to play in spreading good practices. But when the 2002 BPI was released, most comments in the international press not only pointed to the poor performance of major countries such as the United States but also concluded that the OECD Convention had not improved behavior in the private sector. Such a view conflicts with the results of the current study, which shows unambiguously that changes have been dramatic worldwide since the late 1990s. Appendix B

## Table 2.5. Perceptions of Propensity to Pay Bribes Abroad, Ranked from 10 (Best) to 1 (Worst)

| Exporter | BPI 1999 | BPI 2002 | CPI 2001 |
|---|---|---|---|
| Australia | 8.1 | 8.5 | 8.5 |
| Switzerland | 7.7 | 8.4 | 8.4 |
| Sweden | 8.3 | 8.4 | 9 |
| Austria | 7.8 | 8.2 | 7.8 |
| Canada | 8.1 | 8.1 | 8.9 |
| Belgium | 6.8 | 7.8 | 6.6 |
| Netherlands | 7.4 | 7.8 | 8.8 |
| United Kingdom | 7.2 | 6.9 | 8.3 |
| Germany | 6.2 | 6.3 | 7.4 |
| Singapore | n.a. | 6.3 | 9.2 |
| Spain | 5.3 | 5.8 | 7 |
| France | 5.2 | 5.5 | 6.7 |
| Japan | 5.1 | 5.3 | 7.1 |
| United States | 6.2 | 5.3 | 7.6 |
| Hong Kong (China) | n.a. | 4.3 | 7.9 |
| Malaysia | 3.9 | 4.3 | 5 |
| Italy | 3.7 | 4.1 | 5.5 |
| Korea, Rep. of | 3.4 | 3.9 | 4.2 |
| Taiwan (China) | n.a. | 3.8 | 5.9 |
| China | 3.1 | 3.5 | 3.5 |
| **Local corporations** | n.a. | 1.9 | n.a. |

n.a. Not applicable.
*Note:* BPI, Bribe Payers Index; CPI, Corruption Perceptions Index. The countries are listed according to their ranking on the 2002 BPI.
*Source:* Transparency International 2001, 2002a.

provides an alternative reading of the BPI that takes into account the probable bias introduced by differences in country size. It appears that larger exporters are not more bribe-prone and that there is even a plausible positive effect of the OECD Convention. Other things being equal, exporters from countries that are parties to the convention might be less prone to bribery, compared with exporters from other countries, in a proportion that amounts to an improvement of 2 points on the BPI scale of 1 to 10.

Empirical research based on data on trade and foreign direct investment provides strong evidence, both at the macroeconomic level and at the firm level, that international operators tend to avoid corrupt environments. The research gives only weak support to the notion that the firm's home country matters (see box 2.7).

---

**Box 2.7. Research on Avoidance of Corrupt Countries by International Firms**

At least two papers contain empirical assessments of the impact of the U.S. Foreign Corrupt Practices Act (FCPA) on U.S. business opportunities. Graham (1984) looked into the evolution of U.S. market shares before and after the passage of the FCPA, using a two-group classification of competitors' practices as reported by U.S. firms, and found no significant effect on U.S. market shares as a result of the FCPA. Hines (1995) tested for the effect of corruption on four U.S. international business indicators: growth of foreign direct investment (FDI), capital-labor ratios, joint-venture activity, and aircraft exports. The results support the view that U.S. businesses are avoiding corrupt countries and might be losing business to more bribe-prone competitors. (The study does not provide a comparison with other OECD countries.)

Wei has investigated the link between the composition of financial flows and governance at the country level (Wei 2000a; Wei and Wu 2001). His model is based on a gravity determination of investment flows that includes variables such as country size, level of development, distance, and language. The results show unambiguously that FDI flows avoid more corrupt countries. Comparing the United States with Japan, Wei finds that American investors are more averse to corruption than others. Smarzynska and Wei (2001) obtained similar results using firm-level data from Eastern Europe.

Lambsdorff (1998) examined how corruption can affect trade, using trade statistics from 19 major exporters into 87 markets. The underlying hypothesis is the same: international operators avoid corrupt markets, but their aversion to corruption depends on the home country. Unlike Wei (1997), this study uses a simplified gravity equation with market share as a dependent variable, which implies that aversion to corruption is measured only in relative terms. This research points to no significant effect for most countries, including the major East Asian exporters, but it does show that Swedish exporters are relatively more averse to corrupt markets than are their counterparts from Belgium, France, and Italy. (This type of analysis is a rather complex econometric undertaking, and several methodological variants are possible; see Wei 1997. Unfortunately, to our knowledge, this interesting research on trade data has not been supplemented by further work to explore alternative econometric prescriptions and check the robustness of Lambsdorff's findings.)

# Notes

1. The prisoner's dilemma, described in 1950 by A. W. Tucker, is a non–zero sum game in which the players end up developing a "lose-lose" strategy in the absence of cooperation.

2. According to the amendment, the concept of facilitation payments is theoretically more narrow than the practice described in the text. Facilitation payments are not prohibited where they meet certain enumerated criteria, including their "legality" in the place where they are made.

3. This topic delayed by a few years the enabling of the OECD Convention in British law, which does not explicitly make an exception for such payments.

4. Sources of information include press reports (Transparency International offers a good compilation on its Website) and investigative journalism (Backman 1999). Very thorough investigations are conducted by enforcement agencies such as the U.S. Securities and Exchange Commission (SEC) and the Independent Commission Against Corruption (ICAC) in Hong Kong (China). Some of these investigations are public (for instance, the SEC settlement report for violations of the Foreign Corrupt Practices Act, available at <www.sec.gov>) and provide a unique resource of thorough case studies on international bribery. Investigations by bilateral or multilateral agencies of fraud involving official development assistance are also good (but confidential) resources.

5. See, for example, the corruption data of the World Business Environment Survey carried out under the auspices of the World Bank (1999–2000) at <www.worldbank.org/wbi/governance/about.html>.

6. According to Hellman, Jones, and Kaufmann (2000), a signature of state capture is a positive relationship between bribery and firm growth: the capturing firms pay more bribes at the expense of others' business. A negative relationship appears to hold in East Asia and in noncapture countries in general.

7. For instance, in France commissions of up to 5 percent used to be legal, and the real rates on government procurement in many countries are reputedly much higher. Audits of some projects funded under French official development assistance showed that the difference between tolerated and effective rates could be attributed to dubious contracts with third

parties and that direct payments, even when tolerated, were not an important channel of bribes. In the United States, SEC reports on violations of the Foreign Corrupt Practices Act suggest that noncompliant U.S. companies make bribe payments only indirectly, through third parties. (private communication, French Ministry of Finances; U.S. SEC).

8. Some excellent nontechnical digests are available, including Gray and Kaufmann (1998) and Tanzi (1998).

9. See Campos (2002) for an extensive treatment; see also appendix A regarding factors that explain the within-country variability of this perception.

# Chapter 3
# The Spread of Corporate Compliance Programs

After initial skepticism, companies worldwide are now adopting programs to combat corruption. This chapter examines the reasons for the growing acceptance of these compliance programs.

Today's voluntary approach to compliance was pioneered by U.S. companies in response to the scandals that led to the enactment of the 1977 Foreign Corrupt Practices Act. Refinements were pioneered by the U.S. Defense Industry Initiative in the 1980s in the wake of serious irregularities in defense procurement.[1] In the late 1990s, spurred by the OECD Anti-Bribery Convention approved in 1997, companies in other countries started to adopt U.S.-style corporate anticorruption programs, although with important modifications for local use. By then, U.S. corporations were refining the techniques.

Survey data and interviews in East Asia, Europe, and North America confirm that business codes have become a worldwide phenomenon. A Conference Board survey conducted in 2000 that requested information from member companies about their anticorruption programs found such programs in private companies operating in 42 countries, including 7 in the East Asia and Pacific region (Berenbeim 2000: 7–8).[2] Credible anticorruption systems can be found in companies in emerging economies, including India and the Philippines. A Japan Corporate Governance Forum survey of 541 Japanese companies in January 2001 found that 55 percent of the firms surveyed had a code of conduct, 43 percent periodically held ethics training programs, and 37 percent had a department or division dedicated to ethics and compliance systems. Australia's AS (Australian Standard) 3806 codifies the structural, operational, and maintenance elements necessary for an effective anticorruption compliance program: high-level commitment; statements, policies, and operating procedures; management responsibility, supervision, and resources; and record keeping and reporting.

This globalization of business conduct contrasts sharply with the concentration in Anglophone countries found in a Conference Board survey a decade earlier. Except for the systems in North American corporations, all of the programs investigated for the present study were designed and implemented in the 1990s, many of them after 1997.

Another indication of a global trend toward corporate compliance is the growth of supporting initiatives and organizations. For example, the U.S. Ethics Officer Association, created in 1992, now has more than 800 members. The European Business Ethics Network, with a more academically oriented structure, is similar in size. Hong Kong (China) created a very active Ethics Development Center in 1995. A Business Ethics Research Center (BERC) was established in Japan in 1997 with the support of major corporations. In the Republic of Korea 30 leading companies have implemented the 1999 charter of the Federation of Korean Industries.

Until recently, skepticism in non-U.S. companies regarding what was known as the U.S. compliance-based model was rooted in one or more of three widely shared assumptions:

- When operating in different cultures, businesspeople need to tolerate local customs and practices. In many countries lavish gifts and fees for the performance of certain governmental duties are practices that are deeply rooted in the national culture.
- The design of the U.S.-developed compliance model is not adaptable to non-U.S. business organizations; it is too formalized and legalistic.
- In much of the world there is a serious stigma attached to being an "informer." For this reason, outside the United States the "whistle-blowing" information systems on which effective compliance systems rely heavily will not work (Berenbeim 2000: 7–8).

Skeptics have also doubted the effectiveness of the measures taken by U.S. firms, noting that in practice these firms did not seem to be acting more ethically than others, despite their company codes of values. (The poor ranking of the United States in Transparency International's Bribe Payers Index reflects this perception; see table 2.5 in chapter 2.)

Yet company compliance systems are spreading throughout the world. The reasons include changes in the legal framework and within companies themselves.

## Legal Framework

Laws and regulations that have the effect of encouraging company ethics and compliance programs can be divided into sticks (prohibitions) and carrots (incentives). The major developments are (a) the generalization of the extraterritoriality principle and (b) legal mitigation procedures based on company systems.

## *Prohibitions and Extraterritoriality*

Bribery is illegal everywhere in the world, but surveys of international corporations suggest that the most potent antibribery measures are probably regulations in the home country that prohibit bribery in other countries. U.S. companies' pioneering compliance programs were prompted by the 1977 Foreign Corrupt Practices Act (FCPA), under which U.S. companies can be criminally prosecuted for engaging in corrupt practices outside the United States.[3]

The 1997 OECD Anti-Bribery Convention incorporates the FCPA principle that corrupt practices are illegal no matter whether inside or outside the home country.[4] Of the 35 signatories, 34, including four non-OECD countries (Argentina, Brazil, Bulgaria, and Chile), have enacted enabling legislation. Singapore, although not a party to the convention, has also implemented FCPA-type legislation.

Because they must be incorporated into preexisting legal frameworks and traditions, the national laws implementing the OECD Convention cannot be the same across countries. Nevertheless, the text of the convention provides broad principles for application in areas such as jurisdiction, prosecution, and sentencing. The fundamental principle is to put domestic and transnational bribery on the same footing.[5]

Corruption interferes with fair competition. As noted in chapter 2, the motivation behind the OECD Convention was as much to establish a level playing field for firms as it was to uphold ethical values in business. Reflecting this concern, Japan has enabled the OECD Convention by amendments to its Unfair Competition Prevention Law rather than to the criminal law.[6]

The OECD Convention has far-reaching implications. In making companies liable for the behavior of their local branches and affiliates and, to a significant degree, for the conduct of their business partners, the convention provides an incentive for companies to take wide-ranging measures against corruption. Adoption of the convention and, even more, its enabling national laws galvanized the private sector in countries that had reputedly been cool to the compliance model. The French armament industry rushed to implement huge ethics training courses, and Japanese and Korean corporations collectively moved to establish credible programs.

A key clause of the OECD Convention provides for a review mechanism. The OECD secretariat and two other signatories periodically review progress in each country. The review covers not only legal and regulatory measures but also the steps taken by governmental and nongovernmental bodies to promote good practices. As an instrument for promoting improvements and convergence among the signatory countries, the review system is likely to have a continuing effect on antibribery policies and practices, both domestically and internationally. Indeed, such bench-marking exercises (in the form of reports on observance of standards and codes), carried out on a voluntary basis with the help of international organizations, have been increasingly popular for monitoring reforms in the financial or corporate sector.

## Incentives for Developing Compliance Systems

By itself, the Foreign Corrupt Practices Act does not adequately explain U.S. companies' establishment of anticorruption programs. After all, between 1977 and 1995 the U.S. Justice Department prosecuted only 16 bribery cases under the act, and only one person has been jailed for violating it. Furthermore, international experience suggests that investigations can be complex and lengthy, especially in the context of transnational violations, and that proof can be difficult to obtain.

Arguably more important than prohibition have been the legal and regulatory incentives provided to firms based in the United States. The 1991 Organizational Sentencing Guidelines allow for a substantial mitigation (up to 95 percent) of criminal fines and penalties where it can be established that a company has an effective compliance system and thus that any unlawful activity can be regarded as the work of a rogue actor within the firm (see box 3.1).

The U.S. model combining statutory sanctions (sticks) with possibilities for mitigation (carrots) greatly influenced the provisions of the OECD Anti-Bribery Convention. The convention itself stops short of recommending mitigation of sentences for companies breaking the law, but the desirability of consistency across the signatory countries, and the OECD review mechanism, could set up pressure in this direction. In practice, the development of compliance systems in major corporations makes a mitigation process feasible and desirable even in legal traditions very different from that of the United States. In several countries legislators are already following the same dual principle of enforcement and partnership. Some examples, including that of Hong Kong's Independent Commission Against Corruption, are reviewed in chapter 6.

A key to the promotion of self-regulation by the private sector may be the principle of the criminal liability of the legal person, which means that a firm can be tried and sentenced like an individual (see box 3.2). This principle is mentioned in the OECD Convention, but it is not universal. In particular, in much of Europe prosecution still focuses on individual responsibility. CEOs have been routinely incriminated for problems occurring within their supervision, but also at levels sometimes too remote to allow a CEO to have direct knowledge of the facts. Although this potential criminal exposure is a deterrent, experience shows that

---

**Box 3.1.    Mitigation of Culpability under the U.S. Organizational Sentencing Guidelines**

The Organizational Sentencing Guidelines of 1991 consider a firm's culpability in the light of the systems the firm has in place for addressing potential and actual misconduct. Chapter 8 of the guidelines outlines seven key criteria for an "effective compliance program":

- Compliance standards and procedures reasonably capable of reducing the prospect of criminal activity
- Oversight by high-level personnel
- Due care in delegating substantial discretionary authority
- Effective communication to employees at all levels
- Reasonable steps to achieve compliance, including systems for monitoring and auditing and for reporting suspected wrongdoing
- Consistent enforcement, including disciplinary mechanisms
- Reasonable steps to respond to and prevent further similar offenses on detection of a violation.

These are broad principles, allowing companies to design compliance programs that best fit their specific needs and environments.

*Source:* U.S. Sentencing Commission.

---

**Box 3.2.    Criminal Liability of the Legal Person: A Trend toward Convergence?**

Historically, only individuals could be prosecuted and sentenced for a crime. The possibility of making organizations—"legal persons"—criminally liable was pioneered by France in 1690, with the Grande Ordonnance Criminelle—arguably, an early regulatory measure in corporate governance. The principle was scrapped during the French Revolution, but it was rediscovered in the late 20th century in the United Kingdom and the United States. Australia, Canada, and other former Crown colonies followed their example. Japan adopted the principle in the 1980s and is now considering moving toward a mitigation-of-sentencing framework. France and Germany have recently taken up the principle, but with more limited scope. The legal system in China also includes some form of criminal liability of the legal person.

*Source:* World Bank Legal Department.

prosecution is very time consuming, and in recent years it has given rise in some instances to potentially counterproductive relations between business and the judiciary. The principle of criminal liability of the legal person does not automatically exonerate individuals, but it does give benevolent management an incentive to cooperate with the judiciary, and it limits the occurrence of cases of responsible CEOs being incriminated for rogue behavior within the officer's chain of supervision.

Companies are increasingly under pressure to assume a greater share of responsibility for compliance. Using incentives to encourage companies to monitor their own behavior is potentially more cost-effective and more efficient than public enforcement relying on sanctions. The utility of this approach is especially compelling in the many countries that have limited law enforcement resources and capabilities.

## Internal Incentives

Discussions with company representatives highlight the key importance of internal incentives for the adoption of compliance systems—in particular, concern about minimizing the risks associated with the globalization of operations, preventing internal fraud, and avoiding the damage scandal could cause to company reputations. The findings also repeatedly showed the importance of personal commitment by top managers who seek to create strong corporate cultures in which the risks of corruption are minimized.

### Personal Ethical Commitment by Company Managers

Companies are more likely to cite "management leadership and personal convictions" than concern about external forces as a reason for making a serious anticorruption effort. By far the largest number of respondents to the 2000 Conference Board survey ranked "Senior management's leadership and personal convictions" as the most important factor in their companies' decision to develop anticorruption statements or programs. The belief that "bribe payments are wrong" ranked a distant second (see table 3.1). The interviews also show that the leadership's commitment to ethical values translates into a series of goals relating to social responsibility of which corporate programs addressing fraud and corruption are a core but not exclusive component.

### Managing Reputational and Operational Risks

Most companies view fraud and corruption as risks, and there is an overwhelming perception that corrupt practices can have devastating

## Table 3.1. Reasons for the Development of Anticorruption Statements or Programs

| Reason cited as most important | Percentage of responding companies |
|---|---|
| Senior management's leadership and personal convictions | 42 |
| Bribe payments are wrong. | 19 |
| Bribe payments are illegal under host-country laws. | 17 |
| Corruption significantly increases the cost of doing business. | 12 |
| Bribe payments are illegal under home-country laws. | 8 |
| Anticorruption stance is viewed favorably by actual and potential customers. | 8 |
| Anticorruption stance is viewed favorably by the kind of people we want to recruit. | 6 |
| Corruption adds significantly to the amount of time it takes to complete a project. | 4 |

Note: The results are from 146 responding companies.
Source: Conference Board survey 2000.

consequences for a company. In a recent survey by the British invest-ment firm Friends, Ivory, and Sime of 82 companies worldwide in which the firm has interests, 58 percent of the respondents acknowledged that "corruption is a material source of risk for their business."

Reputational risks are much on managers' minds. Gérard Mestrallet, president of the Executive Board of Suez, one of the companies surveyed for the present study, observed,

> In today's world of global, instantaneously transmitted news, a reputation that took years to build can be shattered in minutes. . . . I am convinced that the greatest threat to our Group is not so much a financial or a political crisis as a crisis in our image.

The introduction to the Shell Business Principles states,

> Upholding the Shell reputation is paramount. We are judged by how we act. Our reputation will be upheld if we act with honesty and integrity in all our dealings and we do what we think is right at all times within the legitimate role of business.

In the West, as well as in Japan and Korea, scandal has been the most potent catalyst for developing compliance systems. Scandals have had a more powerful effect when they have had direct repercussions in the home country, regardless of whether or not the problem involved transnational crime. Some European participants in this study referred specifically to incidents in which their company was directly involved. Japanese participants also cited scandals, not necessarily in their own companies. They said that their efforts to install compliance systems had been prompted by the need "to restore or secure corporate integrity" because of a series of corporate scandals that occurred with the bursting of the bubble economy. Fear of scandal due to increased media exposure knows no national boundaries.

Companies also perceive that extending operations into more countries heightens their exposure to the risks associated with corruption. And as large companies increasingly list themselves on more than one stock exchange, their practices come under the jurisdiction of major regulators like the U.S. Securities and Exchange Commission (see box 3.3). An increasing number of firms with top capitalization in the emerging markets of East Asia are also listed on the New York, London, Hong Kong, or Singapore stock exchanges.

---

**Box 3.3.    The Long Arm of the Securities and Exchange Commission: The SEC versus Montedison**

In 1996 the SEC alleged that Montedison, SpA, an Italian industrial conglomerate whose securities (in the form of American depositary receipts) are traded in the United States, disguised hundreds of millions of dollars in payments that, among other things, were used to bribe Italian politicians and other persons. The fraudulent conduct was revealed only after Montedison's new management disclosed that the company was unable to service its bank debt. Virtually all of the former senior managers at Montedison responsible for the fraud were convicted by Italian criminal authorities and were sued by the company.

The SEC charged Montedison with committing fraud and with violating the FCPA's provisions on books and records and on internal accounting controls. All of the alleged violations occurred outside the United States. Five years after the case was filed, and after a further change in corporate control at Montedison, the company settled with the SEC by consenting to pay a US$300,000 civil penalty. This might seem a relatively mild punishment, considering the seriousness of the offenses in Italy, but it set a major precedent.

*Source:* SEC.

---

**Box 3.4.   Geographic Diversity and Anticorruption Compliance Programs: A Practical Response to Increased Risk**

The Conference Board survey in 2000 of 134 large corporations around the world shows that companies which operate in a larger number of countries are more likely to set up specific compliance programs that deal with corruption issues. Companies operating in developing countries are also more likely to have such programs. Those results are consistent with the finding that programs are set up to address corruption proactively.

| Number of countries of operation | Percentage of companies with an explicit anticorruption program |
|---|---|
| Fewer than 10 | 40 |
| 10–24 | 53 |
| More than 25 | 76 |

*Source:* Conference Board survey, 2000.

---

Surveys of large corporations show that the higher the perceived risk, the more likely it is that the corporation has developed a comprehensive system (see box 3.4).

In some companies the push to develop a compliance program has stemmed from a change in business strategy. For example, one of the pharmaceutical companies among the study participants decided that it could use its sales and marketing expertise to substantially increase revenues in East Asia's rapidly expanding economies, relying on distributors to increase sales volume. After reviewing the sources of operational risk (see box 3.5), the company decided that it needed more control over its business practices to pursue this expansion strategy.

Some survey respondents also cited NGO pressures, particularly in Western Europe. Several mentioned shareholders' growing concern about socially responsible investing. In particular, shareholders of Japanese corporations have become increasingly active in proposing reforms of various kinds to management, backed up by legal action.

## Incentives in Large and Small Firms

The larger firms in emerging economies, including transnational corporations headquartered in East Asian emerging economies, face broadly the same incentives as do Western and Japanese firms. Reputational risk is

---

**Box 3.5. Sources of Operational Risk for a North American Pharmaceutical Company in the East Asia and Pacific Region**

The main areas of risk are:

- Clearance of incoming and outgoing shipments through customs. Delay can ruin vaccine products if they are not refrigerated.
- "Incentives" solicited by government hospitals to put products on a formulary list.
- Availability of funds for corrupt activities.
- The regulatory approval process.
- Competition for government tenders for vaccine products. Competitors gain access to the tender documents, which may include confidential and proprietary information (for example, the pricing structure).

Ways of reducing the potential for distributor misconduct include writing an ethical business practices clause into distributor contracts and keeping margins for distributors tight to lessen the amount of money available for undesirable activities.

---

more and more a concern, given a firm's needs to engage in partnerships, access capital markets and, increasingly, invest outside the region, including in the United States and Europe. Within this group of large firms, companies listed on stock exchanges probably have the strongest incentives. Not only do embarrassing incidents affect share value, but there is also increasing evidence that share value and the cost of capital reflect a company's level of transparency and internal control and, more generally, the degree of corporate governance in emerging markets (see box 3.6). Under certain conditions, the development of socially responsible investing brings rewards to listed companies with better compliance and ethics systems (see box 6.9 in chapter 6).

Incentives for good behavior are obviously weaker for smaller firms that do not operate internationally. The probability of being caught is small, and reputational risk is less worrisome. These firms are also more likely to face short-term constraints, including financial distress, that discourage attention to building compliance structures for the long term. As noted in chapter 2, smaller local firms in fact have a harder time resisting extortion—and their managers (in EAP, as elsewhere) consider corruption just as serious an obstacle to development as do international experts or managers of multinationals.

**Box 3.6.   Share Value and Transparency in Emerging Markets: The Evidence**

Whether in developed or emerging capital markets, it is widely expected that increased transparency, disclosure, and compliance at the firm level and, in general, better corporate governance will enhance the share value of a firm in relation to that of comparable firms. There is some evidence that this is true, but it is still not definitive. The connection may be difficult to assess, especially as many factors other than transparency or governance are known to have a strong influence on share value.

An increasingly popular technique is to compare a firm's performance with a comprehensive score, established with the use of a relevant scorecard. This approach was pioneered by Bernard Black (2001), who found a strong correlation between share value and transparency in some emerging markets.

Standard and Poor's has recently provided the most exhaustive scoring database to date. To avoid subjectivity, S&P uses a very strict scoring procedure that is limited to some objective features of transparency and disclosure documents and procedures (a closed, single-choice questionnaire).

To illustrate, the figure shows how the cost of capital, as measured by Tobin's $q$ (the ratio of market price plus debt to asset value), relates to the S&P transparency score for rated utility companies in East Asia and in Latin America, divided equally between regions. (The cross-country comparison makes sense, as utilities are known to be comparable worldwide; see, for example, Bubnova 2000.) According to these findings, the most transparent utilities can raise capital 40 percent more cheaply than the least transparent ones.

**Capital Cost and the S&P Transparency Score: Utilities in Emerging Markets**

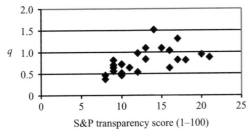

*Note:* The value $q$ is defined as (market price + debt)/asset value.
*Source:* Standard and Poor's 2001; Worldscope; and authors' calculations.

For small firms, perhaps the strongest source of incentives to combat corruption comes from their international connections as suppliers, contractors, and business partners of large operators. Foreign direct investment and contract manufacturing can serve as channels for dissemination of best practices in the area of corporate compliance, as well as in labor and environmental practices. Chapters 4 and 6 and the case studies in Part II of this volume provide examples.

## Notes

1. See <www.dii.org>. An excellent account of the interaction between procurement policy and private sector programs is given by the chief counsel of the U.S. Air Force in Shaw (1999).

2. Forty percent of the respondents to the survey had headquarters outside North America and Western Europe.

3. Under U.S. law, using the concept of the "legal person," organizations, including firms, can be found guilty of criminal conduct in the same way as individuals. A company is criminally liable for an illegal action by employees or suborganizations that is undertaken within the scope of company activities. An organization and its leaders are accountable despite their best efforts to prevent individual deviant behavior in the name of the company.

The SEC, from the very beginning, based its enforcement policy on carrots and sticks. Companies were encouraged to develop internal controls in order to be eligible for a substantial mitigation of criminal fines and penalties. A vivid firsthand account of how the initial measures were designed and implemented is Sporkin (1998).

4. The convention introduced some key principles to ensure the cross-country consistency of national enabling legislations. These include:

- The liability of the legal person—a new concept for some parties to the convention (see box 3.2).
- The principle that sanctions must be proportionate, dissuasive, and comparable to sanctions applicable to bribery at home. (As a result, the severity of punishment varies widely among the signatory countries.)
- Territoriality.

The 35 countries that are participants in the convention and that have committed themselves to transnational prohibition account for 80 percent of the imports of developing countries and transition economies. In principle, the extension of the convention to major Asian exporters (China, India, Malaysia, and Taiwan, China) will raise this proportion to 90 percent.

5. As a result, the convention is also relevant for the issue at home and may spur the introduction of important mechanisms in emerging economies that are parties to the convention.

6. The choice of the Unfair Competition Prevention Law rather than the penal code, which contains domestic antibribery provisions, may be significant. Critics have voiced concern that as a consequence, Japan might not prosecute a Japanese company for a foreign bribery offense unless the behavior results in unfair competition.

# Chapter 4
# Compliance Programs in Practice

Whether in the West or the East, company compliance programs in most countries are built on old rock (see box 4.1). Most business communities have emphasized the value of ethical business behavior since before the industrial revolution.

Today's compliance programs are rooted in statements of company values or codes of ethics, but they go well beyond this. To identify general lessons on what makes for an effective program, this chapter reviews current practice, drawing on company interviews and survey data. The case studies in part II give specific examples.

## Building a Culture of Compliance

Most companies take the view that an effective anticorruption effort is best achieved by institutionalizing a culture of compliance within the firm, backed up by systems designed to reduce the prospect of criminal activity within the company and detect such activity where it exists. Systems and procedures alone will not ensure compliance; Enron had a code of ethics and no shortage of whistle-blowers, but its managers and directors circumvented the code in the most blatant fashion. Of more importance are employees' attitudes and their loyalty to company values.[1] For example, in June 2001 President Oka of Sumitomo sent a New President's message to all employees stating his vision for a global company "whose *Corporate Vision, Management Principles,* and *Activity Guidelines* reach across all the barriers of culture and language to be shared as common values by all employees across the globe, each of whom implements them with confidence and pride."

In building such a culture of compliance, the challenge for international companies is to formulate core principles and implement credible procedures that will succeed in all the business cultures in which the firms operate.[2] Companies also recognize that compliance systems and procedures themselves are most effective in environments of trust where employees feel free to ask questions and, if need be, report possible

---

**Box 4.1. "The Business Principles of Sumitomo," 1891**

Masatomo Sumitomo, who created his company in the early 17th century, left behind a set of family precepts that draws together rules for merchants. A formal document embodying the founder's values, "The Business Principles of Sumitomo," was first compiled in 1891. It states:

1. Sumitomo shall place prime importance on integrity and sound management in the conduct of its business.
2. Sumitomo shall manage its activities with foresight and flexibility in order to cope effectively with the changing times.
3. Under no circumstances, however, shall Sumitomo pursue easy gains or act imprudently to manage its activities as described above.

---

improprieties. A community that is committed to a common set of purposes and values is one in which there is likely to be the highest level of trust.

Philippe de Margerie, general counsel of the Suez Group, has noted,

> Becoming worldwide in scope means becoming multicultural, which in turn means learning and growing from other cultures, and seeking new management modes. . . . Ethical values are precisely where men and women come together, whatever their national backgrounds or other differences. The mutual understanding that comes from shared values is essential to *confidence,* which is at the heart of any business relationship.

## Components of an Effective Program

Companies typically believe that a successful anticorruption effort has four elements (figure 4.1):

- The active engagement of company leadership
- A code of company values and employee conduct, which in turn shapes a set of detailed and consistent statements of policies and operating procedures
- A delivery mechanism to ensure that all employees are familiar with the company's code and ethics expectations
- Warning systems that apply to the supervision and commitment of resources and reporting, and whistle-blowing arrangements.

Each of these is discussed in turn in this section.

## Figure 4.1. Building a Compliance Culture

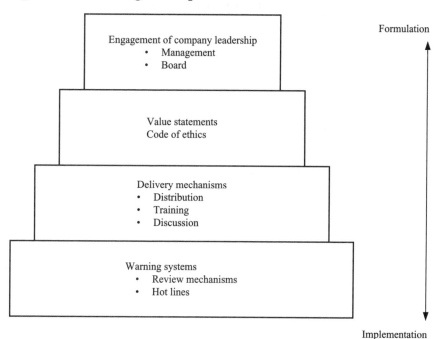

Formulation

Engagement of company leadership
- Management
- Board

Value statements
Code of ethics

Delivery mechanisms
- Distribution
- Training
- Discussion

Warning systems
- Review mechanisms
- Hot lines

Implementation

## *Active Engagement of Company Leadership*

Since the late 1980s, in all regions, Conference Board surveys have documented a steady increase in the involvement of board members and senior executives in the formulation and delivery of ethics programs. For example, the surveys found that only 21 percent of the company boards were involved with ethics programs in 1987 but that by 1999, 78 percent were playing such a role.

Significant involvement by company legal departments, too, is now the rule rather than the exception, reflecting the growing importance of corporate ethics codes as legal documents. General counsels' involvement increased from 41 percent in the 1987 Conference Board survey to 92 percent in 1999. General counsels are playing an important role in company ethics programs even in Japan, where companies used to take pride in their limited deployment of lawyers, particularly in issues involving employee behavior and management control.

Where a company has the kind of focused effort that it is willing to describe as a "program," significant participation by the board and senior managers is especially prevalent (see figure 4.2).

## Figure 4.2.  Share of Senior Management "Heavily" or "Somewhat" Involved in Company Anticorruption Efforts

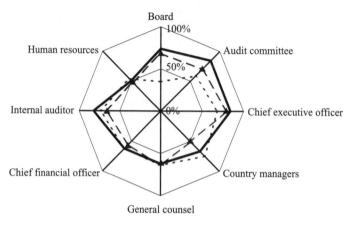

*Source:* Conference Board survey, 2000.

Senior executive engagement in company programs in East Asia is similar to that in North American and European organizations. For example, Hong Kong–based Jardine Matheson's general counsel submitted the draft company code first to the company's board and then to the chief executive officers (CEOs) and chief financial officers (CFOs) of all of the group's major businesses.

## *Values Statements*

A values statement or code of conduct is the foundation for a company anticorruption program. Such a statement provides general guidance for decisionmaking that is in accord with the company's values and beliefs. Increasingly, large companies, particularly those that do business outside their home countries, have adopted values statements regardless of the firm's country or culture of origin.

*Inclusive processes.* Participants in this study say the best way to develop a statement that avoids home-country cultural bias is to involve employees from all regions in the formulation process. Companies are casting an increasingly wide net in an effort to formulate codes that take on-the-ground experience into account—and, in so doing, win the necessary support of local managers. Using inclusive processes that draw on the collective intelligence and experience of company personnel is also the best approach for addressing the company's risk management needs. The firms that take this approach seek comments from all the regions in which they do business. Employees in most, if not all, businesses and job categories participate in surveys, focus group meetings, and discussions to formulate and design the values statements, delivery mechanisms, and warning systems.[3]

Merck engaged in one of the most detailed and thorough formulation exercises. As part of its most recent code-drafting process, the company surveyed a random sample of 10,000 employees (22 percent of its workforce). The East Asian survey response rate of nearly 100 percent was the highest of any region—considerably higher than the overall return of 40 percent. A U.S. pharmaceutical company conducted focus groups in China, Hong Kong (China), the Philippines, and Taiwan (China), using local languages. The focus groups accepted company standards regarding clear instances of bribery, but they expressed concern that the company took an excessively narrow "North American" approach to gifts and entertainment—one that could put them at a competitive disadvantage vis-à-vis other multinational companies. They also wanted better and more consistent training, with a focus on the needs of the region. They had only a limited interest in general anticorruption initiatives in their countries or the region, but they did want to discuss the specific problems that they could and should anticipate, and how to deal with them.

Taking a somewhat different approach, the executive management team of a health care firm designated a committee of its international senior executives and charged the group with identifying the company's core values worldwide. The company then established an Office of Business Practice to provide an infrastructure for implementation and review. The participation of local managers in creating the values statement is seen as essential to program success because it is they who are in the best position to:

- Serve as role models for the company's values and standards
- Promote responsible business practices by employees and agents
- Create an atmosphere in which employees feel comfortable talking openly about business practices
- Respond to employee concerns about retaliation for whistle-blowing.

Most of the East Asia and Pacific companies surveyed have drawn on employee opinions to develop experience-based values statements, policies, and training programs. For example, LG Electronics, a Korean firm, formed a committee that included the CEO and seven business managers.

---

**Box 4.2. When and Why to Retain Consultants**

Participating companies that have used consultants cited the following reasons for doing so:

- To enable the program to develop a truly global orientation
- To implement a large-scale program more effectively
- To obtain more candid employee feedback on specific regional issues
- To utilize the consultants' language services
- To run a confidential 24/7 communications center for a global warning system.

---

This body is served at the working level by the Internal Audit department. Shinsege, a Korean department store company, showed the first draft of its code to all employees above middle-manager level and revised the code on the basis of the comments received. In Japan NEC has surveyed all of its officers on issues of compliance with targeted laws. As part of an effort to develop a comprehensive antibribery program, the Omron Corporation, also headquartered in Japan, is planning a survey to obtain better information on the conditions that give rise to corruption.

Language makes a difference to comprehension and acceptance. As a result of its survey and focus group discussions, the U.S. pharmaceutical company mentioned above decided to expunge "Americanisms" from the text of its code. A North American communications company found that by avoiding legal jargon, it could communicate its broad values in a way that would gain greater international acceptance. Most companies now issue their codes in all languages (and variants) spoken by their employees.

Consultants are not widely used in the formulation, implementation, and monitoring of ethics and anticorruption programs. Recourse to outside consultants, which was virtually nonexistent (2 percent of responding firms) in the initial, heavily U.S.-based Conference Board survey in 1987, rose to only 15 percent in the more global 1998 survey (see box 4.2).

## Delivery Mechanisms

Consistent with the view that every employee's conduct exposes the company to risk, most companies now require all employees to be familiar with company codes, to participate in discussing practical application of the codes, and to follow the codes in practice. Statements of company values and codes of conduct tend to be very widely, if not universally, distributed to employees.

## Figure 4.3. Distribution of Anticorruption Statements by Companies with Active Compliance Programs

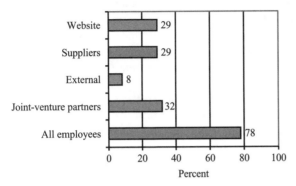

*Source:* Conference Board survey, 2000.

Statements regarding company anticorruption policies are less widely distributed than company codes of conduct. While companies that say they have an anticorruption program are likely to give a copy of the statement to all employees (78 percent do), the practice is not universal. As the Asian compliance manager for the ABB Group put it, "there is no use giving everyone the same message." He drew a distinction between four kinds of employees: senior managers; sales employees who physically meet with customers; white-collar workers (e.g., clerical); and blue-collar (factory) workers.

A growing number of companies now distribute their anticorruption statements to joint-venture partners, governments, vendors, and suppliers. More than a fourth of the companies with active programs that were surveyed post their statements on their public Websites (see figure 4.3).

Some of the participating companies periodically obtain signed disclosure statements from employees. The effectiveness of this kind of certification process as a deterrent to corruption has been questioned (*Economist* 2002). Certification and reporting systems do, however, serve three potentially useful purposes by:

- Emphasizing to employees the importance of their adherence to the company's business conduct standards
- Providing grounds for immediate dismissal if the employee does not disclose violations in which he or she engaged
- Enabling the company to collect intelligence on the business practices issues that it confronts.

Several companies assess their employees' adherence to company values as an integral part of annual performance evaluations. At Sumitomo, for example, the SC Values evaluation applies to all employees, from the rank and file to department heads, and accounts for 20 percent of an employee's total performance evaluation. Because the results of the evaluation affect awards, pay raises, and promotions, employees take it seriously. This appears to be an extremely effective system for inculcating the ethical values of the company.

*Discussion and training sessions.* Discussion and training sessions for staff are increasingly common. For example, 51 percent of the Conference Board survey respondents that have anticorruption programs, but only 17 percent of companies without such programs, complement code distribution with discussion of the anticorruption policy and the administrative structures and procedures that support the policy.

In many companies with active programs, discussions are held only for certain employee groups. In fewer than half (44 percent) of these companies do training and discussion sessions cover all employees, and in only about one-fifth are vendors, suppliers, and joint-venture partners included (figure 4.4).

The Japanese companies surveyed have structures for conducting thorough training programs on business ethics in general, including prevention of bribery, and they stress the importance of general business

## Figure 4.4. Discussion and Training Sessions for Employees: Companies with and without Compliance Programs

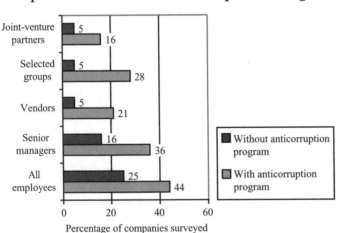

*Source:* Conference Board survey, 2000.

ethics training, rather than training that focuses on prevention of bribery of foreign public officials or on specific laws, ordinances, and rules. Matsushita's approach is typical. The company has no high-profile activities specifically on combating bribery of foreign public officials, but it enjoys a high rating for the management philosophy it has enshrined since its establishment and for its internal education programs, which are designed to apply the philosophy in practice in a thoroughgoing way. Company spokesmen believe that the philosophy is extremely useful in setting and maintaining high business conduct standards for employees.

The Japanese company senior executives who were interviewed for this study stressed the importance of targeting all employees for education and training, citing the prevailing view that all employees are important members of the company and that in important respects even senior managers are no different from other employees.

The Japanese approach to training also acknowledges the key role that senior managers play in limiting the company's exposure to the risk of corruption. Antibribery training is a customary part of each executive's training before taking up a foreign assignment. At present, Japanese nationals usually head the company's foreign offices, but spokesmen from the participating Japanese companies acknowledge that they will need to develop training modules that match the needs of the increasing numbers of local people whom they expect to assume leadership positions in the local headquarters of "overseas group companies."

Companies often prefer to use senior corporate executives to get their local managers up to speed on anticorruption and ethics issues. For example, the ABB compliance director for Asia has a "road show" in which he "trains the trainers."

At a health care firm, in response to criticism from Asian employees that the video vignettes used in discussion sessions were "too American," the Office of Business Practices devised a program tailored to the special requirements of the region, on the basis of recommendations from an Asian training and development committee. The company's business practices officer believes that for training to be effective, there is no alternative to serious, face-to-face discussions of the business conduct issues that the region's employees confront:

> From the beginning, I felt strongly that the best way to train people on responsible business practice is through face-to-face discussions. A lecture style is out of the question. Training needs to be as interactive as possible. In teaching employees how to respond to difficult workplace situations, substantial role playing is beneficial.

*Use of case studies.* Use of case studies, either in training sessions or in written materials that draw on company experience, appears to be less common in Asia than, for example, in the United States. Worldwide, the Conference Board survey found that 22 percent of the program companies use case studies. Two approaches were found: one features a single issue and a brief discussion; the other uses a more complex narrative that covers many issues and does not necessarily include a written "answer."

Korea's LG Electronics is one of the companies that use case study discussions. Its written materials include cartoon depictions of policy issues—not an uncommon practice in Asia. Shell also uses cartoon "lessons" in its Chinese companies.

The health care firm mentioned earlier deemed it important to include some scenario questions designed to be outside the "average" employee's competence. As the business practices officer explained,

> We want employees to feel empowered to make the right decision but we also want them to understand that there are situations where they don't know the best choice. In those cases, the question is, "Do I know where to go for help?"

## Warning Systems

*Hotlines.* Of the typical components of ethics systems, warning systems or hotlines attract the most stubborn cultural resistance when they are introduced. But research and company experience affirm that successful warning systems are at work in most regions and industries and that vague generalizations about the unwillingness of people in certain cultures to use these systems because they might be regarded as "informers" are vastly overstated.

Indeed, the goal of a hotline system is to avoid the need for anyone to "inform." Successful hotline information systems encourage employees to ask questions about sensitive issues and problems before their mishandling can result in a possible informer situation. A list of purposes cited for hotline systems suggests that encouraging informer situations is not the major goal. The hotline is intended to:

- Offer guidance on or interpret the company's policies and standards
- Gather additional information from other resources on behalf of an employee
- Initiate or conduct a business practices inquiry
- Resolve a business practices issue
- Ensure employee confidentiality
- Protect an employee from retaliation.

**Table 4.1. East Asia and Pacific Hotline Calls in a North American Company**

| Topic | Percentage of calls, 2000 |
|---|---|
| Conflict of interest | 45 |
| Gifts and entertainment | 20 |
| Bribery and facilitation payments | 15 |
| Competitive information | 10 |
| Company assets | 5 |
| Harassment | 3 |
| Employee disputes | 2 |

Culture-based resistance appears to be less common in East Asia than in Europe. For example, a Shanghai-based country manager for a European company said, "We have a reasonable utilization of our whistle-blowing system in China. The volume of complaints may not be as high as in the United States, but we do get them. And roughly 40 percent of the informants identify themselves." A North American telecommunications company finds that its East Asian employees are no more and no less resistant to hotline use than workers in any other region. In 2000 the company received approximately 2,000 calls, and 20 percent of them were from the East Asia region (table 4.1).

Of 10 Korean companies with ethics codes, 8 had detailed support processes, including hotline reporting systems and specific ethics policies or regulations. Even among Japanese companies, which feared that hotlines would undermine good labor-management relations, all six participants in the present study have instituted some form of hotline and acknowledge that hotlines are an important part of an effective compliance system. Perhaps because of their short history, these contact points "have not necessarily been used to a great extent" (personal communication by one of the companies surveyed).

Resistance to whistle-blowing systems may be rooted more in the company's own culture than in that of the country in which it is doing business. Where there is an environment of trust and it is understood that the reporting system is a source of advice as much as it is a vehicle for reporting improprieties, the system is likely to be used more and to function for its intended purpose—as an early warning system and a method of preventing, rather than detecting, abuse.

Companies with effective systems report that hotlines or help lines evolve over time, from an initial stage in which employees call in with every kind of complaint, to a stage in which legitimate irregularities are discovered, to the final stage, in which callers seek advice and, in obtaining it, are effectively counseled on how to avoid bad decisions.

Successful warning systems need good logistics, as well as cultural sensitivity. At present, most companies have found it best to provide employees with a list of people with whom they can discuss their concerns and to make certain that they have the necessary contact numbers for doing so. Depending on the situation, possible alternatives include any or all of the following:

- The employee's direct manager
- A functional resource person (human resources, finance, and so on)
- A regional business practice panel or compliance officer
- The corporate global business conduct office
- An external security consultant that maintains a global hotline.

*Other safeguards.* To identify corruption risk factors, one of the companies surveyed for this study divided its bidding process into three phases of review and analysis of cost margins (table 4.2). Through these bid reviews, the company identified facilitation and other unauthorized payments. It found that increased costs could often be attributed to third-party agents and representatives. To reduce its exposure to risk, the company now requires all agents and representatives to certify that they have read and will adhere to the company's code of business practice. Facilitation payments must be recorded, and agents and representatives must report any improper requests. Even so, a company spokesman admits that bribes are still difficult to detect and that there is a limit to the deterrence effect that company policy can achieve: "When people are

**Table 4.2.  Bid Review Process for a North American Company**

| Action | Questions |
|---|---|
| *Phase 1* | |
| Assess initial scope of contract | What are we proposing to do for the customer? |
| | What are the costs (labor, parts, etc.)? |
| *Phase 2* | |
| Examine margins of each cost item | Is the cost of any item flexible? Why is it flexible? |
| | Obtain firmer figures. |
| *Phase 3* | |
| Look for margin erosion | Have initial costs changed? |
| | Which costs have increased/decreased? Why? |
| | Have any of these costs been incurred by a third party (e.g., agent, supplier)? |

committed to doing unscrupulous things, they will find the means and the way. We try to make it as difficult as possible for them to succeed."

Some of the senior executives interviewed say that the best way to control unauthorized payments is to keep extremely tight project and service budgets. Where budgets are tight, unauthorized payments directly reduce profit margins. In a competitive environment, lean budgets are necessary in any event—but by themselves, they may not be enough to enable a company to curb smaller unauthorized payments, whether bribes or facilitating payments.

## Implementation Issues

In the East Asia and Pacific region, employee questions on ethics mainly center on facilitation payments and on how to distinguish them from bribes. Entertainment and gifts also raise complex questions.

### Facilitation Payments, or Bribes?

Facilitation payments are illegal in most East Asian countries, but the prohibitions are rarely enforced, and companies do make such payments. The U.S. FCPA permits these payments where they are not prohibited by local law.[4]

Employees can find it extremely confusing when their companies engage in facilitation payments (see boxes 4.3 and 4.4). The director of the Office of Security and Auditing of one company reported,

> Workshop participants asked me if the following action would be appropriate: "We have completed a government contract and have received 60 percent of what the government owes us. The balance of 40 percent is three months overdue. A small cash payment to a specific official could expedite payment of the balance. Should we make the payment?" Employees unanimously agreed that this was an acceptable example of a facilitation payment. They were surprised when I told them that if they made such a payment, they would be bribing a public official.

Many local representatives of companies taking part in the study believe that maintaining the distinction between facilitation payments and bribes has helped perpetuate the cycle of corruption.

### Entertainment and Gifts

Study participants say that issues frequently arise concerning the entertainment of government clients. East Asian officials often have limited travel

---

**Box 4.3.    Frequently Asked Questions at a North American Company: Facilitation Payments versus Bribes**

Q.: *I do not understand the difference between a facilitation payment and a bribe.*
A.: A facilitation payment is a modest payment that is offered to a government official or employee for the sole purpose of expediting a routine action to which the company has a right. A bribe is a payment intended to influence the decision or action of a government official to benefit an individual or entity. There are many legal issues surrounding facilitation payments and bribes, and no standard or policy can cover every eventuality. You should speak with your manager or the legal department to obtain additional clarification.

Q.: *Bribes are a standard part of doing business in my location. What's more, they can help us improve our market share. So why can't we offer them like our competitors do?*
A.: The company believes that offering bribes contributes to the problems of corruption that countries face. Corruption pollutes the political process, stifles the prosperity of individuals and businesses, and negatively impacts our quality of life. The business that we would obtain in the short term by offering bribes to obtain business is not worth the pervasive effects of corruption on our communities. We strongly believe that those companies who do offer bribes in exchange for business will, in the end, bring about their own demise.

---

**Box 4.4.    Bribery: What Is an "Easy" Question?**

At a company training session in Asia, the business practices officer decided to make the first question "easy":

"A government official asks for $5,000 before a decision can be made regarding our business. Do you pay him?"
    "We gave participants a range of choices including 'don't pay the money,' 'go talk to your manager,' and 'pay the money and get a receipt.' We considered this to be a straightforward bribery question, and the management committee thought that the question was ridiculously easy. During the Asian training sessions, the groups deliberated for 30 minutes before giving an answer. No group responded 'don't make the payment.' Every group picked another alternative: 'speak with your manager,' 'pay and get a receipt,' etc."

---

**Box 4.5.  A Common Issue: Reimbursement for Customer Entertainment**

An employee asked the SGS ethics office the following question:

*Q.: We have invited and provided business-class air transportation and accommodations to a local government official so he could visit one of our branches abroad. When he arrived there, his wife was with him. He explained that he had exchanged the business-class ticket for two economy-class tickets so his wife could accompany him. He expects the company to bear his wife's additional expenses during the trip. What should we do?*

A.: The Code of Ethics clearly states in answer to the question "Is it appropriate to organize technical trips, seminars, or visits to SGS operations for public officials?" that "family members may only be invited at the cost of the participants." . . . It would therefore be the local government official's responsibility to pay for his wife's expenses for this visitation of an SGS facility. You should explain to the official that if the company were to pay for his wife's expenses, this could appear improper to the public—both on the part of SGS and on the part of the government official. With regard to the exchange of the business-class ticket, there is little that the company can do now to rectify the situation. In the future, however, you will want to ensure that we issue tickets that can only be altered with the company's advance knowledge and approval.

---

budgets, and as part of the sales process, some companies have found it necessary to bring groups of Asian government agents to offices in North America. It is not uncommon for these potential clients to use a company's customer reimbursement policy to subsidize or pay for a family vacation (box 4.5).

In some cases, very little of the "entertainment" is related to business activity. A product demonstration may take a half a day, and the rest of a not atypical two-week itinerary in the United States might include trips to Las Vegas or Orlando. Providing the guests with spending money (in one case, US$1,000) is also not uncommon. Although arguably permissible under the FCPA, such courtesies to officials may undermine the reputation of a company's anticorruption program.

## Application to Business Partners

The behavior of business partners is becoming a central issue for the compliance systems of large corporations. In practice, it may not be easy for an individual company to assess on its own the integrity of its partners or to impose sophisticated compliance requirements. This is especially true in joint ventures where the local partner owns a controlling share. Asian corporations operating in other East Asian countries say they feel rather vulnerable to the ethical lapses of their partners.

## Suppliers and Joint-Venture Partners

A significant number of companies with corporate compliance policies and programs have statements regarding supplier (33 percent) or joint-venture partner (16 percent) adherence to these policies and programs. Among these companies is Ondeo Services, the water services management company of the Suez Group, which explains that it "seeks to avoid having the selection of an inappropriate partner lead to behavior contrary to its policy or its ethical values, thereby compromising its reputation and future." Suez applies its Ethics Charter to its own directly controlled subsidiaries, as well as to their subsidiaries and affiliates. Representatives strongly encourage the companies in which they have minority interests to adopt the tenets contained in the Ethics Charter in drafting their own rules of conduct.

In the case of suppliers, Asian trading companies act as agents for customers (for example, clothing manufacturers) who are increasingly concerned about "ethical sourcing." The trading companies, in effect, have a standard contract clause with their customers to monitor supplier compliance with a customer's code of practice for ethical sourcing. Thus, supplier adherence to anticorruption policies is in some instances part of the trading company's monitoring requirements under its contract with its own customers.

Li & Fung, a Hong Kong trading company that participated in this study, conducts training programs in all of its sourcing companies. Although suppliers are not required to participate, the Li & Fung representative noted that a high percentage of them do so: "Indeed, they appreciate training because they will lose business if they fail to comply."

In general, suppliers are more likely than joint-venture partners to be formally bound by company anticorruption policies and to participate in the company's discussion and training programs. But the governance and business structures in East Asia are such that even though the company may not exercise the formal command and control that makes a supplier or joint-venture partner subject to its anticorruption policies, the supplier or joint-venture partner may be accountable de facto for adhering to company policy.

In East Asia management of the enterprise, not majority share ownership, is often the key to exercising compliance oversight. The key question, as James Watkins, general counsel of Jardine Matheson notes, is, "Do you manage the business for the shareholders?" Indeed, it is not uncommon (particularly in capital-intensive oil or water projects in China) for the enterprise to be managed by a company with a minority interest.

Royal Dutch/Shell, for example, has operational control of 19 of its 20 Chinese joint ventures. The Nanhai joint venture, which can be considered a model, has included the Shell Business Principles as part of its articles of association, and Shell has preserved audit rights as a matter of contract. The internal audit program looks at all business processes, including the implementation of the Business Principles.

Besides management of the enterprise, East Asian country managers described other ways of obtaining compliance with the company's business principles. A country manager in the Philippines said that a non-managing minority shareholder company can still exert sufficient control through periodic communication and audits and, perhaps most important, the choice of an external auditor who is acceptable to the parent company.

A local manager conversant with the business practices of Chinese municipal governments took a pragmatic approach, saying that small projects are the best strategy for avoiding corruption. He advised limiting investments to US$15 million–US$25 million, so that a large bribe would not be reasonable; a "nice restaurant" would be the limit.

## Intermediaries

Payments to intermediaries are known to be the principal vector of corruption, especially in the context of international operations (see chapter 2). In many countries a company faces daunting challenges in controlling or simply putting pressure on its partners.

Safeguard procedures vary among companies, but typically they seek to:

- Assess the intermediary
- Have the intermediary commit to an ethical pledge
- Check the adequacy of the remuneration for the actual service provided (especially for agents).

## Recent Initiatives

There is a growing perception that more comprehensive mechanisms are needed to promote awareness and behavioral change among business partners. With this in mind, recent initiatives or proposals include:

- Cooperation between international firms operating in the same industry to exchange information on suppliers (as has been tried in the oil industry).

---

**Box 4.6.   The TRACE Initiative**

Transparent Agent and Contracting Entities (TRACE) is an international nonprofit organization that gives agents, suppliers, and subcontractors the opportunity to commit to anticorruption programs and to submit, on a voluntary basis, to a review of their compliance. Its members are large corporations based in Asia, Europe, and North America that are willing to address supply-chain and third-party issues.

TRACE was created by a few private sector executives who met in Prague in October 2001 during the International Anti-Corruption Conference organized by Transparency International. Part of the impetus came from the realization that many intermediaries have little awareness of international ethics standards and of what they may and may not do when acting under contract.

Within a few months, a truly international network was organized, with a strong focus on East Asia and Pacific and on the Middle East. The services that TRACE provides include training sessions for intermediaries and agents (notably in Korea, where corporations are involved in the program through the Federation of Korean Industries), voluntary review, and independent evaluation of participating intermediaries.

*Source:* TRACE International.

---

- Increased transparency in bidding and contractual documents. For instance, some corporations have proposed that the names of agents and suppliers be disclosed in international bidding documents.

Large companies with strong programs are increasingly involved in dissemination activities targeting their partners and others and helping to reduce their vulnerability (box 4.6).

## Are Compliance Programs Working?

Companies say that they expect their compliance programs to reduce fraudulent practices both inside and outside the company. The crucial questions are:

- Do the programs reduce corruption within the firm?
- Do the programs reduce corruption appreciably in the countries where the firms do business?

Unfortunately, these questions, which are discussed in turn below, are difficult or impossible to answer, given the present state of knowledge. The programs are relatively new, and no independent assessment of their effectiveness is available, so observations must be based on anecdotal evidence and common sense. Companies have data gained from tracking their implementation of programs, but they typically do not have quantitative indicators of program effectiveness. One company has been trying to create a series of indicators of compliance, using statistics on reported incidents, but with difficulties and limitations.

In the future, the credibility and sustainability of programs could be greatly enhanced through monitoring and evaluation using generally agreed techniques.

## Do the Programs Reduce Corruption within the Firm?

A major goal of company compliance programs, as reported in chapter 4, is to reduce the risk of malpractice and fraud by employees. How effective have these initiatives been?

*Implementation.* Most of the companies featured in this study point to measures of their success in implementing their programs. Toyota Motor Corporation, for example, surveys its employees to assess their familiarity with the company's Guiding Principles and Code of Conduct, allowing the company to evaluate the success of ethics communications and training. In April 1999, 15 months after the code was introduced, 91 percent of the respondents were found to have a good or improved understanding of the code; the average score had risen to 3.6 (out of 5) from 3.0 six months earlier. Companies also cite the sometimes huge participation rates of employees in developing company codes of ethics and in related training programs, and the incorporation of compliance standards into employees' performance evaluations.

*Effect on corruption.* The companies interviewed say they have no doubt that their programs are succeeding in reducing the incidence of corruption. Local managers of international corporations frequently state that referring to the company code of conduct empowers them to resist extortion. Shell cites figures for 2000, when 106 contracts were terminated and two joint ventures were divested for incompatibility with Shell's Business Principles. Four incidents of bribery were also identified in 2000, resulting in seven dismissals.

*Effect on the firm.* The genuine commitment to integrity by an increasing number of managers and boards is having effects in the field. Companies increasingly acknowledge that their strict stand on corruption may lose them business, but they are prepared to accept this short-term risk.

---

**Box 4.7.   Third-Party Liability and Corrective Action in SEC Enforcement: An Example from Indonesia**

On September 12, 2001, the U.S. Securities and Exchange Commission (SEC) announced the filing of actions related to the alleged payment by employees of Baker Hughes Inc., for the purpose of influencing an Indonesian tax official. The SEC alleged that the chief financial officer and controller of Baker Hughes made a payment of US$75,000 to its Indonesian accounting firm, with knowledge that the payment was intended for an Indonesian tax official who was reviewing a Baker Hughes tax assessment. The entire payment was inaccurately recorded in the company's books, records, and accounts as a payment for professional services.

The SEC, in a cease and desist order, found that Baker Hughes had violated provisions on books and records and on internal accounting controls. This relatively mild finding apparently took into account the fact that Baker Hughes had uncovered the illicit payment, had taken strong corrective action, had reported the incident to the SEC staff, and had cooperated fully with the staff's investigation.

The SEC also filed the first-ever joint civil action against KPMG Siddharta Siddharta & Harsono and against a local partner at that firm for participating in the alleged bribery scheme. The SEC is litigating charges against two former Baker Hughes officials.

*Source:* SEC.

---

The existence of compliance programs can help reduce the severity of penalties when corruption does come to light. The history of enforcement by the SEC shows that litigation settlements do indeed take account of the quality of compliance arrangements in companies charged with wrongdoing (box 4.7).

## What Effect Do the Programs Have in the Countries in Which Firms Operate?

It is too early to judge whether the programs noticeably reduce corruption in the countries where the firms do business. As regards large-scale corruption, a firm's compliance program can set a powerful example for others. For instance, Jardine Matheson of Hong Kong imposes strict ethical requirements on its suppliers, as does the trading company Li &

Fung. Merck's Korean branch has been instrumental in promoting a code for that country's pharmaceutical industry. Similarly, foreign investors in China tell an encouraging story. Their ventures have in many instances taken over or replaced the operations of state-owned enterprises (SOEs). Customarily, most SOEs did not pay taxes and used other channels to make financial or in-kind contributions to local governments—not always transparently, and often with some degree of corruption. The joint ventures have brought in new managers and fresh practices—including payment of taxes—that have put the private-public relationship on a more transparent footing. Companies say they have overcome initial resistance by appealing to higher levels of government.

The companies interviewed cited examples of lost business due to the enforcement of their codes of conduct. There is, however, a definite belief among them that their stand is beneficial in the long term. One consideration is that corrupt deals are increasingly likely to be voided by new, less corrupt governments (see the section on NATCOM in part II).

Common sense and the anecdotal evidence thus far suggest that corporate programs have good potential for leveraging improvements in supplier and partner firms and that resources, public and private, should be committed to help maximize the effects of these programs beyond the firms that introduce them (see chapter 6).

## Notes

1. At Toyota Motor Corporation, for example, respect for teamwork and spontaneous individual commitment are central to the "Toyota Way." Reflecting these values, the company's Code of Conduct is stated not in terms of "must not do" but "should/should not do," to enhance each employee's sense of spontaneous commitment.

2. In particular, in industries such as extraction, or where substantial local share ownership and even control may be typical or required (as in China), the need to formulate values and adapt processes in accordance with local custom is a necessary part of the give-and-take of the governance process.

3. Turnover is another reason why periodic review of East Asian employee attitudes, through focus and discussion groups and hotlines, can be a critical element in program success. As one company's experience shows, turnover can vary considerably within countries and occupational groups. Turnover figures cited by a Western operator are as follows: China, 13 percent; Korea, 7 percent; Taiwan (China), 9 percent; and

Thailand, 23 percent. (The reason for the larger figure for Thailand is that a group of employees was hired by a competitor.)

4. The restriction in the second half of this phrase is seldom stated with the same emphasis as the permission in the first part.

East Asian managers and employees are not the only people who have difficulty distinguishing between a facilitation payment and a bribe: "Britain's Department of Trade and Industry concedes that there is no clear definition of a facilitation payment or of precisely how it differs from a bribe" (*Economist* 2002: 63).

# Chapter 5
# The Environment for Compliance Programs

Both the design of compliance programs and expectations for their success need to take account of the environment in which companies are working. This chapter looks at three key features of the environment: the adequacy of internal control practices and standards in the area of accounting and auditing; the prevailing standards of corporate governance; and the business culture, which in East Asia is influenced by the traditional practice of guanxi.

## Proper Internal Controls

Ethics and compliance systems are part of a larger set of internal control systems. Internal controls and compliance directly support anticorruption efforts. The link is straightforward because corrupt transactions cannot be accounted for under their real purpose and must be disguised through some form of inappropriate or creative accounting. Proper accounting and auditing (both internal and external) obviously make fraudulent and corrupt practices more difficult and, when they occur, easier to detect.

The OECD Anti-Bribery Convention of 1997 makes extensive references to the importance of proper financial controls to counter bribery. Article 8 requires that a party to the convention take steps "within the framework of its laws and regulations regarding the maintenance of books and records, financial statement disclosures, and accounting and auditing standards, to prohibit the establishment of off-the-books accounts, the making of off-the-books or inadequately identified transactions, . . . for the purpose of bribing foreign public officials or of hiding such bribery." It also requires "effective, proportionate and dissuasive civil, administrative or criminal penalties for such omissions and falsification."

The recent wave of corporate scandals hints that developed economies are by no means immune to the corruption problem, and it underscores the paramount role of the control environment. Greed and unethical

---

**Box 5.1. Enron: A Syllabus of Errors**

The Enron scandal may be the most compelling business ethics failure in a generation. The bankruptcy case that broke in late 2001 is still under investigation, but the scandal has triggered a major reassessment of corporate governance and accounting-related regulations.

Most of the public debate focused on the quality of disclosure and the role of accountants and Wall Street analysts. Although a number of facts have yet to be determined in court, it is acknowledged that misleading financial statements had to be amended when the facts could no longer be hidden. Particularly shocking on ethical grounds was the fact that high-level executives were selling their Enron stock while sending reassuring e-mail messages to employees whose retirement plans relied 60 percent on company stock.

Misguided corporate social responsibility and corporate gift-giving policies resulted in so many beneficiaries of Enron's generosity that it was difficult to find directors who were free from the appearance of conflict of interest. For instance, William C. Powers, dean of the University of Texas Law School, which received US$252,000 in donations, was chair of a special committee to examine transactions between Enron and its partnerships—transactions that were at the core of Enron's problems. Unfortunately, such potential conflicts may not be unusual.

Company officers did not adhere to Enron's code of ethics. Twice, the Enron board "waived" the company's ethics code requirements to allow the chief financial officer to serve as general partner for the partnerships that ENRON was using as a conduit for much of its business. Rather than sell their stock on the market, some managers tendered their shares to the company. In so doing, they deferred considerably the date on which the sale would have been disclosed.

*Source:* Berenbeim 2002.

---

behavior appear to be at the root of the scandals. But it was the collapse of the control environment, including the compliance system, that made possible the development of conflict of interest and of ultimately self-dealing and improper transactions (box 5.1).

The U.S. Sarbanes-Oxley Act of 2002, which was enacted in response to the series of corporate failures, underscores the importance of tools such as codes of ethics and financial control frameworks. The SEC comments refer explicitly to the scheme control framework developed by the Committee of Sponsoring Organizations of the Treadway Commission (COSO) and described in box 5.2. This legislative and regulatory attention will

**Box 5.2. The Importance of the Control Environment: The COSO Internal Control Integrated Framework**

The Committee of Sponsoring Organizations of the Treadway Commission (COSO) was established by the accounting profession and by professional bodies such as the American Institute of Certified Public Accountants (AICPA). In 1992 COSO proposed a framework for internal control that had been prepared by professional bodies from the accounting and auditing profession in the United States. According to COSO,

> the *control environment* provides an atmosphere in which people conduct their activities and carry out their responsibilities. It serves as the foundation for the other components. Within this environment, management *assesses risks* to the achievement of specified objectives. *Control activities* are implemented to help ensure that management directives to address the risks are carried out. Meanwhile, relevant *information* is captured and *communicated* throughout the organization. The entire process is *monitored* and modified as conditions warrant.

© 2003 COSO.

The COSO framework, a reference for the internal audit, is conceptually very close to the compliance system detailed in chapter 4. In practice there are many synergies between the two: the internal audit is usually involved in the implementation of the compliance program.

*Source:* COSO, <www.coso.org>; AICPA, <www.AICPA.org>.

undoubtedly reinforce the role of internal financial control worldwide and of the COSO "cube" as the reference.

Roderick Hills, a former SEC chairman, notes that "in the war against corruption we need armies, and the one readily available, already at the frontline, is the accounting profession." Proper discipline, professional ethics, and capacities are required. In East Asia and in other emerging economies, financial crises and scandals show that there is much to be done. This has become a high-priority area for the reform of the financial and corporate infrastructure. Reforms rely, on the one hand, on the adoption of international standards and, on the other hand, on the strengthening and capacity building of the accounting profession. In most countries the availability and quality of accountants proves to be the stronger constraint on the implementation of sound practices.

In recognition of the link between public and private sector governance, several countries have gone a step farther and have used the development of internal controls in the private sector to support an anticorruption drive at the national level.[1] In Italy, for example, the anticorruption drive, "Mani Pulite" ("Clean Hands"), pushed for better corporate governance with a focus on transparency and disclosure and on internal company systems. Mandatory requirements were included in the Legge Draghi/Codice di Autodisciplina legislation of 1994.[2]

Korea has followed a similar path. An anticorruption act passed in 2001 stresses the responsibilities of all components of society, and article 5 states, "Private enterprise shall establish a sound order of trade as well as business ethics, and take steps necessary to prevent any corruption." This reflects an ongoing trend in the Korean private sector, led by the Federation of Korean Industries, to improve corporate governance (see box 6.2 in chapter 6).

Since the Asian financial crisis of 1997, Korea, Malaysia, and Thailand have taken steps to bring their accounting standards into line with those set by the International Accounting Standards Board (see box 5.3). A key target of those reforms is the accounting profession, which is comparatively underdeveloped in East Asia both in quantity and in quality. Oversight mechanisms have been reviewed and implemented by strengthening professional accountancy bodies (as in Thailand), introducing regulations, and improving the enforcement of the regulations (Nabi and Nowroozi 2002).[3]

## Corporate Governance

Corporate governance—the direction and control of the corporation and its relationship with shareholders and stakeholders—moved to the center of the international development agenda in the wake of the Asian financial crisis. As understood today, sound corporate governance relies on underlying principles of transparency, accountability, fairness, and responsibility (see box 5.4). Corporate governance has become an integral part of the development agenda. International institutions such as the

---

**Box 5.3.   Capacity Building: The Korean Institute of Certified Public Accountants**

The 1997 Asian financial crisis and its aftermath have underscored the need for auditing standards and practices that are transparent and consistent with international standards and practices.

   Prior to the crisis, the Korean Institute of Certified Public Accountants (KICPA) was a not very active professional organization. Its role was fully revisited after 1999 with an emphasis on capacity building. Its main purpose is to improve the skills and knowledge of 3,000 active practitioners in the proper application of the international accounting standards adopted in 1999. Its activities include (a) development of practical interpretations of the Korean Auditing Standards and translation into Korean of international technical pronouncements in auditing; (b) development of educational materials for continuing professional education for practitioners; (c) workshops to promote best practices in audit; and (d) seminars to enhance understanding of the respective roles of the audit committee, the internal audit, and external auditors; and (e) best practices and interrelationships between the various intervening bodies . This initiative was supported by the World Bank and by a grant from the ASEM Trust Fund.

---

OECD, the World Bank, and the Asian Development Bank are actively supporting reforms in this area.

## Link between Corporate and Public Governance Agendas

The connection between public and private governance is widely recognized, especially since the financial crises of the late 1990s revealed the

---

**Box 5.4.   OECD Principles of Corporate Governance**

The 1999 OECD principles of corporate governance target five key areas:

- The rights of shareholders
- Equitable treatment of shareholders
- The role of stakeholders in corporate governance
- Disclosure and transparency
- The responsibilities of the company's board.

---

Box 5.5.    Corporate Governance and Countrywide Corruption

Corporate Governance and Corruption Ratings, Selected Economies, East Asia

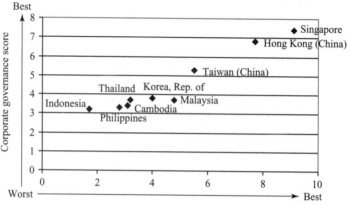

Crédit Lyonnais Securities Asia (CLSA) rated 25 main emerging markets, mostly in Asia and Latin America. The results are shown in the figure. The rating, on a 1–10 scale, weighs five factors: rules and regulations, quality of enforcement, political environment, adoption of international accounting and auditing practices, and mechanisms for promoting good corporate governance.

Source: Crédit Lyonnais Securities Asia, Emerging Markets (April 2001).

pervasive effects of combined failures in both (Backman 1999). Country by country, the quality of corporate governance appears to be highly correlated with the prevalence of corruption in the country at large. Academics, analysts, and financial institutions are issuing a growing number of tentative ratings of the quality of corporate governance at the country level. Not surprisingly these ratings are closely aligned with ratings of countrywide corruption (box 5.5).

This connection is consistently emphasized by policymakers and by international institutions such as the World Bank, the OECD, and the Asian Development Bank, to the point where making a contribution to the fight against corruption is a rationale for the corporate governance agenda. This is clearly reflected in the priorities of the Global Corporate Governance Forum, an advocacy organization sponsored by the OECD, the World Bank, and bilateral development institutions (see <www.gcgf.org>). The same view is promoted by NGOs, both regional (notably, the institutes of corporate directors established in some Asian countries) and global, such as Transparency International and the Center for International Private Enterprise (see Sullivan 2001).

Indeed, both public and corporate governance reforms rely, loosely speaking, on the same set of principles and values: transparency, fairness, and accountability. They target groups of people that are most often closely related (business and government elites). For listed companies, internal controls are the nuts and bolts of good governance. And the requirements for transparency and disclosure that are fundamental to sound financial markets and responsible private sector development directly support anticorruption efforts through compliance programs. Regulatory reforms and capacity building in accounting have direct relevance for the implementation of the corporate governance agenda when it comes to transparency and disclosure.

## At the Company Level, a Less Than Straightforward Relationship between Governance and Business Ethics

Strictly, corporate governance focuses on the publicly held corporation and the relationship between management and shareholders, with a strong practical emphasis on the role of the board and the protection of minority shareholders. These concerns of corporate governance are only remotely related to the design and management of systems to deal with fraud or resist extortion.

Corporate governance reforms target only the tip of the corporate iceberg—that is, publicly held companies. Furthermore, the design and implementation of ethics and compliance programs is clearly a managerial responsibility. But the research reported here proves unambiguously that company programs can be implemented under any form of ownership (widely or closely held publicly owned corporations, privately held corporations, and family-owned businesses). It also shows that internal controls are not directly the consequence of the management-shareholder relationship and are universal in scope and principles.

Ideally, a culture of compliance and smooth corporate governance should go hand in hand at the company level, but this is not always the case. Within the past few years, companies with respected and exemplary compliance and ethics systems have been embroiled in major corporate governance controversies, particularly with regard to the compensation and retirement benefits of current or former executives. Another illustration of this difference in perspective can be found at the country level in Korea, where the public and private agendas are backed by different constituencies. The Federation of Korean Industries has developed an effective initiative to promote compliance programs in large corporations, while at the same time, shareholder activists who are active in urging the corporate governance agenda are targeting the same organizations. [4]

## The Role of the Board in Listed and Nonlisted Corporations

Despite the important differences in focus and audience, ethics and compliance are usually strongly linked with some good corporate governance practices. This is especially true for governance principles that are independent of the ownership structure—in particular, the duties and responsibility of the board.

Boards and their committees are increasingly involved in promoting ethics and monitoring compliance worldwide, as noted in chapter 4. Among the companies surveyed by the Conference Board, only 21 percent of the boards were involved in drafting ethics codes in 1987, but 78 percent were playing such a role by 1999.

In Japan corporate governance improvements, especially at the board level, have gone hand in hand with the development of integrity systems. During the 1990s, in many large corporations the role of the board was reasserted, with the visible result being drastic reduction of board size for the sake of effectiveness. At the same time, ethics became an area of board involvement. In most instances programs have been developed under board supervision and, in a few cases (notably, that of Sumitomo), with significant leadership by a board member.

In this context proper director education is considered key, especially by a number of leaders in East Asia, to the promotion not only of sound corporate governance but also of corporate ethics. Institutes of corporate directors are the crucial organizations. Their role is to bring more professionalism into directorship, focusing both on trust and duties and on ethical standards. In countries such as the United States, the United Kingdom, and Australia institutes of this kind have existed for decades. The services they provide include:

- Research and independent policy advice to government
- Education and professional development
- Information services
- Networking (exchange of views and sharing of experiences among professionals).

Such institutes have been established in most emerging economies in East Asia and have created an active network for exchanging information, carrying out regional research, and harmonizing training content (see box 5.6; see also box 6.11 in chapter 6).

---

**Box 5.6.  Thailand Institute of Directors**

Thailand was the first crisis-affected country in East Asia to create an institute of corporate directors as part of the reform of the corporate sector. Created in 2000, the Thai institute can be considered a pioneer in EAP and in emerging economies. Its success is largely attributable to several factors: the competence of its president and its excellent staff; technical assistance from the Australian Institute of Corporate Directors; and strong support by the Thai Securities and Exchange Commission, particularly its commissioner, and by the Stock Exchange of Thailand (SET). For example, SET has provided space in its building to the institute free of charge for the past few years and is subsidizing 75 percent of the Directors' Certification Program.

The training program targets 4,000 directors with a solid five and a half day class. Several hundred directors and executives had completed the course by the end of 2002.

---

The quality of corporate governance in affiliates is critical to the effectiveness of a company's anticorruption strategy, particularly in the common case of minority joint ventures. This is an obvious concern for a large oil, mining, or utilities corporation (see chapter 4 and case studies in part II for specific examples), but it is also a challenge for companies with intra-Asian investments, especially if their headquarters are in countries with little or no corruption. As a Singaporean businessperson observed, it is important "to continually push the limits" but at the same time to be realistic about the prospects for improvement, especially when the prevalent business culture does not traditionally rely on codified ethics and governance standards.

Finally, listed companies experience more pressure to adopt sound internal systems. Increasingly, corporate governance–related codes and guidelines applicable to listed companies in emerging economies refer to compliance systems or, more generally, to business ethics (box 5.7).

## Business Culture and the Example of Guanxi

As outlined in chapter 4, many international companies seek to build their own corporate cultures, instilling values and norms of behavior that apply across all countries of operation and that are to be followed by employees no matter what their national or cultural backgrounds. At the same time, companies recognize that a code of ethics and the associated compliance system must accommodate to some extent the cultural

---

**Box 5.7.   Compliance and Ethics in Corporate Governance Guidelines in EAP**

The Pacific Economic Cooperation Council (PECC) is a nongovernmental economic advisory body to Asia-Pacific Economic Cooperation (APEC) that brings together businesses, public organizations, and academic experts from APEC countries. In 2002 PECC issued corporate governance guidelines that adapted the OECD guidelines to better take into account some typically East Asian features such as the concentration of ownership under family control. Among the nine missions cited for corporate boards is "ensuring ethical behavior and compliance with laws and regulations." PECC also recommends that boards approve a code of ethics and monitor compliance with the code.

In April 2002 the Philippines Securities and Exchange Commission issued a code of corporate governance for listed companies. The code does not explicitly refer to a program of ethics, but it does promote strong oversight, by a corporate board and the board's audit committee, of the internal control mechanism and environment, as well as of the company's compliance.

---

features of the countries in which the company operates. Hence the strenuous efforts made by many companies to involve a broad range of employees in the *formulation* of their ethics codes, not just to train them in the application of the codes.

To highlight some of the cultural issues companies face in East Asia Pacific, this section looks at the widespread practice of guanxi (more fully described in part II) and explains how companies, Western ones included, are adapting to it and using it.

Guanxi relationships link millions of Chinese firms throughout the region in a social and business network. Guanxi has been described as an "I scratch your back, you scratch mine" type of give-and-take, but it is also akin to a two-way line of credit, to be drawn on in time of need. No formal account of a person's "indebtedness" is maintained, but guanxi ties are considered binding. Someone who fails to return an obligation risks loss of face, personally and for the members of his or her network. Since guanxi networks often comprise generations of family members, the social pressure to deliver on guanxi commitments—and avoid family embarrassment—can be intense. Maintaining face, or *mianzi*, for oneself and one's family is important because a person must possess a certain amount of personal prestige to be considered trustworthy, which in turn is the basis for cultivating and maintaining guanxi.

Studies have shown that companies gain a competitive edge by building and maintaining a strong guanxi network. Guanxi helps individuals and companies to:

- Mitigate external political and socioeconomic risk
- Navigate opaque bureaucracies
- Cope with absence of rule of law
- Access reliable information, resources, and infrastructure and predict market changes
- Recruit trustworthy employees.

The prevalence of guanxi raises several business conduct concerns. Although Chinese culture draws a sharp distinction between guanxi and illegal corruption, the prevalence of guanxi can help create the conditions in which corruption can take root. Chinese businesspeople naturally wish to work with those they know and trust—which is all the more understandable, given the difficult and (outside China) often hostile conditions in which Chinese businesses operate—but this preference can lead to cronyism and nepotism. Whistle-blowing and transparency are only slowly accepted in environments influenced by the guanxi tradition.

Chinese society believes that guanxi should operate in compliance with the laws and within a legal framework. Engaging in misconduct for personal benefit not only results in a loss of face for the individual but also brings shame to the group or network. In this respect, guanxi acts to discourage improper behavior.

Yet the fact that a trusted individual can hold a tremendous amount of discretionary power with little oversight creates an environment conducive to misconduct. When an individual engages in wrongdoing not for self-enrichment but for the ostensible benefit of the company, the link between guanxi and misconduct becomes more complex. And by discouraging whistle-blowing, guanxi lessens the likelihood that illegal behavior will receive public attention.

As China strives to comply with international business norms and compete globally, the guanxi practices of Chinese firms and the behavior of their foreign counterparts are becoming less distinct. With the spread of internal and external monitoring and enforcement of policies, the professionalization of management, increased transparency of laws and regulations, and increased use of (and faith in) legal contracts, many of the environmental factors that enable guanxi to facilitate misconduct are eroding.

Whereas in the past guanxi was essential at every point in a transaction, this is no longer the case in China today. Procedures, laws, and regulations have become more standardized and conform more closely to international norms. Most important, there has been a distinct evolution away from the "gentlemen's handshake" and toward contracts as an accepted means of making business commitments.

Both Chinese and Western firms are taking a new, strategic, more flexible approach to guanxi. They increasingly recognize the value of guanxi with other firms and stakeholder groups, not just with government officials. And they are making efforts to transfer the personal guanxi of employees to the firm level.

In China today, Chinese and successful foreign firms share similar attitudes toward guanxi. Both see guanxi first and foremost as a competitive advantage. Neither would shy away from hiring an individual based solely on the value of the guanxi he or she brings to the firm. Both sometimes grapple with the business conduct issues that result from improper use of guanxi, just as they also actively seek to capitalize on the benefits and efficiencies to be derived from it.

# Notes

1. As explained in chapter 3, the SEC was the first regulator to promote a company system as part of good corporate governance, and it was instrumental in the passage of the Foreign Corrupt Practices Act. Section 30A of the Securities Act of 1934 explicitly makes foreign bribery a breach of the securities law but also suggests the implementation of a compliance system by the issuers.

2. According to experts, the law has had visible results for large corporations. Dissemination of best practices has been slower among small and medium-size enterprises, which contribute a bigger share of output in Italy than in any other industrial economy.

3. The International Monetary Fund (IMF), the OECD, and the World Bank are sponsoring Reports on the Observance of Standards and Codes (ROSCs). ROSCs are country-specific. They target a given component of the financial and corporate infrastructure and benchmark it against international standards and practices. One series of ROSCs looks in great detail at accounting and auditing practices, while others concentrate on corporate governance of listed companies. Accounting and auditing ROSCs are available for some Asian countries, including the Philippines and Thailand, at <www.worldbank.org/ifa>.

4. The protection of minority shareholders and shareholder activism have had an unexpected downside. There is anecdotal evidence that in some countries listed companies have been blackmailed for illegal

payments by individual shareholders in exchange for those individuals' not making an abusive use of shareholder rights. One of the Japanese companies in the sample set up its code of ethics after it was found that shareholders' meetings were controlled by organized crime groups that extorted the management. This is apparently a real concern in a few emerging markets in Asia (the case of the Philippines has been mentioned to the authors) and also in the recent past in European countries such as Italy.

# Chapter 6
# Building Knowledge and Resources for Better Business Ethics: Current Initiatives

Firms that espouse ethical business standards can help spread these standards by raising their expectations for ethical behavior among their employees and business partners and by codifying and exchanging good practices. A company's ethics program is, first of all, a matter of individual choice and commitment. But to develop sound tools, a company needs to access appropriate resources and to assess itself against benchmarks provided by the experience of others.

This chapter examines the activities being pursued to disseminate good practices in compliance and ethics in the region and the initiatives being taken, beyond the firm level, to help improve corporate ethics. Such efforts are being made in the private sector but also in the context of private-public partnerships. (A list of relevant Websites is given in appendix D.)

The following inventory (as of late 2002) demonstrates that not only is there a wealth of initiatives in East Asian countries or relevant for East Asia but also that this is a fast-moving area. There are many possible vectors of dissemination, depending on the partnerships involved. The content of the resources available is very diverse: while large international corporations are looking for increasingly sophisticated benchmarking tools (discussed in some detail here), other programs that focus on values and awareness of the issues target a larger audience of smaller firms, agents, and other players such as the media.

## Raising Awareness about Ethics and Corporate Responsibility

Initiatives to increase awareness of ethics and corporate responsibility of the local private sectors in developing and transition economies have been undertaken worldwide by various organizations, including NGOs, business groups, and the World Bank Institute. The goal is not only to provide basic training but also to foster discussion and experience sharing among the participants.

---

**Box 6.1.   The World Bank Institute's Use of New Technologies for Capacity Building**

**A Web-based course on corporate social responsibility**
The WBI's Corporate Social Responsibility (CSR) program has developed a fully Web-based course designed as an introduction to ethics and CSR theory and practice. The course is a capacity-building exercise that seeks to promote formal recognition of the positive role the private sector can play in sustainable and more equitable development. All course materials are accessible online, making "classes" available according to the individual's pace and schedule. Participants can discuss the contents and ideas with one another on the course discussion boards, which are also online. As of June 2003, 56 sessions have been held, involving 5,000 business leaders, academics, and journalists from more than 100 countries, including emerging economies in East Asia. A similar program conducted earlier focused on corporate governance at the regional level in East Asia. In some cases courses have been delivered at the country level using distance learning facilities at the World Bank Institute.

**Global online CSR conferences**
Expert moderators of the CSR e-conferences provide relevant and up-to-date background readings and guidance leading to focused, high-quality discussions that translate into action plans aimed at tangible change in client countries. Participants are asked to prepare team contributions from their countries and then develop action plans that will translate the recommendations by participants and moderators into concrete agendas for sustainable development. Since the program was started in March 2002, five online conferences have taken place, drawing thousands of participants. Among them was the "E-Conference on Business Ethics and Corporate Accountability: The Search for Standards," September 9–27, 2002.

*Source:* World Bank Institute; further information is available at <www.csrwbi.org>.

---

To maximize its coverage, the World Bank Institute makes use of modern techniques such as the World Bank global distance learning facilities (box 6.1). In other cases local ethics centers have been established to support independent sustainable programs. The Washington-based NGO Ethics Resource Center has helped create such resources in Colombia, Russia, South Africa, Turkey, and the United Arab Emirates, with the assistance of various corporate sponsors and international organizations. As yet, East Asia does not have independent centers of this kind.

In Hong Kong (China), the Hong Kong Ethics Development Center (HKEDC), established under the umbrella of the Independent Commission Against Corruption (ICAC), provides many materials and supports training activities targeting small and medium-size enterprises (box 6.2). The HKEDC is increasingly extending its cross-border cooperation with the mainland provinces. Having a government agency directly involved in the dissemination of business ethics is quite exceptional worldwide and reflects the very strong policy of prevention implemented in Hong Kong (see box 6.7, below).

---

**Box 6.2.   The Federation of Korean Industries: Promoting a Generic Model**

In early 1996 the Federation of Korean Industries (FKI) developed a Charter of Korean Business Ethics. The charter provides a basic structural outline for a company ethics program on issues such as duty to customers, fair competition (the subject under which bribery policy is discussed), fair transactions, employee conduct, company relations with employees, and corporate citizenship. Since releasing the charter, the FKI has also:

- Produced a practical guide that includes exemplary cases of ethical management (1999)
- Established a roundtable of business ethics officers from 32 domestic companies (2001)
- Founded a Center for Business Ethics (2001)
- Developed a manual and conducted surveys on business ethics practices
- Surveyed difficulties and discussed solutions to business ethics problems with member companies
- Promoted cooperation with international organizations, including the OECD and Transparency International.

An FKI survey in July 2001 found that the percentage of companies adopting the charter had grown steadily:

|  | 1999 | 2000 |
|---|---|---|
| All companies | 21.8 | 42.3 |
| 30 leading companies | 33.3 | 69.4 |

*Source:* FKI.

## Dissemination of Good Practices within the Private Sector

Good practices can be disseminated in three ways: by companies themselves to their suppliers and other business partners; through the work of business, academic, and professional networks dedicated to promoting good governance; and through business schools.

### Company Efforts

Corporate ethics codes and compliance systems designed to prevent corruption are most developed in large corporations, which face issues of compliance not only within their own immediate operations but also within firms in their supply chain and in local business partners and intermediaries. These corporations have strong incentives to disseminate best practices directly or to help dedicated organizations. Evidence suggests that this virtuous process is spreading.

### Networks

Whereas North American and European companies have been inclined to rely on their own resources when designing anticorruption programs, East Asian corporations, both large and small, have tended to draw on one another for models and sometimes to take a collective approach. Examples from Korea and Japan illustrate this mutual benchmarking by companies. For example, in the mid-1990s the Federation of Korean Industries designed a generic program model drawing on U.S. experience that has been adopted by growing numbers of Korean firms (box 6.2).

In Japan corporate and academic cooperation has catalyzed the implementation of ethics codes and socially responsible practices in large corporations. Coalitions of motivated executives with international exposure, some of whom serve in academic capacities, have been key to the recent proliferation of ethics programs supported by the Business Ethics Research Center (box 6.3).

Under the umbrella of the Pacific Economic Cooperation Council (PECC), the institutes of directors in East Asian countries have created IDEAnet, a network for exchanging experiences and promoting knowledge about compliance and corporate social responsibility, among other topics (see box 6.4). Given the role of executive boards in establishing and monitoring company ethics systems, the institutes plan to work together and include compliance and ethics in country based curricula. The corporate governance guidelines recently promoted by PECC include ethics and compliance as explicit principles (see box 5.7 in chapter 5).

---

**Box 6.3.  Corporate and Academic Partnerships for Ethical Business in Japan**

After Japan was shaken by corporate scandals in the 1980s, the Federation of Economic Organizations of Japan (Keidanren) produced in 1991 the Charter for Good Corporate Behavior and strongly appealed to member companies to respect business ethics. In 1996 the charter was revised, and a guidebook was issued. But a new wave of corporate scandals in the late 1990s signaled the failure of this first initiative.

The reengineering of corporate ethics in Japan was taken over by a number of new and active groups that involved private sector executives and academic institutions and that focused strongly on implementation. A Business and Society Committee was launched in 1997 by the Kansai Economic Federation, a business organization. In its final report in May 1999 the committee urged Japanese companies to improve their internal control systems by making use of an ethical and legal compliance management system standard, ECS 2000.

The project to launch the ECS 2000 was initiated in 1998 under the leadership of Iwao Taka, a professor at Reitaku University. This project eventually led to the establishment of the Business Ethics and Compliance Research Center (R-BEC) hosted by the university.

Meanwhile, the Business Ethics Research Center (BERC) was established in 1997 by a small number of major Japanese corporations with the cooperation of the Japan Society for Business Ethics, an academic association. BERC is an independent nonprofit organization dedicated to promoting ethical business practices that serves as a vehicle for the exchange of information and strategies among corporate ethics officers. The center cooperates closely with academic groups such as R-BEC. By the end of 2002, 53 companies were affiliated with the center.

In Japanese corporations the implementation of ethics and compliance systems was closely correlated with changes in corporate governance, especially as regards board activity. The Corporate Governance Forum of Japan, established in 1994, played a leading role in raising awareness of corporate governance issues in the Japanese business community. After years of discussion among members, including the top management of leading Japanese corporations, scholars, and lawyers, the forum in 1998 published "Corporate Governance Principles," which included specific proposals for achieving good corporate governance and business ethics. Recent worldwide surveys have highlighted the consistent quality of socially responsible reporting in Japan (KPMG 2002).

Part II of this volume provides further details on compliance laws and programs in Japan.

---

**Box 6.4.    Institute of Directors in East Asia Network (IDEAnet)**

In recent years, several East Asian countries have established institutes of corporate directors as a tool for the promotion of better corporate governance, especially at the board level. Although inspired by established institutes in Australia, the United Kingdom, and the United States, these institutions take varied forms. Some are independent, while others are associated with academic, private, or governmental organizations. Whatever their type, they are at the forefront of corporate governance reform in their economies.

IDEAnet was organized in 2000 with the objective of coordinating initiatives and sharing information between and among institutes of corporate directors in East Asia. It currently has members in China, Hong Kong (China), Indonesia, Korea, Malaysia, the Philippines, Singapore, Taiwan (China), and Thailand. It is collectively working toward providing a wider range of globally recognized training courses, networking opportunities, and more aggressive and relevant advocacy and policy reform initiatives in each of the member economies and in the region as a whole.

The group has started to broaden its reach by working with counterparts from outside the region. Multilateral organizations such as the World Bank's Global Corporate Governance Forum have been primary supporters of such initiatives.

To date, IDEAnet has conducted several working meetings and joint conferences. In addition, several members, working under the auspices of the Pacific Economic Cooperation Council, developed the Guidelines for Proper Corporate Governance Practices, which were adopted by Asia-Pacific Economic Cooperation (APEC) in Shanghai in 2001. Most members of IDEAnet are currently working on a corporate governance scorecard initiative for their respective economies and eventually for participating economies in the East Asia region.

*Source:* Global Corporate Governance Forum.

---

At the global level and in Western countries, organizations dedicated to improving corporate ethics include:

- The Ethics Officer Association (EOA), created in 1991 in the United States. Today, more than half of all Fortune 100 companies belong to the EOA, and there are many nonprofit members. The EOA network holds conferences and smaller meetings and also conducts research.

- The European Business Ethics Network (EBEN) and the International Society for Business, Economics, and Ethics (ISBEE). These institutions bring together academic research and practical perspectives.
- Knowledge-oriented institutions such as the Conference Board's Global Business Ethics Network (box 6.5).

---

**Box 6.5.   The Conference Board's Global Business Ethics Network**

The Conference Board, founded in 1916, has over 2,500 members in more than 60 countries. From its earliest days, the board's work in business ethics and related issues has been part of a broad-based research program in economics and management practices. Today's program has evolved out of the earlier research activities.

The Conference Board's Global Business Ethics Network, established in 1997, facilitates an exchange of views between different sectors of society regarding business principles and promotes a better understanding of the practical issues in formulating and implementing principles for the conduct of global business. The goals and research focus of the group are to:

- Define standards for global business practice
- Apply core principles in diverse political, social, and cultural environments
- Obtain the support of and promote cooperation with nonbusiness institutions.

To date, the network has supported five research projects, including the one underlying the present study. It has held meetings with company, government, academic, and NGO participants in Africa, Asia, Australasia, and North and South America. Other participating institutions include the World Bank, the Wharton School at the University of Pennsylvania, the business school INSEAD (with centers in France and Singapore), the Fundação Getulio Vargas in Brazil, Japan's Business Ethics Research Center, Transparency International, and the International Labour Organization.

Three times a year, the Global Business Conduct Council convenes senior executives who exercise responsibility in multinational companies to discuss common concerns. Although there is no formal relationship between the Global Business Ethics Network and the council, the council's discussions illuminate members' interests that have been integrated into the research conducted by the Conference Board and the network.

An Asian Business Conduct Group has been formed; its first meeting was held in December 2002.

With active support from member corporations, and in connection with other stakeholders, these organizations have supplemented and reinforced company anticorruption initiatives by gathering and disseminating knowledge and promoting new directions. Such groups for sharing knowledge and experience catalyze the dissemination of best practices and help in the process of benchmarking.

Groups of professional experts in ethics and compliance have been formed in Japan, Korea, and Hong Kong (China). Thus far, their membership is still small compared with their Western counterparts. The Japanese organization of ethics officers, BERC (see box 6.3), has a few dozen members, while its counterparts in Europe and North America have several hundred. The latter, however, are a decade older.

## Business Schools

In East Asia business school curricula have begun to focus on ethics issues, holding out the hope that ultimately corruption will be drastically reduced by a new generation of businesspeople with a less tolerant perspective. In some business schools, the issue of corruption is discussed as part of courses in professional responsibility. In others, ethical issues are integrated into the standard curriculum.

Even so, by no means all business schools cover the subject of ethics or, more generally, corporate social responsibility. This study did not systematically investigate the curricula in EAP countries but it seems that except in Japan, only a few institutions in the region provide an in-depth course, even in the most developed economies, such as Hong Kong (China) and Singapore. Noteworthy exceptions are the Asian Institute of Management in the Philippines, with its Center for Corporate Responsibility, and Hong Kong Baptist University.

This is probably an area in which further progress can be expected, catalyzed by regional and international cooperation in the field of curriculum development and by coupling education with research that can directly benefit companies at the country level. Such coupling has been a common practice in Western countries, where ethics centers or societies are usually hosted by business schools.

## Operational Initiatives

Some initiatives target specific professions and industries, either globally or at the country level. In the consulting engineering profession, for example, the International Federation of Consulting Engineers has developed an integrity management framework to be applied worldwide by

---

**Box 6.6.   Business Integrity Management in the Consulting Industry**

The International Federation of Consulting Engineers (Fédération Internationale des Ingénieurs Conseils, FIDIC) is an international professional organization. Consulting engineering is a major industry worldwide, with firms in both developed countries and emerging or transition economies. FIDIC's constituents are national associations in those countries. One of the organization's mandates is to provide guidelines on standards and practices to help engineers and their clients worldwide.

Consulting engineers confront extortion in their everyday work, particularly on government contracts. But as the industry becomes increasingly global, firms from all countries increasingly expect fair procedures.

In the mid-1990s FIDIC concluded that a long-term global strategy was needed to disseminate best practices and that the work should involve stakeholders, including the financing institutions. The World Bank provided support for FIDIC's Integrity Management Task Force, which was mandated to implement the strategy. The task force combined a global approach and grassroots experience. It was headed by Felipe Ochoa of Mexico, himself a company CEO. Many of its members were from other emerging economies, and all had applied ethical management principles in their own companies.

The task force produced a set of Business Integrity Management guidelines, which became official in 2001. In essence, the guidelines contain the ingredients described in chapter 4 in this volume—active engagement of the leadership, a company code of conduct, delivery mechanisms, and warning systems—but customized for the industry.

The FIDIC is working with its national associations to disseminate the guidelines to end users, through, among other methods, multilanguage, multimedia training programs. It is working with government agencies to have integrity principles taken into account in project and procurement procedures. And it is promoting the inclusion of business integrity principles into the International Organization for Standardization's ISO 9001:2000 certification principles for quality management in the consulting industry.

*Source:* FIDIC and World Bank.

---

its component national associations (box 6.6). The TRACE initiative (see box 4.6 in chapter 4) is aimed at agents and intermediaries through country-based training. Given the sector-specific features of corruption, this targeted approach can be very valuable.

## *Integrated Efforts with the Public Sector*

The primary role of the public sector in the battle against corruption is to reduce opportunities for corruption in public procedures, promote transparency, and safeguard a level playing field for the corporate sector. Priorities include reforms in areas such as public procurement, taxation, and customs. But experience shows that public agencies and regulators can also engage more directly with the private sector and play a critical role in promoting ethical practices by:

- Creating a legal and regulatory framework that provides incentives to corporations for ethical behavior.
- Supporting organizations that participate in the dissemination of good practices.
- Making explicit use of ethics and compliance in public procedures. For instance, in public procurement, bidders may be required to have a relevant compliance system.[1]

Such interventions, which ultimately have the agency or regulator establishing ethical and compliance standards in the country, can be undertaken only by strong and efficient public bodies. The first type has been discussed extensively in previous chapters. Reference to compliance in public procedures such as procurement can be a powerful tool for leveraging agencies but is still underdeveloped.

Hong Kong's ICAC provides a unique example of public-private partnership in all these dimensions (boxes 6.7 and 6.8).

## The Case for Standards

Whether formally agreed international standards would facilitate the dissemination of ethical business practices and compliance with these practices in the private sector is a question that is being actively debated at the global level.

Certification by the International Organization for Standardization (ISO) might prove useful by requiring that compliance by an organization be assessed against a benchmark. In principle, certification could also be used as a reference in legal or regulatory procedures or by investors seeking to invest in socially responsible corporations.

The Ethics Officer Association and the Conference Board take different approaches with respect to business conduct standards. The EOA is exploring the possibility of developing, through the ISO process, a business conduct management system standard that would be mutually compatible with ISO 9000 (quality) and ISO 14000 (environment).

**Box 6.7.   Hong Kong: Public-Private Partnerships against Corruption**

Hong Kong's legal and enforcement frameworks have two components:

- The Prevention of Bribery Ordinance (1971)
- The Independent Commission Against Corruption (ICAC, 1974).

ICAC is independent of any other government branch, including the police, and has considerable latitude to carry out its investigations. Its work force of 1,300, mostly investigators, is huge by any standard. Two other important distinctive features of ICAC are:

- A recognition that public corruption and private corruption are entangled and should be dealt with simultaneously. ICAC takes a comprehensive approach toward corruption that addresses not only misconduct by public officials and bribery by private companies but also fraud and corruption in the context of purely private transactions.
- An increasing emphasis on prevention. This results in interactions with government agencies and private firms, as well as in the systematic promotion of ethics and compliance systems.

To carry out its prevention mission, ICAC relies on a Corruption Prevention Department and a Community Relations Department. Both are increasingly involved in private sector–oriented activities, which combine dissemination, advice, and regulatory incentives.

An Advisory Services Group (ASG) within the Corruption Prevention Department works in collaboration with the investigating unit. It helps companies that are referred to it by the investigators—mostly small and medium-size enterprises—with designing compliance systems. The ASG is also responsible for analyzing patterns of corruption within the private sector. To remedy identified problems, the ASG prepares and leads sectorwide and thematic initiatives.

The Hong Kong Ethics Development Centre (HKEDC), created in 1995, is hosted by ICAC; the major business associations in Hong Kong are also actively involved. The HKEDC is Hong Kong's primary resource center in business ethics. It disseminates manuals and multimedia products and organizes ethics training for companies and professions. Recently, along with regulators and professional bodies, HKEDC has been promoting professional ethics in areas such as banking, accounting, and fund management.

---

**Box 6.8.   Fighting Corruption in the Hong Kong Construction Industry: An Integrated Approach**

Hong Kong's construction industry has been tarnished in recent years by a combination of private and public corruption, resulting in substandard quality. For instance, three years ago it was discovered that the foundation piles of some new buildings were not laid to required depths. There were several causes for the problems:

- Inadequate and ineffective site supervision, exacerbated by collusion and corruption (mostly excessive socializing) between supervisors and contractors.
- A hands-off approach by employers who appointed consultants to manage their projects. As a result, underperforming consultants were not tracked down in time for management action to be taken.
- Lack of independence of materials-testing laboratories, which were appointed by the construction contractors instead of by employers.
- Multilayer, unproductive subcontracting, which meant that the final subcontractors could not realize a substantial profit without resorting to substandard work.

Recognizing that the problem called for a large-scale, integrated effort, in 2000 ICAC organized a construction conference attended by industry stakeholders, including private and public clients, professionals (surveyors, engineers, and architects), and contractors. A responsible construction approach was initiated that includes actions to enhance accountability and other administrative control measures.

To promote good practices, the government has implemented requirements that the lead contractors be registered and abide by certain guidelines. A critical element is the commitment to quality supervision requirements for foundation work, which specify the level of professional input at critical stages of the construction process.

In parallel, a huge ethics training effort has been mounted under the supervision of the Hong Kong Ethics Development Centre. More than 12,000 people (contractors' staff, public officers conducting supervision at government project sites, and tertiary students in construction-related faculties) have been trained so far. At the site level, awareness that corruption is a high-risk crime is promoted through various media, from posters to newsletters issued by construction-related trade associations and workers' unions.

*Source:* ICAC.

Proponents think that the standard would be a useful tool for bench-marking the business conduct systems of companies and business partners.[2] To allay one of the most frequently expressed company concerns, the EOA states that it "plans to take every possible step to ensure that the management system is not intended for third-party certification." The Conference Board, for its part, does not propose standards a priori but instead emphasizes the exchange of information on good practices (see, for example, Berenbeim 1999, 2000).

This latter approach wins more support from senior executives of large companies. They argue that common standards:

- Are too numerous, onerous, and inefficient and generate a welter of confusing requirements that are difficult to manage
- Are drafted with little or no input from the business community
- Do not approach the issue from a process or management point of view
- May lead to third-party certification that is costly without adding value (Berenbeim and Muirhead 2002).

In conversations, senior executives have said that three conditions could make it easier to accept common standards:

- Reasonable reporting and disclosure requirements
- Compliance terms that are open to a broad range of interpretations
- A governing structure in which companies participate.

Companies are open to the implementation of good-practice systems. Such systems would consist of a series of general principles, suggested but not mandatory performance elements, and pertinent evidence on the existence and effectiveness of the performance elements.

Third-party verification may offer an efficient and relatively inexpensive way of substantiating that a company has an effective compliance system. This process will attest that a company has institutionalized policies and programs that could help minimize exposure to corruption, but it does not determine whether or to what degree a company has engaged in corrupt practices. Companies could find such substantiation useful for sentence mitigation under the U.S. Organizational Sentencing Guidelines or similar standards (for example Australia's AS 3806). Despite pervasive resistance to third-party verification processes thus far, this approach might gain acceptance through use in due diligence reviews of potential agents and partners and in internal audits that are disclosed because of growing emphasis on transparency.

---

**Box 6.9.  Business Principles for Countering Bribery**

A set of principles developed over a two-year period of discussions by a group of companies, nongovernmental organizations, and trade unions offers support for enterprises in developing effective approaches for combating bribery.

Use of the Business Principles for Countering Bribery, developed by Transparency International and Social Accountability International, will enable companies to comply with the OECD Anti-Bribery Convention, the Rules of Conduct to Combat Extortion and Bribery of the International Chamber of Commerce (ICC), and the antibribery provisions of the revised OECD Guidelines for Multinationals.

Field-tested for practical application by a medium-size company in countries perceived as difficult (as indicated by high ratings on the Corruption Perceptions Index), the Business Principles are designed to be used by small, medium-size, and large businesses. They offer advice on difficult issues—for example, facilitation payments, gifts, hospitality, and expenses; business relationships with agents and subsidiaries and in joint ventures; implementation practices (training, and internal and external communications); and board and senior management monitoring and review.

Support activities (discussion and orientation) and advice for individual companies will be available to organizations that elect to use the Business Principles in their management policies and processes.

---

For the local private sector in emerging and transition economies, certification is probably not a realistic goal for the near future. Less binding procedures for benchmarking, such as scoring by research or commercial organizations (as is being done in Japan), might prove more practicable and effective (see box 6.9).

## Investors' Assessments as a Benchmarking Tool

Investors' assessments of integrity management can provide a company with an independent benchmark of its own system against relevant standards. The increased popularity of socially responsible investing (SRI) provides a framework for evaluating how companies are doing business, with a scope that goes far beyond integrity to address social and environmental concerns. There are now more than 200 SRI funds in the United States, and they are developing rapidly in Europe.

The SRI standard methodology utilizes negative or positive screening—that is, exclusion of certain industries from the portfolio or, conversely, selection of certain industries or companies with socially responsible performances. SRI is usually based on outcome (or product) rather than on processes and does not provide information about the quality of the corporate system of internal control and compliance.

A recent initiative to develop SRI in Japan took precisely the opposite view and promoted an "integrity screening strategy" focusing on integrity management instead of the products and services delivered (box 6.10). This approach yields a rating that makes benchmarking possible and offers a better way of having markets contribute to the promotion of integrity than traditional screening. In addition the methodology is free

---

**Box 6.10.   IntegreX: A Breakthrough from Japan in Socially Responsible Investing?**

In 2001 a private rating company, IntegreX, was launched in Japan with a view to putting the integrity screening method into practice and helping further promote socially responsible investing (SRI) movements. IntegreX methodology uses a screening procedure, R-BEC001, proposed by the Business Ethics and Compliance Research Center of Reitaku University (R-BEC). The procedure is based on a checklist of company characteristics that financial or institutional investors are expected to take into account in their choice of socially responsible investments. The focus is on whether a company is aware of the risks of infringement of relevant laws or codes and whether it is in a position to control those risks in a reasonable and accountable manner. Its key measures are related to the implementation of an effective compliance system.

IntegreX surveyed 3,500 listed companies in Japan to gather data concerning the self-control mechanisms each company has established to prevent malfeasance by directors, officers, and employees. Using the results of the survey, the company selected the best 100 companies. According to a report by the *Nihon Keizai Shimbun* newspaper, released in early July 2002 (Taka 2002), the share value of those 100 companies outperformed that of TOPIX, a broad-based Tokyo Stock Exchange index. The margins became conspicuous especially after 1997, when a number of business scandals broke out. These data show that the performance of ethical companies can ensure stable and sustainable performance in the long run. The growing popularity of SRI-related products will likely put pressure on Japanese companies to become more concerned about business ethics and compliance issues.

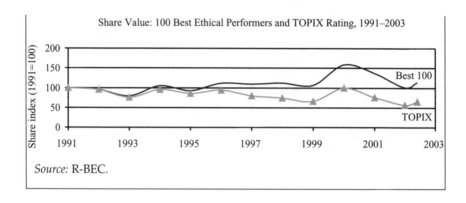

Share Value: 100 Best Ethical Performers and TOPIX Rating, 1991–2003

Source: R-BEC.

**Box 6.11.    Anticorruption Action Plan for Asia and the Pacific**

In East Asia the OECD and the Asian Development Bank took the lead in organizing a number of regional conferences involving governmental and nongovernmental organizations. Following consultations with experts and government representatives, a regional action plan was endorsed in Tokyo in 2001. The plan provides members with an analytical framework that facilitates benchmarking and comparisons and ultimately helps these countries design their next steps. Although the contribution of the private sector has been identified, so far most activities focus on public sector reforms. The plan rests on three pillars:

I. Developing effective and transparent systems for public services
II. Strengthening antibribery actions and promoting integrity in business transactions

  • Effective prevention and enforcement: legislation; antibribery agencies and judiciary; international cooperation
  • Corporate responsibility and accountability: promotion of internal controls and compliance; adequate sanctions

III. Supporting active public involvement.

Extensive country-based case studies were discussed through the World Bank's Global Distance Learning Network. The case studies, which focus on public sector reforms, will be presented in a companion volume to this book.

Source: OECD and World Bank.

from ideological and political considerations—a factor that could ease SRI development in Asia and elsewhere.

## Potential for Increased Regional Cooperation

In recent years steps have been taken to look at anticorruption initiatives in a regional perspective (see box 6.11). Economic integration, common culture, business culture, and administrative practices underscore the relevance of the approach, which also provides an opportunity for policymakers and advocacy groups to exchange ideas and information on experiences and practices.

Unlike public governance and corporate governance, business ethics and compliance does not yet have organized regional activities or a network. There is now a core of business, academic, nongovernmental, and governmental organizations pursuing these activities at the country level. To better leverage this expertise and to catalyze dissemination in new countries or sectors, it would be worthwhile establishing a regional network, whether formal or not. The network should make deliberate use of the potential synergies with existing networks active in related areas, such as the Institute of Directors in East Asia Network (IDEAnet), described in box 6.4, above. The network concept has gained support not only from regional experts and leaders but also from foundations outside the region that are willing to bring financial support to it.[4]

## Notes

1. An example is the U.S. Defense Industry Initiative (DII), which is closely associated with the department's procurement procedures. For good resources on the DII, see <www.dii.org>. See also Shaw (1999).

2. For a full discussion of the EOA initiative, see Essrig (2001).

3. The Fund for the Study of Corruption, established by Carla Hills, a former U.S. trade representative, and Roderick Hills, a former SEC chairman, has expressed interest in extending its support to the regional anchor of the proposed network. A practical proposal was put forward by Roderick Hills at a July 2002 roundtable in Singapore, "The Role of the Private Sector in Fighting Corruption: An Implementation Agenda," hosted by the Institute of Policy Studies (Singapore), Transparency International, and the World Bank. At the time of publication of this volume, implementation was being actively discussed by business leaders in Southeast Asia.

# Chapter 7
# The Current Agenda

Company efforts to promote ethics and compliance are now a reality worldwide. In East Asia growing numbers of multinational and regional corporations are adopting programs to fight fraud and corruption. In the future those techniques are likely to gain wider acceptance as a result of the deepening of globalization and the emergence of new generations of businesspeople more sensitive to governance issues. Thus, the private sector is poised to make a significant contribution in the war against corruption, even if its impact cannot be instantaneous.

This study points out a number of key findings and directions.

*Private sector programs are a "glocal" (global + local) answer to the problem that corruption poses to business development everywhere.*

- Large corporations are better able than small ones to develop strong systems, as they have more resources and greater bargaining power to resist extortion. In turn, they have an interest in raising awareness and disseminating good practices among their suppliers and business partners, and a legal and moral responsibility to do so.
- The national and the international perspectives cannot be disentangled. International trade and investment are blamed for spreading corruption, but they are also important vectors for disseminating good practices. This interconnectedness is especially important in East Asia, with its high degree of intraregional integration in trade and investment.

*Private sector initiative cannot substitute for actions and reforms by the public sector.*

The contribution of the private sector is to leverage measures undertaken by the public sector. This has been demonstrated in the international arena, where the 1997 OECD Anti-Bribery Convention has given a strong impetus to the recent proliferation of programs in multinational corporations.

- The perception that corruption is an obstacle to business is now universal, although with some nuances. Also universal are the techniques and ingredients being used in company programs: active engagement of the leadership, a company code of conduct, effective implementation through training, and discussion and warning systems. This similarity across companies and countries is likely to increase as globalization progresses.
- Cultural differences will continue to raise serious implementation issues. This point is especially germane in East Asia, where guanxi, the traditional Chinese way of doing business, although compatible with a high degree of integrity, relies on personal trust and nonformalized relationships. Considerable country-specific customization in compliance programs may be needed if companies are to resist corrupt practices effectively.
- Better business ethics and internal control systems are part of today's corporate governance agenda. Transparency and disclosure practices that conform to international norms greatly help internal systems to resist extortion. Good practices in the governance structure of a company interact positively with the implementation of corporate ethics programs; for example, boards of directors are increasingly involved in formulating and monitoring these programs. In turn, ethical practices and internal control help a company's governance structures to function well.

*Although the design and implementation of a corporate system depend mainly on choices by the company itself, the company cannot do it all.*

The promotion of good practices will be spurred by a number of external factors, including the incentives provided by laws and regulations, partnerships involving individual firms or organizations, and the resources available to the firm in the form of knowledge, training, and benchmarks. Both public and private capacities are still scarce, and the following proposals aim at using them to best advantage.

1. *Make appropriate adjustments in the legal and regulatory environment.* A country's laws and regulations should provide incentives for disseminating norms for business ethics and should encourage corporations headquartered in the country to adopt internal compliance systems. These are not necessarily straightforward steps, and the

agenda is long term. It includes:

- *Incorporation of references to ethics and to companies' internal systems into laws and guidelines applicable to the corporate sector.* Two obvious means for doing this are (a) guidelines, established by securities commissions or eventually embodied in securities law, for the governance of listed companies, and (b) anticorruption laws, especially those that establish anticorruption bodies, as in Korea. Such references are far from systematic today, and for clarity's sake it is important that these texts define, at least broadly, the appropriate content of a company system— as is the case, for instance, in the United States (the Sarbanes-Oxley Act) and Australia (AS 3806). The same references to ethics and internal control should also be made (if they are not already there) in laws and guidelines targeting the professions that play important roles in the corporate governance agenda, particularly the accounting profession.
- *Consideration of a company's compliance system when enforcing the law or administrative procedures.* As a first step, regulators and public agencies can mitigate fines and penalties on an experimental basis when confronted with breaches of the law in a few areas. Ultimately, taking this stance may lead a country to adopt some form of sentencing guidelines that will mitigate sanctions according to the quality of a company's compliance system. Pending a systematic legal framework, mitigation can be used case by case as a means of leveraging the administrative procedures enforced by regulators or public agencies. An obvious precondition is that the agency be strong and honest—which suggests the need for limited and gradual experiments. Potential areas are (a) securities and exchange commission enforcement, and (b) public procurement (e.g., qualification or debarment procedures). The FIDIC proposal and the account of the construction industry in Hong Kong described in chapter 6 are examples.
- *The extension of the OECD regime to non-OECD countries in East Asia and Pacific.* The OECD regime is relevant for emerging economies because it puts national and transnational corruption on the same footing. Asia, unlike Latin America, has no non-OECD participants in the OECD Anti-Bribery Convention, yet the intensity of intraregional trade makes the convention relevant in the East Asian context. Although the extension of the OECD regime might not trigger an overnight change, the regime and the review procedure that are built into the convention might help countries design good frameworks.
- *The introduction of core legal principles that encourage effective internal control systems.* These include (a) the principle of corporate criminal liability, which is a necessary basis for introducing provisions for mitigation of sentencing, and (b) the protection of whistle-blowers—a measure

that should be applied in both the private and the public sectors. Those are probably long-term changes; not all the advanced OECD countries have implemented them yet.

2. *Promote partnerships to catalyze the dissemination of good practices.* These partnerships should leverage scarce expertise, resources, and enforcement capabilities in both the private and public sectors.

Forms of private-private partnerships include:

- *Large companies working together* (through ethics associations or existing organizations)—at the country level, as has proved successful in Korea and Japan, or in connection with a global working group, such as the Conference Board's working group on Global Business Ethics Principles, or on both country and global levels.
- *Large companies, both international and regional, working with suppliers and intermediaries* to raise awareness, provide training, and ultimately improve standards. Some promising experiments are under way in this key area, including the TRACE initiative described in box 4.6 in chapter 4.
- *Dialogue with other stakeholders.* Thanks to a number of very active NGOs, civil society is involved in the fight against corruption. Although it is not realistic for individual company programs to be scrutinized by civil society organizations, it is important that large-scale partnerships in the private sector be known and recognized by stakeholders, as is usually the case.

Public-private partnerships are also essential. Public agencies may be directly involved in promoting good practices, as in Hong Kong. Anticorruption agencies elsewhere may not yet have the resources to develop a dialogue with private sector organizations with the same intensity. But to ensure the consistency of public and private efforts as private sector programs gain momentum, it will be important for the public entities in charge to develop capacities to work operationally with the private sector.

3. *Create and disseminate resources and knowledge* for individual corporations that are willing to develop anticorruption programs.

*Training* is a priority area in which there is a huge gap. Some potential vehicles are:

- Inclusion of the principles of professional ethics in the curricula of institutes of accountants.

- Courses offered by institutes of directors, which are now very active in East Asia and have expressed willingness to include ethics and compliance in their curricula.
- Ad hoc training for some industries.
- Inclusion of ethics subjects in business school courses. This step is of the greatest importance for the longer term, since, ultimately, the agenda will be implemented by future generations of business leaders.

*Knowledge concerning facts and trends* can be developed through such means as:

- *Experience-sharing* between professionals involved in the area (for instance, through the creation of ethics associations).
- The development of *academic research capabilities.* An ethics research center, as Japan's experience has shown, can be very useful in developing case studies and helping monitor problems. Such research can support business schools, business organizations, professional institutes, and anticorruption agencies alike.

*Benchmarking instruments* can be developed for individual corporations. East Asia has recently seen a number of private initiatives for providing cross-company assessmesnts of transparency, compliance, and corporate social responsibility. This is a promising area, although the methods are still being elaborated.

# Part II
# CASE STUDIES

The names of some companies have been changed to preserve anonymity. Also, personal titles are given as they were at the time of the interview (2001 or 2002) and may no longer be current.

# Business Ethics Programs and Antibribery Initiatives of Japanese Companies: Changes in Legislation and Corporate Efforts

Business ethics has become a widely recognized concern in Japan over the past 10 years. In February 1999 Japan amended its Unfair Competition Prevention Law to implement the provisions of the Organisation for Economic Co-operation and Development (OECD) Anti-Bribery Convention. Japanese businesses were thus compelled to tackle the issue of bribery of foreign public officials. This development coincided with a renewal of efforts by businesses and business organizations to restore or secure corporate integrity in the wake of a series of corporate scandals. Japanese corporations have undertaken reforms of corporate governance, and there is growing debate on business ethics and compliance issues within the business community and in government departments.

## Social and Institutional Influences

Many Japanese companies lost their integrity in the bubble economy of the late 1980s. "The end justifies the means" had become the order of the day, and in increasing numbers of companies the traditions of Japanese-style management, with its stress on the management *process*, were undermined.

The term "business ethics" did not gain currency in Japan until after the bubble burst. In 1991 the Federation of Economic Organizations of Japan (Keidanren) established its Charter for Good Corporate Behavior and strongly appealed to its member companies to respect business ethics. But the early 1990s saw the revelation of unlawful practices involving securities companies, including the Big Four—Nomura, Daiwa, Yamaichi, and Nikko—while banks and their borrower companies drew tough condemnation for having managed irresponsibly. In 1996 Keidanren revised the charter and issued a guidebook containing detailed instructions.

In 1997, however, further scandals came to light. A number of Keidanren member companies were found to have given payoffs to corporate racketeers in violation of Japan's Commercial Code. These developments discredited Keidanren as the leader in business ethics in Japan.

Since then, several business organizations have played important roles in promoting better business ethics. The Kansai Economic Federation took over from Keidanren in conducting full-fledged discussions on business ethics. It launched the Business and Society Committee in 1997, and in its final report, in 1999, it urged Japanese companies to build management systems for complying with laws and ordinances relating to ethics.[1]

In 1997 the Business Ethics Research Center (BERC) was established, with the cooperation of the Japan Society for the Study of Business Ethics, as an independent nonprofit organization dedicated to promoting ethical business practices. By the end of 2002, 53 companies were affiliated with the center. BERC serves as a vehicle for the exchange of information and strategies among corporate ethicists through educational activities and resource assistance.

The Corporate Governance Forum of Japan, established in 1994, has played a leading role in raising awareness of corporate governance issues. After years of discussion among its members—including top managers of leading Japanese corporations, scholars, and lawyers—in 1998 the forum published "Corporate Governance Principles," which included specific proposals for achieving good corporate governance.

Also noticeable is a rising tide of shareholder activism, making shareholder relations a subject of increasing concern among boards of directors. The shareholder profile of Japanese companies has been changing: as cross-holding of shares among Japanese companies has declined, foreign investors have increased their share of company stocks, and many have been active in proposing corporate governance reforms to management. The 1995 amendment to the Commercial Code made it easier for shareholders to file a lawsuit against directors of corporations, requiring a payment of only 8,200 yen, or US$63, to go to court. Since then the number of suits filed by shareholders has grown. Some lawsuits implicate the directors of several general construction companies in bribery scandals; others accuse major securities companies of making illicit payments to racketeers. Among the companies surveyed for this study, directors of Kobe Steel and Sumitomo Corporation have faced litigation.

Recent legal judgments have also spurred concern among company directors about corporate governance. One such judgment, in September 2000, shocked directors across the nation: the court ordered the directors of Daiwa Bank to pay 82.9 billion yen in compensation to shareholders. The court found that the directors had not exercised "due care" in that they had failed to prevent one of their employees from losing huge sums of money in fraudulent trading. This case triggered similar lawsuits focusing on directors' lack of due care. More often, shareholders have won court judgments that compensated them for losses or have reached out-of-court settlements in their favor. In several cases shareholders have induced companies to pledge to establish a compliance system in order to prevent a recurrence of irregularity.

Shareholders' growing concern for socially responsible investing (SRI) is another trend with implications for corporate governance. Recently, IntegreX, Inc., an institution dedicated to evaluating SRI, surveyed all 3,500 listed companies as to the status of their efforts in business ethics and compliance. A database of the survey findings will be released soon. There is little doubt that this type of study and the resulting publications will further encourage individual companies to tackle compliance issues.

Meanwhile, the Japanese government is making efforts to promote compliance and ethics efforts. First, in 1999 the Financial Services Agency started undertaking comprehensive financial inspections, targeting financial institutions. Financial institutions are subject to strict inspections in regard to their compliance status, and if they fail to satisfy the compliance requirements, they may be ordered to suspend operations. The authorities have reduced the inspection burden for those financial institutions in which internal controls are functioning adequately.

Second, there is a new trend in the government not only to oblige companies to observe laws and ordinances but also require them to build a framework to observe the laws. Discussions on compliance started in 2001 in the Social Policy Council, an advisory body to the government, and similar discussions have begun in the Environmental Standards Division and the Product Safety Division of the Ministry of Economy, Trade, and Industry.

Third, a cabinet meeting in December 2000 adopted the Outline of Administrative Reform, which obliges companies to build a framework for assuming responsibility for their own acts, for the purpose of ensuring people's safety and a fair society. This is explicitly stated as an issue that needs to be tackled simultaneously with the promotion of regulatory reform. Companies are also required to disclose information relating to such activities.

Fourth, attempts are under way to revise the country's Anti-Monopoly Law so as to enhance the authority of the Fair Trade Commission of Japan (JFTC). Unlike the United States, with its Federal Sentencing Guidelines, and the United Kingdom, which has the Competition Act of 1998, Japan has no governmental provisions to reduce penalties for companies that have compliance systems. The proposed revisions would empower the JFTC to take account of a company's anticorruption systems when deciding on penalties for breaking the law.

## Actions by Companies

Japanese companies have started to refine their ethics programs and internal control structures. About 55 percent of them have established a corporate code of conduct, ethics guidelines, compliance manuals, and other such documents; 37 percent have a department or division dedicated to ethics and compliance issues; and 43 percent periodically hold ethics-related training programs targeting employees.[2]

A growing number of Japanese businesses have taken steps to reinforce oversight functions—for example, by engaging independent outside directors. In 1997 Sony Corporation took the initiative of cutting its executive board from 38 to 10 directors while introducing the new post of executive officer. Other companies, including Omron and Kobe Steel, followed suit, and by 2000 about 240 businesses had reportedly made similar structural reforms.

Even so, the image of company ethics held by the market and the general public remains far from favorable. For example, in a survey of students' views of the Japanese business community, conducted in autumn 2000, 68 percent of the respondents agreed that "honest companies are not rewarded, while dishonest companies are making profits"; 63 percent believed that "there is hardly any information as to which companies are honest"; 84 percent believed that "penalties against scandals are too lenient"; and 62 percent agreed that "many companies believe it is worth engaging in unlawful practices." If this is the new generation's perception of reality, it means that Japanese companies have little incentive to tackle ethical and compliance issues internally. Certainly, companies whose business performance has deteriorated as a result of scandals have made greater efforts to deal with ethical and compliance issues. But such efforts are not long-lasting if a company fears they will reduce its competitiveness.

## Antibribery Provisions: The Unfair Competition Prevention Law

After signing the OECD Anti-Bribery Convention in May 1997, the Japanese government amended the Unfair Competition Prevention Law (UCPL) to implement the provisions of the convention. The amended law took effect in February 1999, when the convention entered into force.

The amendments have two key features:

- *A new clause prohibiting bribery of foreign public officials.* This antibribery clause states, "No person shall give, offer, or promise any pecuniary or other advantage, to a foreign public official, in order that the official act or refrain from acting in relation to the performance of official duties, or in order that the official, using his position, exert upon another foreign public official so as to cause him to act or refrain from acting in relation to the performance of official duties, in order to obtain or retain improper business advantage." In this context, "foreign public official" is defined as (1) persons engaged in public service for a national or local government in a foreign country; (2) persons engaged in service for an entity constituted under foreign special laws to carry out specific tasks in the public interest; (3) persons engaged in service for a government-backed public corporation which conforms to a certain set of requirements; (4) persons engaged in public service for an international organization; or (5) persons exercising a public function, which belongs to the authorized competence of a national or a local foreign government or an international organization and is delegated by them.

• *New provisions on the sanctions for the offense:* a maximum penalty of three years' imprisonment or a fine of up to 3 million yen for an individual violator and up to 300 million yen for a corporate violator.

In 2001 the Japanese government further amended the UCPL in response to suggestions made by the OECD Working Group on Bribery:

• The phrase "in relation to international business transactions" was inserted to limit the scope to improper business advantage to be obtained through acts of bribery.

• In the definition of foreign public officials, especially those engaged by an enterprise controlled by a national or local foreign government, the phrase "other individuals specified under government ordinances as corresponding to such persons" was added.

• The "main office" clause was deleted. Before the latest amendment, the UCPL contained a provision stating that the antibribery clause would not be applied if the main office of the person offering a bribe was in the home country of the public official being bribed.[3] The deletion of the "main office" clause eliminated the alleged loophole.

Despite these measures, critics are still voicing concern over Japan's implementation of the OECD Convention. They make the following points:

First, the Japanese government has prohibited the act of bribery of foreign public officials through amendments to the law on competition rather than through changes in the Penal Code. No other signatory to the

OECD Convention has used such an approach, and some critics suspect that a Japanese company might not be actively prosecuted for foreign bribery unless unfair competition resulted.[4]

Second, Japan is one of only two signatories of the convention that have not applied the nationality principle to the foreign bribery offense. This means that prosecution cannot be conducted purely on the basis of offenses committed abroad. The adoption of nationality-based (versus territory-based) jurisdiction can be interpreted as mandatory under the convention, and some countries have even enacted aggressive legislation applying their own antibribery provisions to a foreign bribery offense committed by a foreigner in a foreign country. Although the OECD Working Group had suggested such an amendment, the Japanese government has not yet implemented it.

Third, the punishment for foreign bribery is relatively mild. Although it complies with the provisions of the convention, which stipulates that it "shall be comparable to that of the Party's own public officials," it is light in comparison with penalties in other countries.[5] The OECD Working Group points out that the corporate sanctions available in Japan are not "sufficiently effective, proportionate, and dissuasive" in view of the large size of many of its corporations.

No Japanese company has thus far been punished for foreign bribery. Not much time has elapsed since the law was amended, but the lack of prosecutions is suggestive of the law enforcement agencies' stance on this matter. In future, Japan must actively absorb the recommendations made by the OECD Working Group and develop a structure to effectively accomplish the mission of the Anti-Bribery Convention it has signed.

## Antibribery Initiatives by Japanese Companies

Six major Japanese companies with business ethics programs were surveyed for this study to examine what efforts they have been making to combat bribery of foreign public officials: Kobe Steel, Matsushita Electric Industrial Co., NEC Corporation, Omron Corporation, Sumitomo Corporation, and Toyota Motor Corporation. The six companies all began introducing antibribery initiatives following the enactment or entry into force of the amendments to the UCPL in 1999. Business efforts to combat the bribery of foreign public officials have just begun in Japan. The six companies surveyed in detail are all relatively advanced in the introduction of business ethics, compared with other Japanese companies.

## Status of Internal Regulations

Toyota, NEC, Omron, and Sumitomo have relatively detailed provisions targeting bribery of foreign public officials. The specifics vary:

- Toyota Motor Corporation was the first to engage in activities to combat bribery of foreign public officials. In the Toyota Code of Conduct, established in January 1998, the company obliged employees to refrain from engaging in acts of bribery overseas.
- Under its Corporate Ethics Guidelines, established in October 1998, Omron prohibited the entertainment of foreign public officials. Omron has detailed provisions to prevent bribery of foreign public officials, extending the principle of developing a healthy relationship with government officials.
- NEC issued its Code of Conduct when the amended UCPL became effective in February 1999. The code prohibits acts of bribery of foreign public officials, such as officials of foreign governments and local authorities, and payoffs aimed at gaining improper business advantages.
- Kobe Steel issued its Code of Conduct at the same time. The code forbids payoffs to either domestic or foreign public officials.
- Matsushita has no specific provisions against bribery of foreigners, as it believes that the overall provisions covering bribery apply to foreign bribery as well.
- Sumitomo added an item on "prevention of unlawful payoffs to foreign public officials" in its Compliance Manual, introduced in April 2001.

## Education and Training Programs

Since the amended UCPL entered into force in February 1999, the six companies have conducted intensive education and training programs to stamp out acts of bribery overseas. Each company spends considerable time raising its officers' awareness of the issue of bribery of foreign public officials. As in many Japanese companies, subsidiaries and offices abroad tend to be managed by Japanese officers, and officers to be stationed overseas usually receive antibribery training in Japan before leaving for their posts, to control the risks associated with overseas subsidiaries and offices. In the future, as more senior positions are opened to natives of host countries, training schemes will need to be tailored to local staff.

## Comprehension Surveys

Although the companies are refining their internal regulations and conducting staff education and training programs, they are not fully aware of the trends in their subsidiary companies, especially those overseas. NEC conducts a survey on the observance of laws by all its officers and assesses the evolution of the corporate culture on the basis of a time-series model. Omron is planning a comprehensive review of its efforts to prevent bribery of foreign public officials.

## Scope of Internal Controls

The companies have various checking mechanisms to prevent unlawful payoffs, and these systems are believed to help prevent bribery of foreign public officials as well. NEC, for example, has established an independent Corporate Auditing Bureau that records ex post transactions with foreign governments and carefully examines the nature of the transactions. Sumitomo has prepared monitoring guidelines and a checklist for preventing unlawful payoffs relating to transactions with foreign governments, and it uses them in carrying out control tasks. All six companies have established some kind of hotline or contact point, although these are not much used, perhaps because they are so new.

## General Observations

1. Virtually all the six companies developed their compliance structures by themselves, rather than with the help of consultants.
2. The companies appear to believe that "a sense of business ethics must be acquired first by the management," but they require their codes of behavior and compliance manuals to be observed by everyone—employees and managers—in cooperation with each other. This may be attributable to the Japanese custom of regarding directors and executives as employees and all employees as important members of the company, rather than as mere labor.
3. Most companies conduct education and training programs that target all employees, including executives. Most attach great importance to education at turning points for employees, such as joining the company and promotion.

The companies surveyed have structures for conducting thorough training programs on business ethics in general, including prevention of bribery, and they stress the importance of general business ethics training, rather than concentrating on the prevention of bribery of foreign public officials or on specific laws, ordinances, and rules. Matsushita's approach is typical. Matsushita has no specific high-profile activities regarding bribery of foreign officials, but it enjoys a high rating for the management philosophy it has enshrined since its establishment and for its internal education programs, which are designed to apply the philosophy in practice in a thoroughgoing way. The management philosophy is believed to be extremely useful in improving and maintaining the integrity of the company.

## Unresolved Issues

Separately from the survey of six companies, R-BEC conducted a survey among businesspeople from a wider set of enterprises. Some of the respondents expressed their frustration about high-profile visitors from other countries who make unreasonable demands for recreational travel and parties. One businessperson said that his company analyzes such demands and allows those that are not too extravagant to be met, provided that they are judged not to be directly related to business. That judgment, however, is not always easy to make. Another businessperson, discussing participation in large projects involving the government of a developing country, said that ordinary public officials do not often exercise much influence—it is politicians' demands that raise the more problematic issues.

## Looking Ahead

To be successful, measures to prevent bribery overseas need to be undertaken in the context of a broader business ethics and compliance structure. Companies engaged in activities for combating bribery of foreign public officials do appear to have some form of framework for general business ethics and compliance.

The criminal and administrative sanctions imposed on companies involved in scandals are extremely lenient in Japan compared with those in other industrial countries. Tougher sanctions are needed to ensure that companies make greater efforts to improve business ethics.

It is presumed that some Japanese companies have no programs for combating bribery of foreign public officials. Such companies should be approached in one way or another. A Japanese branch of Transparency International is to be launched in the near future. Its formal establishment would help promote Japanese companies' efforts at compliance.

# Notes

This section was prepared by Profs. Iwao Taka and Toru Umeda of Reitaku University.

1. The model management system advocated by the Kansai Economic Federation is based on the ECS2000 corporate responsibility standard issued by the Business Ethics and Compliance Research Center of Reitaku University (R-BEC) in May 1999.

2. These figures are from a survey undertaken in October 2000–January 2001 by the Corporate Governance Forum of Japan on corporate governance and business ethics in listed companies. Complete replies were received from 541 companies, or 22 percent of the total number polled.

3. This meant, for example, that if an employee of a company having its main office in the United States bribed a U.S. public official in Japan, the employee could not have been charged or prosecuted under Japanese law for bribing a foreign public official.

4. The Ministry of Economy, Trade, and Industry, which is in charge of implementing the UCPL, argues that the goal of making foreign bribery an offense is to ensure fair competition in international business transactions and that foreign bribery raises different issues from domestic bribery, which is dealt with under Japan's Penal Code.

5. In Australia, for example, foreign bribery is subject to a maximum of 10 years' imprisonment.

# Kobe Steel

Kobe Steel was founded in Japan in 1905 and began independent operations as Kobe Steel Works, Ltd., in 1911. In fiscal 2000 the company ranked 5th in Japan and 27th worldwide in gross steel production. Aside from steel, the company's principal businesses are welding materials, aluminum, and copper, along with machinery, construction equipment, and electronics and information-related industries. The Kobe Steel Group comprises 187 subsidiaries and 67 affiliated companies. Group revenue in fiscal 2000 was 1.37 trillion yen, and in March 2001 the group was capitalized at 213.6 billion yen. The group has more than 30,000 employees.

Overseas bases include 14 firms in the United States, 5 in Singapore, 4 in Malaysia, 3 each in Thailand and the Netherlands, 2 each in China and Venezuela, and 1 each in Korea, Australia, and Switzerland. Operations outside Japan provided about 23 percent of the group's revenue in 2000.

## Origins of the Ethics Program

Kobe Steel presents a classic case in which a scandal led a company to initiate efforts to change its corporate culture. In the course of a corporate restructuring in 1999, Kobe Steel discovered a violation of Japan's Commercial Code. Three Kobe executives were suspected of having paid *sokaiya* racketeers in return for their help in ensuring that the 1997 shareholders' meeting went smoothly. In November 1999 the executives concerned were subpoenaed for investigation by the police, and the company was subjected to police inspection. According to newspaper reports, the executives had made illicit payments for at least 11 years, for a total of about 210 million yen. It was also reported in the same month that a total of 160 million yen of "political contributions" had been transferred through a Venezuelan ambassador to Japan to a candidate running in Venezuela's 1998 presidential election.

The company reacted quickly. It established a Corporate Ethics Committee, transferred control over shareholders' meetings and stock affairs from the General Affairs Department to the Legal Department, and created the position of legal affairs management officer within the Legal Department. In 2000 a New Year's address by President Mizukoshi stressed the commitment of top management to corporate ethics. The president declared, "To restore lost trust from society as soon as possible, and to prevent another occurrence, we will devote our full efforts to improve the corporate culture of the company," which would become a "highly transparent corporation with a law-abiding spirit." In fiscal 2001 the company undertook to strengthen the role of external auditors and to improve the disclosure of matters relevant to shareholder meetings.

The makeup of Kobe Steel's Corporate Ethics Committee was unusual for a Japanese company. President Mizukoshi assumed the task of committee chair, joined by three board members and three experts from outside the company. In this structure the president exercises leadership while respecting views from outside the company and limiting participation from within the company. The Legal Department has administrative responsibility for the work of the committee.

The committee proposed a plan to establish a corporate ethics, or compliance, system by the end of fiscal 2002. Specific measures were to include the drafting of a code of ethics, the establishment of an ethics consultation office, the enhancement of internal controls, the implementation of compliance training, and the compilation and distribution of manuals. A compliance-related reporting and consultation system for early prevention or minimization of risks was also to be put in place.

## Corporate Code of Ethics

The Corporate Code of Ethics was drafted by middle management, reporting to the Corporate Ethics Committee, and was released in June 2000. In its preparation, some recourse was made to the codes of other companies. Despite its history of more than 90 years, Kobe Steel had nothing resembling a specific company code or statement of corporate philosophy.

The code now forms the center of Kobe Steel's approach to corporate ethics. Its introduction states that for a company to be ethical, individual employees must be mindful of the ethics of the company. The code is divided into Principles of Corporate Ethics, the Code of Conduct, and Guidelines for Implementation (box CS.1).

Part 2 of the Code of Conduct includes elements concerning gifts or graft:

- *Relationships with clients.* Entertaining and gift giving shall be within socially acceptable parameters. Employees are prohibited from giving

---

**Box CS.1.   Kobe Steel's Corporate Code of Ethics**

**A. Principles of Corporate Ethics**

- Observe the laws and regulations, as well as the standards of society, and conduct business in a fair and sound manner.
- Contribute to society by providing excellent products and services.
- Respect each employee's personality and individuality and create an open work environment.
- Respect stakeholders.
- Be a good corporate citizen and contribute to the community.
- Contribute to protecting the environment and building a more affluent and comfortable society.

**B. Code of Conduct**

*Part 1. Business activities*
- Provide excellent and safe products and services.
- Foster healthy and good relationships with customers and other parties.
- Promote fair and free competition.
- Protect intellectual property rights.

*Part 2. Kobe Steel and its employees*
- Respect each employee's personality and individuality.
- Protect privacy.
- Protect human rights and prohibit discrimination.
- Maintain a safe and healthy work environment.

*Part 3. Kobe Steel and society*
- Observe laws and regulations.
- Sever ties with antisocial elements.
- Disclose information.
- Protect the environment.
- Contribute to the community.

**C. Guidelines for Implementation**

The guidelines lay out the measures needed to implement the Principles of Corporate Ethics and the Code of Conduct and to monitor the state of compliance:

- Familiarization/establishment inside and outside the company.
- Implementation system for the Corporate Code of Ethics.

- Treatment of individuals violating the Code and the Principles.
- Means for consultation on laws and regulations described in the Code of Conduct, company regulations, manuals, and so on.

clients rebates, commissions, and other forms of compensation that would enable the clients to benefit personally or that are made discretionally. When employees must officially give gifts to customers, they must follow the rules approved by their departments.
- *Relationships with suppliers.* Suppliers should be selected on the basis of rational criteria such as price, quality, and terms of delivery. Employees may be entertained by or receive gifts from suppliers as long as these are within the parameters of what is socially acceptable. Employees must report such activities to their managers. If suppliers provide entertainment or gifts that go beyond the norm, employees must refuse such entertainment or return the gifts.
- *Relationships with affiliated companies and partner companies.* Transactions with Kobe's affiliated companies and partner companies should be as fair and transparent as third-party transactions. Entertainment and gifts must be within socially acceptable limits.
- *Relationships with ministries and local governments.* With regard to civil service personnel, employees must respect the National Civil Service Personnel Ethics Law (Law No. 129 of 1999) and the National Civil Service Personnel Ethics Regulation (Cabinet Order No. 101 of 2000).

The introduction to Part 3 of the code states that "Kobe Steel shall conduct business following the laws and regulations, as well as the norms and rules, of society. Employees shall be aware that violations of the law may jeopardize the existence of the Company."

Severance of ties with antisocial elements is of concern for the company because of its involvement in past scandals. The relevant part of the code reads as follows:

Kobe Steel shall not become involved with any individual or group that has an adverse influence on the social order or on the sound business activities of the Company. In particular, Kobe Steel's management should not fear such people and should become a role model in correct behavior. . . . If racketeers or other criminal elements attempt to extort money from the Company by making a claim against its products or any other reason, such act will be regarded as a civil violence case. On the principles of not being afraid, not giving any payoffs and not taking advantage of others, Kobe Steel shall systematically fight against such intimidation. The Company shall not isolate any employee.

# Implementation System

The main points of interest in the implementation of Kobe Steel's compliance system are the responsibilities of the Corporate Ethics Committee, the company's communications and training activities, and the work of compliance managers and the Ethics Consultation Office.

## Corporate Ethics Committee

Although not much time has passed since its launch, the Corporate Ethics Committee has already played an important role in establishing a corporate ethics program. The committee is responsible for monitoring compliance with laws and regulations governing business activities. Specifically, it coordinates matters relating to the Corporate Code of Ethics, ethics consultation channels, enhancement of internal auditing, compliance training, and compilation of compliance-related manuals. These tasks are carried out by the Legal Affairs Management Office, which has a staff of seven. (The Legal Department as a whole has a staff of 22—a relatively small number for the size of the company.)

The Corporate Ethics Committee meets four times a year. The issues discussed in the committee are reported to the Board of Directors as needed.

## Communications and Training

To familiarize officers and employees with the behavior expected of them, the company has created and distributed a Corporate Ethics Handbook. In a commendable step unusual for a Japanese corporation, the full text of the Corporate Code of Ethics has been made public, in Japanese and in English, on the company Website.[1] Booklets on risk management regulations and on general principles of risk management have been issued to staff.

Compliance education and training to increase awareness of the ethics program is conducted at various levels—for new employees, general employees, and managers—and in a variety of facilities. Those in charge of the training have the impression that work group leaders at each site have a higher awareness of the company's ethics code than do the other categories of workers.

Training covers overall compliance and particular issues, laws, and regulations—for example measures against organized crime, the Antimonopoly Law, and the Subcontractor Law. Specific manuals on such topics are prepared for use in training.

The head office does not implement education and training in ethics and compliance for overseas facilities or subsidiary companies. Whether to carry out such training is left to the discretion of the planning and administration department in each constituent division.

## Compliance Managers

Compliance is the responsibility of the general manager of each department, who appoints a compliance manager to deal with practical issues in this area. Compliance managers are required to make periodic reports on implementation to the Corporate Ethics Committee.

## Ethics Consultation Office

An Ethics Consultation Office for employees has been established in the Office of the Corporate Ethics Committee. The office can be reached by telephone, fax, or electronic mail, but it has not been contacted very often. More frequent are consultations with officers responsible for human rights matters, who are placed in each facility to field reports and provide consultations on matters such as sexual harassment and gender discrimination.

## Prevention of Bribery of Foreign Public Officials

Among the ethics and compliance topics that are of concern to Kobe Steel, preventing bribery of foreign public officials may not be receiving the highest priority. Although the company could have incorporated a specific rule explicitly prohibiting bribery of foreign public officials in the Code of Conduct, it did not. Part 3 of the code stipulates that "the Company shall not give illegal remuneration or other benefits to Japanese and overseas government officials related to their official services."[2] Routine business audits are conducted, but there is no specific oversight system designed to prevent corruption.

The offices responsible for antibribery initiatives are the central Legal Department and the planning and administration departments of each of the six international units that make up the corporation. The Legal Department does not organize companywide training and seminars specifically on preventing overseas bribery, but the issue of bribery is covered in general compliance training and seminars. Seminars focusing on overseas bribery will be held, if necessary, with a clear focus on managers of the departments that undertake international business. For example, immediately after the entry into force of the amended Unfair Competition Prevention Law, several training sessions were carried out in the Overseas Engineering Department.

It is questionable whether Kobe Steel has invested sufficient effort in addressing the issue of overseas bribery. Slackened demand for plant business will not immunize the company from the risks associated with bribery of foreign public officials. It is recommended that Kobe Steel introduce more extensive and inclusive antibribery measures as a form of risk management.

# Notes

This section was prepared by Profs. Iwao Taka and Toru Umeda of Reitaku University and by Mr. Takaji Hishiyama.

1. The Kobe Steel Corporate Code of Ethics is available at <http://www.kobelco.co.jp/column/topics-e/messages/53.html>.

2. The amended Unfair Competition Prevention Law, which criminalizes the bribery of foreign public officials, came into effect in February 1999. Kobe Steel's Corporate Code of Ethics, including the Code of Conduct, was established after that date.

# Sumitomo Corporation

The Sumitomo Corporation is one of Japan's leading *sogo shosha*, or integrated trading companies. The history of Sumitomo began in the early 17th century when Masatomo Sumitomo opened a book and medicine shop in Kyoto. The Sumitomo Corporation now conducts worldwide commerce in products, services, and technologies. It has 30,715 employees (including those of consolidated subsidiaries) in nine business units and operates in 88 countries. Annual sales are about US$80 billion.

A scandal stemming from improper copper transactions that involved the corporation gave impetus to the recent efforts to address corporate governance. These efforts have included the introduction of an ethical compliance system and the development of a present-day form of the "Sumitomo Business Spirit," which has been handed down in an unbroken line for 400 years (see box 4.1 in chapter 4). The principles are now incorporated in Sumitomo's Management Principles, Activity Guidelines, Sumitomo Corporation (SC) Values, and Compliance Manual. The corporation has also introduced comprehensive measures to prevent bribery of foreign public officials. A number of unique measures have been devised, including the incorporation of the SC Values into personnel records, the Speak-Up helpline system, a verification system for preventing improper payments; and reform of the corporate climate through direct dialogue. New employees are instructed about the Sumitomo Business Spirit at the very beginning. Framed copies of the Business Principles hang in the corporation's offices.

## Managerial Commitment

Since 1996, Sumitomo's presidents have expressed strong personal commitment to good corporate governance, greatly influencing what has been accomplished. For example, in June 2001 President Oka sent a New President's message to all employees stating his vision for a global company "whose *Corporate Vision*, *Management Principles*, and *Activity Guidelines* reach across all the barriers of culture and language to be shared as common values by all employees across the globe, each of whom implements them with confidence and pride." He observed that, as the basis for this vision, the highest priority must be given to "integrity and sound management" and "compliance." The following month, he stressed to staff that "comprehensive compliance is tantamount to the practice of our management principles."

## Corporation Management Principles and Activity Guidelines

The Sumitomo Corporation embarked on major corporate reforms in 1996 in response to a scandal. A former department manager had been engaging in improper copper transactions, and Sumitomo was forced to record a loss of approximately 285 billion yen. As a result, fiscal 1996 was the company's first unprofitable year since its founding. Incoming president Miyahara stressed that "we must return to the origins of the Sumitomo Business Spirit [and] must use this incident as a spur to build a company imbued with tension and activity, one that imparts energy and vitality, and one worth working for."

As part of this effort, Sumitomo established its Management Principles and Activity Guidelines with the intent of building better corporate governance. The values expressed by these two statements together form the SC Values, which, it was stipulated, "are to coexist as the basis for conduct and judgment in the course of duties." The SC Values are a modern-day paraphrase of the Sumitomo Business Spirit (see box CS.2).

The Management Principles, Activity Guidelines, and SC Values apply to both domestic and overseas group companies. Cards, handbooks, intranet sites, and other resources are used to promote employees' thorough knowledge of these statements.

## Implementation System

Sumitomo began reinforcing its ethics compliance system in 2000. In November of that year a Compliance Committee was established, with three functions: to promote and coordinate compliance, to share information and prevent duplication, and to handle problems that surface through the Speak-Up system. The members of the committee include the chairs of the corporate groups (Internal Auditing, Legal, Personnel and General Affairs, Planning and Coordination, IT Planning and Promotion, Accounting, and Risk Management), advised by a consulting attorney. Administrative services are provided by the Legal Group. After each meeting, the results are reported to the Board of Directors, as needed, and to the Board of Corporate Auditors. The committee meets every three months.

---

**Box CS.2.    Statement of the Sumitomo Corporation Values**

Our intention is to be a global organization that is constantly a step ahead in dealing with change, creates new value, and contributes broadly to society.

**Management Principles**
To achieve prosperity and realize dreams through sound business activities.
To place prime importance on integrity and sound management with utmost respect for the individual.
To foster a corporate culture full of vitality and conducive to innovation.

**Activity Guidelines**
To act with honesty and sincerity on the basis of the Sumitomo Spirit and in keeping with the Management Principles.
To comply with laws and regulations while maintaining the highest ethical standards.
To set high value on transparency and openness.
To attach great importance to protecting the global environment.
To contribute to society as a good corporate citizen.
To achieve teamwork and integrate corporate strength through active communication.
To set clear objectives and achieve them with enthusiasm.

**Pillars of the SC Values**
Integrity and sound management
Integrated corporate strength
Vision
Change and innovation
Commitment
Enthusiasm
Speed
Human development
Professionalism

---

## Communications and Training

Since April 2001, a Compliance Manual has been issued to all employees. Compliance is treated as the responsibility of each employee, including executives. The manual provides guidelines on such topics as adherence to the antimonopoly law and prohibition of unfair competition, prohibition of bribery, prevention of improper payments to foreign public officials, restriction of insider trading, and bans on conflicts of interest. It also includes specific advice for applying the guidelines.

At present, the Compliance Manual applies only within Sumitomo Corporation itself. Its situations do not apply to the various subsidiary firms within Japan and abroad or to affiliated companies. The Compliance Committee, however, makes requests and provides guidance to these companies to create systems that enhance compliance. To this end, the Compliance Manual is distributed to managers at overseas locations. A U.S.-specific manual has been created for U.S. subsidiaries, and a manual for Europe is being prepared. Manuals for Asia are in the study phase.

Meetings to explain the Compliance Manual to all managerial employees began in July 2001. The corporation holds practical training sessions whenever laws or regulations are newly enacted or revised.

Compliance education is incorporated into various employee training courses, including courses for new managers (directors) and administrators. Legal compliance chapters are included in a basic book for employees with fewer than five years' employment and in a career training book for employees who have been with the firm one or two years.

## Personnel Evaluations

A pioneering practice that deserves mention is Sumitomo's annual evaluation of employee performance with regard to the SC Values (see box CS.3). This evaluation applies to all employees, from the rank and file to department heads, and it accounts for 20 percent of an employee's total personnel evaluation. Because the results affect awards, pay raises, and promotions, employees take the evaluation seriously. This appears to be an extremely effective system for inculcating the ethical values of the company. In the future, the system will cover all officers, including the president.

## Reporting and Warning Procedures

The Speak-Up system, a help line for consultation and reporting, was put in place for use when employees do not feel they can use normal managerial channels. In principle, information with attribution is communicated to the administrative body of the Compliance Committee, which then handles the issue in strict confidence. The system began operation in November 2000. At the time of writing, it had handled no noteworthy matters.

---

**Box CS.3.   Evaluation on Values at Sumitomo**

Each employee of the Sumitomo Corporation is asked to evaluate his or her own performance, judging it as "good" or "needs improvement" for each pillar of the SC Values, and to make an overall assessment of performance, graded as A, B, or C. The employee's supervisor then assesses the employee's performance and meets with the subordinate for discussion.

At the same time, employees are observers of how their supervisors conduct their jobs, including their compliance with the SC Values. Employee assessments of the supervisor's job performance are gathered and tabulated by the division manager, who in turn feeds back the results to his subordinate—that is, the supervisor in question. This system provides useful material for reflection by supervisors on their own performance. This mixture of self-evaluation and evaluation by the superior (multifaceted evaluation) is expected to promote communication in the workplace.

---

# Prevention of Bribery of Foreign Public Officials

The Activity Guidelines charge employees "to comply with laws and regulations while maintaining the highest ethical standards." Accordingly, internal training instructs employees that bribery is clearly prohibited.

The February 1999 amendment to the Unfair Competition Prevention Law gave the corporation an opportunity to specify and activate a specific policy against bribery, especially of foreign public officials. At that time, revisions were made to the Compliance Manual:

- Section 9 of the revised manual stipulates that "actions constituting bribery or actions having that appearance are never to be taken, and exchanges of gifts, entertainment, or similar activities with public officials are in principle prohibited."
- Section 10, "Prohibition of Improper Payments to Foreign Public Officials," takes a strong stance against bribery of foreign public officials: "Employees must not provide payments or other gain to foreign public officials improperly for the purpose of obtaining business, nor may they promise or suggest the same."[1]

Compulsory instructions were also issued on Essential Safeguards for Preventing Improper Payments, and administrative procedures were strengthened to help prevent bribery.

Since February 1999, the corporation has run seminars on bribery for all departments and divisions engaged in foreign trade to promote thorough knowledge of the issue, and the topic is part of the basic course for young employees at Sumitomo Business College.

## Note

This section was prepared by Profs. Iwao Taka and Toru Umeda of Reitaku University and by Mr. Takaji Hishiyama.

1. To this are added the following three specific guidelines adapted to the activities of the trading company itself:

- "When exchanging gifts, making a contribution, entertaining, inviting, or engaging in a similar activity with a foreign public official, or when paying a commission or other such administrative fee in connection with receipt of an order or similar activities, the separately established 'Essential Safeguards' and 'Checklist for Preventing Improper Payments' must be used as the basis to ascertain that the payment complies with domestic and foreign laws and regulations, customs, and other such stipulations.
- "When executing a contract relating to payment of an administrative fee or the like, the several points listed in the 'Essential Safeguards' must be checked and obeyed, regardless of the name of the contract concerned, such as Sales Agent Contract or Consultant Contract.
- "If you have concerns, questions, or other inquiries in a particular transaction, consult the Legal Group or other related departments or divisions well in advance."

# Toyota Motor Corporation

Toyota Motor Corporation was established in 1937 through the determination of Kiichiro Toyoda, the son of Sakichi Toyoda, renowned as the inventor of the automatic loom. Toyota's current production base includes 15 plants in Japan and 42 companies in 25 other countries. In 1999 Toyota produced roughly 5.4 million automobiles worldwide. Other company businesses include housing, information and communications, finance, intelligent transit systems, marine business, and biotechnology and afforestation. Consolidated fiscal 2000 figures showed 211,000 employees and nearly 13 trillion yen in revenue.

Toyota has a well-established reputation for productivity growth and the creation of economic value. It is also held in high regard internationally and domestically in the social realm, placing third in the Ranking of the World's Most Socially Responsible Companies and tenth in the Ranking of the World's Most Respected Companies (*Financial Times*, Dec. 15, 2000). In the 2001 Ranking of Corporate Social Contributions by Leading Companies, published by the Asahi Shimbun Foundation, Toyota ranked first in "Harmony with Community," tenth in "Family Orientation," and tenth in "Environmental Protection."

## Basic Philosophy and Top Leadership

The basic philosophy expounded by Sakichi Toyoda continues to play a key role in the company's management and is one of its distinctive features. It underlies the Guiding Principles at Toyota, which were elaborated in 1992 and revised in 1997 (see box CS.4). Successive chairmen of the company have personally involved themselves in updating the company philosophy for changing times and in elaborating guidance for employees.

In 1997, under the leadership of then-chairman Shoichiro Toyoda, the company revised the Guiding Principles to better reflect the company's globalization and the expanded social role and responsibilities it had taken on.

---

**Box CS.4.  Guiding Principles at Toyota**

1. Honor the language and spirit of the law of every nation and undertake open and fair corporate activities to be a good corporate citizen of the world.
2. Respect the culture and customs of every nation and contribute to economic and social development through corporate activities in the communities.
3. Dedicate ourselves to providing clean and safe products and to enhancing the quality of life everywhere through all our activities.
4. Create and develop advanced technologies and provide outstanding products and services that fulfill the needs of customers worldwide.
5. Foster a corporate culture that enhances individual creativity and teamwork value, while honoring mutual trust and respect between labor and management.
6. Pursue growth in harmony with the global community through innovative management.
7. Work with business partners in research and creation to achieve stable, long-term growth and mutual benefits, while keeping ourselves open to new partnerships.

---

In 1998 the company introduced the Code of Conduct for Toyota Employees with the aim of putting the Guiding Principles in a functional form that gives specific guidance on conduct. In 2001, under the leadership of President Cho, it introduced Toyota Way 2001. This effort reflected a perceived need for a more explicit worldwide affirmation and sharing of the Toyota beliefs, values, and techniques that had been handed down tacitly, including "continuous improvement" and "respect for people."

The Guiding Principles are embodied in Toyota's 2005 Vision and the associated plans and policies. Efforts to impart a thorough knowledge of principles and policies have been made down to the divisional and departmental levels so that coherent, unified action can be undertaken throughout the company.

## Corporate Code of Ethics

Each item of Toyota's Code of Conduct for Toyota Employees contains a theme and a subtitle that describes its essence, a basic philosophy section, specific conduct guidelines, and a consultation section concerning the theme (see box CS.5). In line with the respect for teamwork and

---

**Box CS.5.  Outline of the Code of Conduct for Toyota Employees**

Guiding Principles at Toyota
President's Message

Chapter 1  Employee Code of Conduct for the Company Relationship
Includes "Creating a Vibrant Workplace"

Chapter 2  Employee Code of Conduct for Company Activities
Includes procurement, overseas projects, and other operational activities

Chapter 3  Employee Code of Conduct for Societal Relations
Includes relationships with government offices

Chapter 4  Employee Code of Conduct for Personal Activities
Includes illegal activities and antisocial activities

---

spontaneous individual commitment that are part of the Toyota Way, the tone of the Code of Conduct is not "must not do" but "should/should not do"—an expression that is meant to give each employee a sense of spontaneous commitment.[1]

## Implementation System

Toyota's general approach, based on traditional management principles and manufacturing experience, is that responsibility for corporate ethics and for adherence to the Unfair Competition Prevention Law resides at the local level, where the issues are thoroughly familiar. In 2000 Toyota's Corporate Conduct Ethics Committee decided to work out specific codes of conduct for application in each group. Groups that are currently developing these codes include Domestic Sales, Overseas Relations, Production Technology, Quality Assurance, Production and Distribution, General Affairs and Personnel, Public Relations, Environment, Legal, Information and Communications, and Housing.

### Corporate Conduct Ethics Committee

The Corporate Conduct Ethics Committee is the highest organization responsible for overall coordination of corporate ethics-related activities. Reflecting Toyota's concern for corporate ethics, the committee includes 11 senior management people: the company president, who serves as chairman, and the company executive vice presidents. The committee meets two or three times a year, and its proceedings are reported to the Management Meeting and then companywide through appointed officers. The Legal and Accounting Divisions serve jointly as the administrative body.

A coordinating post for activities related to corporate ethics has been established in each division, and each of these coordinating posts is responsible for establishing and implementing specific measures for progress within the division.

## Communications and Training

The Code of Conduct is distributed to all company officers and employees, both those in Japan and those transferred overseas. Its essentials are described to all department heads, who are instructed to make them thoroughly known in their departments. The code is accessible on company intranets.

To evaluate the success of communications and training, the company surveys employees to assess their familiarity with the Guiding Principles and the Code of Conduct. In April 1999, 15 months after the code was introduced, 91 percent of the respondents were found to have a good or improved understanding of the code; the average score was 3.6 out of 5.0, as against 3.0 six months earlier.

When Japan's Unfair Competition Prevention Law was revised in February 1999, Toyota's Corporate Conduct Ethics Committee heard a summary of the legal revision and a description of its background. Since the committee then included officers at the rank of managing director and higher (it is now made up of vice presidents and higher-ranking officers), top management can be said to have taken the initiative in receiving training.

The Code of Conduct, in conjunction with the Guiding Principles and the 2005 Vision, is incorporated into training for new employees and into periodic internal company training. Practical training courses are carried out as needed; examples include seminars for new officers, which explain the responsibilities of officers under commercial law; training for advancing employees, to address their expanded authority and responsibilities; seminars for overseas appointees, to explain the legal systems of individual countries; and antimonopoly law seminars covering particular issues.

## Warning Procedures

The Legal Division manages intranet homepages that provide readily accessible information on appropriate conduct. This information includes question forms that allow any employee to seek advice by e-mail about an ethics problem. The thinking is that this service can help nip problems in the bud.

# Prevention of Bribery of Foreign Public Officials

Before the 1999 revision of the Unfair Competition Prevention Law, Toyota's Code of Conduct already gave examples of corruption likely to arise in various circumstances and clearly prohibited corrupt actions, at home or abroad. After the revision of the law, explicit measures were taken to prevent bribery of foreign public officials. With the assistance of the Legal Division, Toyota's Overseas Planning Division issued guidance to promote knowledge of the law:

- An explanatory manual, "Prohibition on Providing Improper Gains to Foreign Public Officials," presents the foreign and domestic background leading to revision of the Unfair Competition Prevention Law, the essentials of the manual, a summary of the law, the compliance system in Toyota, and contacts for help.
- A question-and-answer supplement to the manual with examples of specific problems is designed to increase understanding of the bribery issue. It covers definitions of concepts and policies; views on facilitation payments, entertainment, and gifts; and application of the principles to foreign subsidiary companies, partners, and company employees.

# Application to Subsidiaries

To the extent that Toyota employees assigned to a foreign subsidiary company are engaged in daily production activities at a plant, the possibility for involvement in on-site corruption seems comparatively low. Nonetheless, Toyota takes comprehensive measures that spare no effort. These measures are administered by the Overseas Planning Division, which is responsible for promoting legal compliance by posts that oversee foreign subsidiary companies or are in direct contact with foreign public officials. It also requests those posts to report on the status of legal compliance and responds to inquiries and reports that it receives from them. The Legal Division provides support to the Overseas Planning Division.

Within the Overseas Project Group, the relevant posts are responsible for making their employees thoroughly familiar with the content of the manuals, for checking on the extent of compliance, and for providing guidance as needed. They consult the Overseas Planning Division on questions or uncertain issues, including those posed by employees. When posts learn of actual corruption or determine that an illegal action may have occurred, they report to the Overseas Planning Division immediately.

The Overseas Project Group has clear responsibility for preventing corruption, with the Legal Division in a supporting role. At present, 8 legal specialists from the Legal Department (which currently has 64 staff members) are on assignment in various regions of the world. In the East Asia and Pacific region, one specialist is posted in Singapore and one in China. Under the motto "Local resources for local sites," local information and experience are shared in consultations regarding legal problems, and functional communication is carried on with the Legal Division at headquarters.

The Legal Division holds an annual global business and legal meeting for those responsible for overseas legal issues. This meeting provides an opportunity for seamless cooperation and exchange of information.

Considerable training covering ethics matters, among other subjects, is directed toward the corporations that make up the Toyota Group. The Toyota Legal Affairs Meeting, which provides training on new rulings, laws, and regulations, holds classes for officers and department heads in the 13-company group. There are numerous other examples, including courses on antimonopoly law and lectures on legal issues in sales that provide training on laws bearing on topics such as debt collection and sales.

# Note

This section was prepared by Profs. Iwao Taka and Toru Umeda of Reitaku University and by Mr. Takaji Hishiyama.

1. Reflecting this encouragement of individual commitment, when Toyota began production through NUMMI (a joint venture with General Motors) in the United States, it built teams, encouraged original thinking, and promoted *kaizen* ("continuous improvement") plans. The reported result was that productivity nearly doubled (Shimada 1988).

# The Chinese Art of Guanxi
# in Business

Over the past two decades, China and much of Southeast Asia have enjoyed unprecedented economic growth. One of the key factors behind the region's rapid development is Chinese *guanxi* relationships, which link literally millions of Chinese firms throughout the region into a social and business network.

What is guanxi and how does it work? Why is it of such vital importance in the context of Chinese business? What business conduct concerns does guanxi give rise to? And how can we expect practices to evolve, given China's increasing integration with the global economy and the country's publicly expressed desire to adhere to international business norms?

## What Is Guanxi?

Guanxi is generally defined as a connection or relationship, but it is an oversimplification to equate it with conventional business networking. It can only be properly understood in a cultural context, as a concept deeply rooted in Confucian Chinese tradition.

Confucius identified five key social relationships (ruler/subject, father/son, husband/wife, older brother/younger brother, and friend/friend) and outlined the obligations that members of each set have to the other party. The individual is valued as a person only to the extent that he or she is a member of one or more such groups. Guanxi is the bond of trust that ties an individual within these long-term relationships. Guanxi bonds are characterized by reciprocity and mutual obligations.

Guanxi has been described as an "I scratch your back, you scratch mine" type of give-and-take. Although this characterization captures the reciprocity inherent in guanxi, the relationship is rarely in balance at any point in time. Rather, the balance tends to shift between the parties over the long term, as needs arise. Thus, I could be scratching your back for a good while before the need arises for you to reciprocate. Perhaps a more apt comparison is a two-way line of credit, to be drawn on in time of need.

Unlike such banking arrangements, however, no formal accounting of "indebtedness" is maintained.

Despite the absence of a contractual commitment, guanxi ties are considered binding. Someone who fails to return an obligation risks loss of face, personally and for the members of the network. Since guanxi networks often comprise generations of family members, the social pressure to deliver on guanxi commitments—and avoid family embarrassment—can be intense. Maintaining face, or *mianzi*, for oneself and one's family is important because one must possess a certain amount of personal prestige to be considered trustworthy, which in turn is the basis for cultivating and maintaining guanxi.

## Why Is Guanxi Important and Relevant in the Context of Chinese Business?

Guanxi networks have enabled Chinese companies to transact business efficiently and to operate in high-risk environments. In fact, the strength of guanxi ties is generally recognized as being a key determinant of business success in China. Studies have shown that companies gain a competitive edge by building and maintaining a strong guanxi network.[1] This is particularly important for smaller companies, which often depend on guanxi to survive. Guanxi is important for a number of reasons, which are discussed next.

### *Mitigating External Political and Socioeconomic Risk*

Many Chinese companies operate in environments with a high level of political and societal risk. In a number of countries in Southeast Asia, for example, ethnic Chinese constitute a small minority of the population and control a disproportionate share of the national economy. This has periodically made them the focus of resentment and backlash by the ethnic majority. Maintaining close-knit guanxi ties enables the groups to survive and operate in hostile environments. In addition, guanxi networks can be relied on to help companies raise capital—which is especially important when national lending institutions discriminate against ethnic Chinese.

### *Navigating Opaque Bureaucracies*

Although the situation has been improving in recent years, the Chinese government is known for its enormous and difficult-to-navigate bureaucracy. Challenges take various forms. For example, China has a number of internal, or *neibu*, regulations that are not publicly accessible. Guanxi with appropriate individuals can help a company become aware of and properly interpret such rules. In addition, there may be situations in which the jurisdictions of government agencies overlap or where their expectations conflict. Guanxi can help a company clarify the government's expectations and secure necessary approvals.

## Coping with the Absence of Rule of Law

It has been said that guanxi fills the gap between the law and its enforcement. Historically, guanxi has been especially valuable for businesses operating in countries without a stable legal and regulatory environment or without an independent judiciary.

Although the situation in China has been improving with the country's entry into the World Trade Organization (WTO), there is still a perception that laws are not completely or impartially enforced.[2] Furthermore, cultural considerations play an important role in discouraging individuals from seeking legal recourse. "The first response . . . is to seek guanxi when disputes arise."[3] And "rather than depending on an abstract notion of impartial justice, Chinese people traditionally preferred to rely on their contacts with those in power to get things done" (Luo 1997: 54). If laws are open to interpretation, it makes sense to have strong ties to people in a position of power who have the authority to interpret laws in your favor.

## Accessing Reliable Information, Resources, and Infrastructure

Guanxi can be helpful in acquiring reliable information, coping with shortages of goods, and overcoming difficulties with communications and transport. In the past one could not acquire necessary materials or get business done without strong guanxi ties. Today, guanxi expedites the flow of information and resources by circumventing bureaucratic obstacles that slow the process.

Guanxi is also important in helping businesses predict market changes. Because information flows freely and efficiently among members of a network and guanxi networks know no national boundaries, businesses can respond swiftly to changing market demand and conditions. Thus, many Chinese companies are able to meet market demand quickly without having to wait for formal market research.

## Recruiting Trustworthy Employees

Traditionally, Chinese companies have hired employees using guanxi networks. While this practice occasionally results in hiring based on reliability rather than competence, Chinese employers often believe that having highly loyal and committed employees makes up for any loss in efficiency.

As this list implies, the use of guanxi has far-reaching implications for how business is conducted by Chinese firms, touching on legal, financial, marketing, and human resource issues, as well as the personal and family sphere. It is a remarkably streamlined and efficient system of decentralized networks that has enabled Chinese businesses to operate effectively for centuries.

## What Business Conduct Issues Arise Concerning Guanxi?

Given this background, several questions arise: To what extent does guanxi promote a *fair* competitive edge for business? Do the honestly gained advantages of guanxi outweigh the potential for abuse or misconduct? The business conduct issues raised by guanxi are discussed next.

## *Corruption*

It is important to note that tapping relationships to facilitate business, while sometimes controversial, is not the equivalent of corruption. The Chinese tend to draw a clear line between appropriate use of guanxi and abuse in the form of bribery or corruption.

Guanxi has several characteristics that differentiate it from corruption (Luo 2002: ch. 4):

- *Time orientation*. Corruption is based on a short-term, transaction-based exchange, whereas guanxi is a long-term relationship. Furthermore, no time limits are expressed for guanxi-related favors; corrupt activities generally have explicit deadlines that must be met.
- *Morality*. Guanxi is an ethically accepted practice in Chinese society, whereas corruption is considered immoral.
- *Legality*. Guanxi is legal and admired in Chinese society; corruption is illegal and is widely condemned.
- *Nature of transaction*. Guanxi involves an exchange of favors, as opposed to a monetary exchange. Moreover, guanxi is inherently a social transaction—the cost of noncompliance is a loss of face. Corruption, by contrast, is an economic transaction that has legal consequences.
- *Transferability*. Long-term guanxi ties (and obligations) can be transferred to other members of a network, whereas corruption is generally a transaction-based covert relationship between two individuals.

---

**Box CS.6.    Letting in the Light in a Trade Office**

In his memoirs, N. T. Wang, a Harvard-educated economist, recalls that he was offered his first job—in China, after World War II and before the Communist Revolution—through "the Chairman," with whom he had personal guanxi. He accepted the position without any knowledge of the position or even a discussion of salary. On relocating to China, he learned that he was to become chairman of the Economic Commission for several northeastern provinces and that he would be responsible for all the region's imports and exports.

Given the lucrative business at stake, both the position and the department were susceptible to corruption. Wang notes that there was no system of checks or balances, nor were there clear lines of authority or oversight. He recounts one occasion when he was offered a six-figure U.S. dollar sum to grant a license to an individual. Although he walked out on the person, he did not feel comfortable taking legal action: he felt that there was insufficient evidence to pursue the case legally, and he was concerned that the person would turn the tables and accuse him of soliciting a bribe. Thus, he saw no benefit to blowing the whistle.

Wang describes the policy of "complete transparency" that he followed to ensure that his department remained free of corruption. He made all policies and procedures public information, posted licenses for public inspection, and invited journalists to ask questions about commission decisions. He found this Western-style "sunlight" approach effective in combating bribery.

*Source:* Wang (2001).

---

These distinctions notwithstanding, in some instances guanxi helps create conditions in which corruption can take root (see box CS.6).

## Cronyism

Two companies are competing for a contract. The company that makes an inferior bid is awarded the deal. The key decisionmakers share close guanxi ties. Is this a clear case of cronyism? While cronyism is a possibility, it must also be remembered that the Chinese generally prefer to do business with people they know and trust because this can lead to long-term business benefits and better deals in the future. Although such situations may elicit allegations of cronyism or favoritism, it is not valid to say that such use of guanxi is a de facto case of cronyism. As with corruption, however, guanxi ties can be used to facilitate cronyism, even though that is viewed as an improper use of guanxi in Chinese culture.

## Nepotism in Hiring

The Chinese preference, particularly in smaller family-owned firms, for hiring people who are known and trusted raises concerns about nepotism when candidates who are professionally more qualified are rejected in favor of a candidate with good guanxi. In addition, recruitment decisions are sometimes influenced by the guanxi that a potential new hire brings to the organization. Since guanxi is primarily rooted in interpersonal relationships, employees bring their guanxi with them when they join a new organization.

## Gift Giving and Entertainment

Gift giving and entertainment are important cultural traditions and play a key role in building and cultivating guanxi. Such practices are generally seen as a sign of goodwill and respect and are viewed as legitimate investments in the relationship. It is important to note that the Chinese generally distinguish between genuine guanxi and superficial attempts to influence a relationship by "wine and meat friends." Similarly, inappropriately lavish or impersonal gifts may be viewed not as legitimate guanxi building but as improper attempts to influence the outcome of a business decision. This is exemplified by the case of Beijing's former mayor, Chen Xitong, whose extensive collection of Rolex watches and other luxury gifts was widely publicized on Chinese television and who was sent to prison for corruption.

## Lack of Financial Transparency

Just as guanxi centers on bonds of trust, it is also true that those with whom one does not have guanxi are often viewed warily, or at least with a healthy dose of suspicion. Chinese businesses, much like private companies elsewhere, are reluctant to share information about their companies with unaffiliated outside parties.

When one considers the often hostile environments within which Chinese firms operate, this reluctance is understandable. Interestingly, it has been noted in the Asian press that an Enron-type massive deception of investors could not happen in Southeast Asia, where investors are much less likely to assume when they review public information that they are receiving a full and accurate reflection of a company's financial performance. Nonetheless, disclosure practices are gradually evolving in the direction of transparency as more Chinese companies go public on international stock markets.

## Whistle-Blowing

Whistle-blowing is relatively rare in guanxi-based cultures. This is because delivering on one's obligations in the relationship generally takes precedence over fulfilling personal and societal perceptions of fairness, integrity, and the public good, lessening the likelihood that a person will make the difficult moral choice of reporting misconduct to outside authorities. In addition, there are sometimes legitimate concerns that the other party will turn the tables and counteraccuse.

## Does Guanxi Facilitate or Impede Misconduct?

To what extent does guanxi foster conditions in which misconduct can take root? Is corruption, which is endemic among Chinese companies, both in China and abroad, attributable to guanxi?[4] Does guanxi lead to a suspension of moral judgment?

These questions defy easy response because guanxi has dynamics that pull in both directions. On the one hand, Chinese society distinguishes between proper and improper use of guanxi and condemns the latter. Nonetheless, there are numerous gray areas that are open to interpretation. Drawing a clear line can be frustrating for firms and employees alike, but there is one parameter that remains black and white: guanxi should operate in compliance with the laws and within a legal framework. Furthermore, guanxi is rooted in morality and is based on social relationships and prestige. Engaging in misconduct for personal benefit not only results in a loss of face for the individual but brings shame to the group or network with which that individual is associated. In this respect, guanxi acts to discourage improper behavior.

On the other hand, a trusted individual can hold a tremendous amount of discretionary authority with little oversight, and this creates an environment conducive to misconduct. When an individual engages in misconduct not for self-enrichment but for the ostensible benefit of the company, the link between guanxi and misconduct becomes more complex. In such a situation, should impropriety become public, does the imperative to deliver on obligations within one's guanxi network outweigh the potential opprobrium of the greater society? Furthermore, by discouraging whistle-blowing, guanxi lessens the likelihood that improper behavior will receive public attention. In these respects, it can be argued that guanxi promotes misconduct.

How these competing dynamics ultimately balance out is open to debate. But with the spread of internal and external monitoring and enforcement of policies, the professionalization of management, increased transparency of laws and regulations, and increased use of and faith in legal contracts, many of the environmental factors that enable guanxi to facilitate misconduct are gradually eroding.

## How Will Guanxi Evolve in the Future?

There are two schools of thought with respect to the future evolution of guanxi in China's fast-paced business environment. Some feel that the role of guanxi is declining in the face of market forces and expect that both within China and abroad, businesses will compete on a level playing field based on arm's-length transactions. The recent case of Citic Pacific and its head, Larry Yung, is cited as an example (box CS.7).

The second school of thought, which is more generally accepted, maintains that despite economic advances, guanxi is more entrenched than ever. Although there have been periodic efforts by the Chinese government to communicate the demise of guanxi in business, it remains a deeply embedded part of Chinese culture and will, in all likelihood, continue to heavily influence business conduct in the future.

Even so, the practice of guanxi has been evolving. Whereas in the past guanxi was essential at every point in a transaction, this is no longer the case in China today. "It's absolutely necessary to open doors in the

---

**Box CS.7.   Is Guanxi Declining in China? Hints from a Recent Case**

Larry Yung, the son of China's former vice president Rong Yiren, was widely known for his formidable guanxi ties in China. His personal reputation as someone who could get things done helped send Citic Pacific's stock surging in the 1990s.

In a sign that even Yung's guanxi has limitations, in January 2002 Citic Pacific announced that it was selling a fiber-optic network that it had acquired in 2000. The company failed to circumnavigate China's law barring foreign companies from getting licenses to operate in China. This was interpreted by some to mean that "Beijing may be telegraphing a message that guanxi capitalism is dead" (Balfour and Einhorn 2002).

beginning. But once the initial foundation is established, guanxi is less important than it used to be," according to Mitchell Presnick, managing director of Edelman Public Relations in China.

Furthermore, the rule of law is growing in China. "The role of guanxi is still there for Chinese and foreign companies, but the role of contracts has also expanded. There is more reliance on contract specifications and stipulations," says Yadong Luo of the University of Miami School of Business. In recent years procedures, laws, and regulations have become more standardized and now conform more closely to international norms. Most important, there has been a distinct evolution away from the "gentleman's handshake" and toward contracts as an accepted means of making business commitments.

There have also been structural changes in how guanxi is used today. Whereas in the past guanxi with government officials in China was considered of primary importance, businesspeople are increasingly recognizing the value of guanxi with other firms and stakeholder groups. Firms are viewing guanxi more strategically and flexibly than formerly. Thus, efforts are being made to transfer the personal guanxi of employees to the firm level. This new strategic approach to guanxi is being pursued in Chinese and Western firms alike.

In China today, Chinese and successful foreign firms share similar attitudes toward guanxi. For example, neither would shy away from hiring an individual solely on the basis of the value of the guanxi that person brings to the firm. For both, guanxi is first and foremost seen as a competitive advantage.

As China strives to comply with international business norms and compete globally, there are fewer areas that distinguish the guanxi practices of Chinese firms from those of their foreign counterparts. Both sometimes grapple with the business conduct issues that result from improper use of guanxi, just as they also actively seek to capitalize on the benefits and efficiencies to be derived from it. It seems certain that Chinese guanxi will continue to evolve to suit new environmental realities and will remain a defining characteristic of Chinese business conduct well into the future.

## Notes

This section was prepared by Ms. Kris Day, Calico Consultants.

1. Several studies link guanxi with improved business performance and competitive advantage. See, for example, Fan and Ambler (1998); Leung, Wong, and Wong (1996); Yeung and Tung (1996); Abramson and Ai (1997); and Luo (1997).

2. For example, many regulations that are inconsistent with WTO rules have been abrogated.

3. Zhongzhi Gao, a Chinese attorney and legal consultant to the World Bank, personal communication, 2001.

4. In the Transparency International's Bribe Payers Index released in May 2002, Chinese companies were considered highly likely to pay bribes. Of 21 countries evaluated, China ranked second to last. (See <www.transparency.org> for details on the Bribe Payers Index.)

# Jardine Matheson

Jardine Matheson, which was founded in the 19th century in Hong Kong (China), is a multinational enterprise with a portfolio of seven core businesses concentrated mainly in the Asia and Pacific region. Although Jardine Matheson is active in 30 countries, 77 percent of its profit comes from Asia. Within Asia, 75 percent of this total is in Hong Kong and 5 percent in mainland China. The company's activities include supermarkets, consumer marketing, engineering and construction, insurance brokering, automotive sales, property, and hotels. Companies in which Jardine Matheson has a substantial or controlling interest employ about 150,000 people.

## Origins of the Ethics Program

Jardine Matheson's current ethics program began in 1997 with a charge to James Watkins, the new director and general counsel of the group, to review and update a code that the company had issued in 1993–94. His approach was "to look at other company codes" and to develop business conduct guidelines relevant for "particular businesses and geographic areas" (personal communication, 2001).

A draft statement was submitted to and approved with minor changes by the Jardine Matheson board and the CEOs and chief financial officers (CFOs) of all the company's major trading businesses. The code is the same for all businesses and countries.

The code was reissued in February 2001 with a cover note from the new managing director. At this point, major changes are not likely to be made. As Watkins recalls, "The former CEO wanted it to be like the Ten Commandments. He would not be happy if it were subject to repeated amendments or changes."

The code addresses antibribery policies, and the group policy manual that was designed for management use provides a more detailed discussion. Giving or receiving "illicit payments," defined as "a secret payment to any person," is banned. Employees must report to any senior staff member any proposal or suggestion to make or receive such a payment. Failure to comply with this condition is grounds for dismissal.

Senior staff approval is the key to determining what payments are acceptable. The policy permits "small facilitative payments in exchange for routine administrative tasks as long as such payments are not made to obtain preferential treatment."

## Implementation System

Code distribution proceeds on two tracks. Managers receive the "long-form" Group Policy Manual, and all staff at the clerical level and above receive copies of the Code of Conduct. In addition to English, the code has been translated into Chinese, simplified Chinese, Thai, Malay, and Indonesian.

Training is not formal or structured, and it is limited to a 30-minute presentation by the group general counsel in the induction program for executive staff. Case studies are not discussed, but the general counsel does give examples of the kinds of situation that senior managers might confront.

## Reporting and Warning Procedures

The company has no whistle-blowing or hotline system. Persons who become aware of improprieties are encouraged to report such incidents to senior staff managers and, if need be, to bypass the person to whom they report.

Instead of a hotline, Jardine Matheson depends on quality management and self-discipline. Having introduced a code, it relies less on public or third-party exposure. Commenting on changes since promulgation of the code, Watkins says, "We get more enquiries asking whether activities are permissible because there is now greater need for compliance and more attention to whether particular acts are allowed under the code."

Fear of detection and exposure is not the only reason for seeking advice when confronted with questionable requests. The group audit requirement that senior managers submit a compliance letter with regard to activities under their direction and control is another important incentive for seeking clarification before making a decision that might contravene the code.

Watkins says that among managers there are differences in the degree of compliance, commitment, and diligence but that these are not rooted in cultural resistance. For example, with regard to the management team, he says,

> They are there as a resource. We rely on them to help us get new business and for management control. We want them to encourage compliance. Some

do, others take it less seriously. Whatever the situation may be, the reasons are due to personal rather than cultural distinctions.

It is also harder to judge program effectiveness in remote locations than it is in Hong Kong, where corporate staff have regular contact with local managers. Nonetheless, Watson says, there is "no reason to believe that there are serious disparities."

## Application to Joint Ventures

There are three different circumstances in which Jardine Matheson can apply its compliance standards in joint-venture situations:

- The company has a majority position and is able to insist on its compliance system (examples include Dairy Farm and Mandarin Hotels).
- The venture is jointly managed, and the other company's code is used. For example, the Schindler Lifts (Hong Kong) venture uses the Schindler code. When, however, Schindler bids on Hong Kong public works, it is required to use in tenders the Hong Kong business conduct standards, which are comparable to those of Jardine Matheson.
- The company is a minority shareholder and does not exercise management control, but the venture has its own code that is the same or similar (for example, Jardine Lloyd Thompson).

In the event that Jardine Matheson has neither equity control nor a partner with comparable business conduct standards, the key, Watkins emphasizes, is "whether the company manages the business for the shareholders." If it does, it is likely that the company's compliance system will be adequate.

# CLP

CLP is the largest electrical utility in Hong Kong (China). The company also invests in and operates power projects in mainland China, where it is the biggest private sector investor, and it develops and invests in projects throughout the Asia and Pacific region. In addition, CLP holds interests in generating assets in Malaysia, Taiwan (China), and Thailand.

## Origins of the Ethics Program

CLP promulgated its code of conduct in 1994. As one participant in that exercise said, "we codified a series of things that have been around." In this effort, CLP's Human Resources and Internal Audit Departments cooperated with Exxon (now ExxonMobil), its joint-venture partner in mainland power projects. Jack Vlastica, an Exxon employee seconded to CLP, was involved in the compliance program and helped coordinate the effort with Exxon policies and practices.

Bribery was specifically addressed in 1998 as part of an effort to codify good business practices with respect to gifts and entertainment. This addition was not made because of a specific incident, nor was it in response to the OECD Anti-Bribery Convention that was enacted in 1997.

## Application to Joint Ventures

Much of CLP's business is done through joint-venture agreements. The company has three methods of ensuring that its business conduct standards are met in these situations:

- *Participation in boards of joint ventures.* Where CLP has representatives on boards of joint ventures, it is often able to obtain approval for its code or for one with comparable standards.
- *Secondment of CLP personnel to joint ventures as deputy general managers working with local staff.* CLP managers say that CLP personnel see these arrangements as providing an opportunity for managers in

local companies to gain expertise in technologies that are new to them. Chinese partners are especially receptive to this approach because of corporate governance provisions mandated by the securities and exchange regulator.

- *Audit rights in the construction phase.* The audit terms in the construction phase of a contract are often sufficient to ensure that CLP's business conduct standards are met.

## Implementation System

CLP posts its code on the company Website and conducts companywide training every three or four years. In March 2000 the company issued a manual with a detailed description of training procedures. All 4,000 employees, including managing directors in China, go through training courses that are led by their managers. A session of the course is devoted to employee questions; those questions that cannot be answered on the spot are referred to a group internal auditor. Training programs do not use case studies but do discuss frequently asked questions.

The giving and receiving of gifts is the most common employee concern. Rather than rely on mechanistic applications of company policy, participants are asked to analyze a particular situation by using a four-step screening test:

- Is it legal to give or receive the gift?
- How would third parties view acceptance or giving of the gift? (That is, would you be comfortable with having others read about this action on the front page of the newspaper?)
- If you are the recipient, do you have the status or authority to reciprocate?
- What is the company's policy?

CLP has encouraged similar training programs in joint ventures. The Daya Bay power company has formulated a comparable code and is working through its board to communicate it to employees. Suppliers' compliance with CLP business conduct standards is obtained through contracts. Major contractors are audited, and the key ones have adopted codes similar to CLP's. In addition, some of CLP's long-term contractors participate in training programs.

## Advice and Learning Systems

CLP has found that the practice of discussing frequently asked questions in the course of training sessions provides useful information on troublesome problems that the company confronts. The compliance statement that every employee above a certain level must sign is a second source of information. Managers are asked to certify that their area is in compliance. If the necessary compliance level has not been achieved, the manager must state what the problem is or was and whether it has been or is being fixed.

# LG Electronics

LG Electronics (LGE) is a Korean company whose products and services include digital displays, appliances, media systems, handsets, and networks. Each of its component enterprises is managed autonomously. LGE has more than 70 subsidiaries in 40 countries. In 2000 more than two-thirds of its US$13 billion in sales revenues came from exports. China took nearly a fifth of these exports, and the rest of Asia accounted for roughly one-fourth.

## Corporate Code of Ethics

LGE's anticorruption policies and practices have evolved from the company's Code of Ethics, the fundamental purpose of which is to ensure fair competition. In 1993, looking ahead to 2000, top management saw that commitment to "free and fair competition" was critical to establishing and maintaining credibility in global business and that attention to corporate ethics and to building a culture of transparency must be a key element of the company's business plan. "Without fair transactions, we cannot be an excellent company," the leadership group argued.

The main obstacle to achieving these "fair transactions" was a pattern of exploitative supplier relations. Employees in procurement departments were asking for gratuities from suppliers. Sometimes they did not have to ask—they were offered gifts. Abuses in other areas were common, if less egregious: they included discrimination and favoritism in human resource decisions and occasional theft, embezzlement, and improper use of proprietary information by employees.

The Ethics Code was drafted by a committee consisting of the chief executive officer (CEO) and seven or eight business managers, supported by the Internal Audit Department. For benchmarks, the authors looked at best-practice companies in similar industries (for example, General Electric) and at high-profile examples such as the Singapore Government Law.

Bribery was an implicit code violation from the start, since it contravened the company's commitment to "free and fair competition." But

LGE introduced explicit anticorruption policies and practices into the code in 1998, when Korea adopted new legislation against bribery to conform to the OECD Anti-Bribery Convention. The code now provides that:

> Employees should comply with the Act on Preventing Bribery of Foreign Public Officials in International Business Transactions, a Korean law that prohibits any direct or indirect promising, giving or offering bribes to a foreign public official in relation to his/her official business in order to obtain improper advantage in the conduct of international business transactions.

Significantly, the company put this language into the Fair Competition section of the code. The company's leadership believes that the most serious consequence of bribery is that it results in an unfair competitive process and damages the company's reputation with competitors, consumers, and the public for fairness in its business practices.

## Implementation System

Notable elements of LGE's implementation system are communications and training, and written acceptance of the code by employees.

### Communications and Training

All employees hired in Korea, regardless of where they are posted, receive copies of the code. Code orientation is part of the training curriculum for all new employees. The training includes discussions of problems that the company and its representatives typically encounter. As in some other East Asian companies, such as Matsushita and Shell, these dilemmas are sometimes presented in cartoon format. Certain frontline employees—salesmen, and service and procurement employees—take part in these exercises at least twice a year.

### Employee Certification

Every year, each employee must sign a "pledge of action" reading, "I pledge my strongest support to the Code of Ethics and the Practice Guideline for the Code of Ethics of LG and affix my signature to that effect."

## Warning Procedures

The ethics program is monitored regularly for compliance. The company's Internal Audit Department makes periodic checks of employee compliance and retains consulting companies for formal reviews of supplier practices.

Procedures for obtaining advice or reporting questionable conduct are set forth in the code. Section 2, clause 2, instructs employees to discuss questions of code interpretation with an "executive" (most likely, the person to whom the individual reports). If the executive is not helpful, the code allows the employee to refer the case to the formal ethics committee head of the particular unit (usually, the head of Human Resources). If there is no resolution at this point, the case could go to the Administrative Office of the Ethics Committee, that is, LGE's Internal Audit Department.

The company recognizes the limits of its formal procedures, and it maintains a Website and telephone number for anonymous complaints. The senior auditor interviewed said, however, that thus far he was unaware of any specific inquiries or reports regarding the bribery of public officials. It is possible but unlikely that employees have called the CEO directly to report irregularities because in that event the CEO would probably have asked the Internal Audit Department to investigate such complaints.

## Beyond the Company

Independent third parties such as subcontractors, distributors, consultants, agents, and brokers that deal with LGE are "encouraged to comply," and in fact, "lectures" and "explanations" from company managers extend the process beyond mere encouragement. The company has terminated contracts for violation of the code.

# Government-Led Ethics in Singapore and Its Transborder Impact

*In Singapore, it is within our control. We want to make sure that business is done in a clean way so that there is a level playing field for everybody.*

*In the public sector, we cannot tolerate any corrupt behaviour. In the private sector too, if it comes to the notice of the anticorruption agency, action will be taken.*

*Outside, we would not encourage our business people to involve themselves in such practices as winning contracts through bribery.*

Prime Minister Goh Chok Tong, speaking to visiting Filipino journalists in 1999 (Corrupt Practices Investigation Bureau, CPIB)

The key to Singapore's success in implementing good governance and a strong anticorruption ethos has been the clear determination of its political leaders to weed out corruption. In the period just after World War II, corruption was widespread in Singapore, as in other parts of Asia. Early measures taken by the colonial administration failed to rally public support. Yet today Singapore is considered one of the most corruption-free countries in the world and, by a wide margin, the least corrupt in Asia [1]

This achievement is to the credit of the postindependence government and political leaders, who were progressively able to rally public support for their anticorruption drive. As then–prime minister Lee Kuan Yew told Parliament in 1987, "the strongest deterrent is in a public opinion which censures and condemns corrupt persons" (CPIB). The political leaders took it on themselves to set a good example for civil servants, in part by creating a group of young, highly motivated technocrats in the bureaucracy who are imbued with a strong belief that corruption must not be allowed to fester in Singapore. With rising standards of education and wages, this belief became sufficiently anchored in the Singaporean psyche to become its new policy and a benchmark for the republic.

---

**Box CS.8.    Some Features of Singapore's Prevention of Corruption Act**

- The Corrupt Practices Investigation Bureau (CPIB) is independent of other agencies and reports to the prime minister. It has extensive police powers to investigate and make arrests.
- The CPIB, like Hong Kong's Independent Commission Against Corruption, is competent to investigate corrupt practices in both the public and private sectors. It encourages private firms to report fraudulent kickbacks in private transactions.
- Section 36 of the act provides very good protection for informers. At the same time, false statements, including malicious complaints, are offenses punishable by up to one year in jail (sect. 28). Nonreporting of knowledge or presumption of corrupt behavior is also a punishable offense.
- On conviction, the offense of corruption is punishable with a fine of up to 100,000 Singapore dollars, jail terms of up to five years (up to seven years for the most serious offenses such as cases involving members of Parliament), or both.

*Source:* CPIB.

---

Not only does the law severely punish corruption in Singapore; it is strictly and swiftly enforced. This combination acts as a real deterrent to corrupt practices by Singaporean nationals and by foreigners living and working in Singapore. The credibility of the country's anticorruption infrastructure was confirmed by its ability to bring to court not only cases of low-level corruption but also a number of high-profile cases involving high-ranking officials and prominent businesspersons.

The first legislation, the Prevention of Corruption Act of 1960 (box CS.8), considerably re-enforced an agency dedicated to fighting corruption created under British rule, the Corrupt Practices Investigation Bureau (CPIB). The legislation was revised over the years to make it more effective and to take into account new issues. The latest amendment, in 1998, included a form of transnational reach (as discussed below). In addition the Corruption, Drug Trafficking and Other Serious Crimes Confiscation of Benefits Act, introduced in 1989 and revised in 1999, enabled the courts to freeze assets or confiscate offenders' properties.

Today, Singapore's corporate sector is very diversified. Singapore hosts a dynamic sector of family-owned corporations, as well as large, publicly owned corporations. Temasek Holdings, a wholly government owned corporation, manages corporate state assets, including shares in a number of the largest listed companies. Both privately owned and publicly owned companies endorsed the national ethical spirit and adopted good practices of internal control. In addition, in recent years the Singapore Stock Exchange has promoted for its listed companies reforms in corporate governance that resulted in the adoption in 2002 of one of the most comprehensive codes in the world.

In this context, fraud and corruption are hardly major issues for companies operating in Singapore, and neither private sector organizations nor public agencies feel the need to engage in active promotion of the ethics and compliance model. This contrasts with the situation in other advanced Asian economies such as Hong Kong (China), the Republic of Korea, and, to a certain degree, Japan, where initiatives have been developed in recent years primarily in response to problems at home.

The ethical challenge faced by the Singaporean private sector is not so much on the home front as with operations in other countries in East Asia. Large and small corporations are massively engaged in trade and investment in countries, such as neighboring Indonesia, where governance standards and practices are very different from those prevalent in Singapore. The Singaporean private sector is thus confronted with a situation that has no equivalent in other advanced economies.

On the one hand, there is a clear temptation to apply double standards when operating abroad, if only to maintain a level playing field vis-à-vis local firms. Singaporean corporations are sometimes perceived by their nonregional competitors as not always acting properly. This perception is reflected in the 2002 release of the Transparency International Bribe Payers Index, in which Singapore fares much worse than countries with similar levels of corruption at home (see chapter 2 and appendix B).

On the other hand, there is a broad consensus in Singapore that this regional contrast is detrimental to Singapore's economy in the long term and that in the short term it endangers Singaporean corporations operating abroad. On moral grounds, the Singapore community believes that it is not right to apply double standards and that Singaporean citizens and corporations should promote and share, when feasible, the Singaporean ethos with their neighbors. The government and the private sector have taken a number of steps in this direction.

1. The law in Singapore has been modified to ban foreign corrupt practices. Singapore is not a party to the OECD Anti-Bribery Convention, but its law against transnational bribery carries very harsh penalties (see box CS.9).

---

**Box CS.9.    The Extraterritorial Reach of Singapore Law under the Prevention of Corruption Act**

The latest version of the Prevention of Corruption Act stipulates, in section 37, that an offense of corruption committed by a Singaporean citizen outside Singapore with foreign officials carries the same liability and sanction as if it had been committed in Singapore:

"(1) The provisions of this Act have effect, in relation to citizens of Singapore, outside as well as within Singapore; and where an offense under this Act is committed by a citizen of Singapore in any place outside Singapore, he may be dealt with in respect of that offense as if it had been committed within Singapore.

"(2) Any proceedings against any person under this section which would be a bar to subsequent proceedings against that person for the same offense, if the offense had been committed in Singapore, shall be a bar to further proceedings against him, under any written law for the time being in force relating to the extradition of persons, in respect of the same offense outside Singapore."

This provision has been upheld as constitutional by the Court of Appeal.

---

2. The government and some Singaporean organizations are active in promoting principles of good governance in other Asian countries. Singapore is a hub for various conferences on corruption or corporate governance. The government is also supporting the work of international organizations active in the area, such as the World Bank and the Asian Development Bank, through voluntary contributions.

A major challenge for corporations is that the preferred mode of operation of Singaporean businesses is through minority partnerships with local businesses. In most cases the Singaporean partner does not have a direct hand in the investee's internal controls. As a Singaporean business leader said during the interviews, it is important "to continually push the limits" of insisting on compliance with ethical standards. At the same time, he warned, it is necessary to be realistic about the prospects for improvement, especially when the prevalent business culture in some other countries does not traditionally rely on codified ethics and governance standards and when socioeconomic conditions do not favor these standards.

Procedures and codes of conduct addressing the ethical issue are found primarily in large, listed corporations. The general approach is to rely on governance mechanisms and especially on the board, as is clearly acknowledged by state-owned Temasek Holdings (see box CS.10).

## Box CS.10.  Corporate Stewardship at Temasek Holdings

Temasek Holdings' "investee" companies are partly or wholly owned by the government of Singapore. They are fully independent entities; they have performance benchmarks, based on their corporate visions and goals, which they set independently; and they are accountable directly to all shareholders, not just to Temasek. They set their own financial and business targets, strive for operational excellence, and are supposed to be commercially competitive. Of these firms, commonly known as government-linked companies, seven are publicly listed, and Temasek holds a significant stake in them. Examples include Singapore Telecoms (67 percent held by Temasek), Singapore Airlines (57 percent), SembCorp Industries (51 percent), and DBS Group Holdings (13 percent). Fifteen, including PSA Corporation and Singapore Technologies, are nonlisted and are wholly owned by Temasek. The listed companies in the Temasek stable currently account for approximately 21 percent of the Singapore Stock Exchange's total market capitalization, or about US$38.8 billion. The role of Temasek Holdings in Singapore and among Singaporean companies thus cannot be overstated.

Temasek Holdings follows the strict code of conduct and the anticorruption ethos of Singapore. Because anticorruption is "a given" and "a national policy in Singapore," the promotion of those values is cited in the corporation's charter as one of Temasek's missions. As a relatively small holding corporation, with 200 government employees, Temasek does not have a specific code of its own, but it is seriously promoting good corporate stewardship (of which corporate governance is a part) in all its investee and wholly controlled companies. A specialized division within Temasek has been created to implement this policy. Temasek expects its investee companies to follow closely such practices as establishing good, professional boards, having good audit committees, and strictly following best practices. Temasek specifically emphasizes the role of the board and the quality of directors in the implementation of sound internal controls and good practices. Through its own board, Temasek maintains a dialogue with the boards of its investee companies and expects them to be just as stringent in ensuring good governance and adherence to the anticorruption ethos as is Temasek itself. This is crucial to Temasek, which works on the fundamental premise that good corporate governance and a good code of ethics will enhance shareholder value.

The implementation of internal controls and codes, however, is the responsibility of the individual company. Temasek Holdings' control of its investee companies is not direct, especially when it comes to second-tier corporations outside Singapore. Investee companies are expected to implement their own "regional" programs in corporate governance, based on their own boards' directions and stringent controls.

# Note

This section is based on research and analysis conducted by Dr. Eric Teo, managing director of Savoir Faire Consultants, Singapore.

1. In the August 2002 release of the Corruption Perceptions Index, Transparency International gave Singapore a rating of 9.3 on a 1 (worst) to 10 (best) scale. Singapore was tied with Sweden as fifth best among 102 countries.

# "ABC Healthcare Corporation"

(*Note:* The real name of this corporation has been withheld to protect confidentiality; all the other facts reported in this case are unchanged.)

"ABC Healthcare Corporation" is a multinational Fortune 500 health care company headquartered in North America. It has been in business for more than 70 years. It currently has operations in more than 110 countries and employs about 45,000 people worldwide. Annual sales revenues for fiscal 2000 were about US$7 billion, more than half of which came from outside the United States.

The ABC Corporation has been in Asia for almost 30 years, and its sales revenues in Asia for fiscal 2000 exceeded US$500 million. In the East Asia and Pacific region the company maintains sales offices in China, Hong Kong (China), India, Indonesia, Korea, the Philippines, Singapore, Taiwan (China), and Thailand and has manufacturing facilities in China and Singapore. Almost all of ABC's business is contracted with governments. Since in some Asian countries the government will only enter into contracts with locally owned enterprises, ABC must often partner with local enterprises to establish operations within a specific country. Because of this, ABC has both wholly owned subsidiaries and joint ventures in the East Asia and Pacific region.

Because the East Asia region represents almost 30 percent of the world's population, ABC is keenly interested in expanding its operations there. It is confident that as the East Asian market matures, people will devote more of their individual resources to health care. By 2010, the company hopes to increase revenues in the region by a factor of five.

## Origins of the Ethics Program

In the late 1980s ABC explicitly identified the values under which it had always operated, irrespective of country of operation. An important value—and the one most relevant to anticorruption—was "integrity." The company began taking steps to ensure that it had business practices, standards, and policies in place to support this key value.

Soon after this, ABC experienced a business ethics crisis (not in the East Asia and Pacific region). An ABC official had broken the law while conducting business on behalf of the company. A large fine was levied against the company, and a lesser fine against the official in question. But because ABC had already made great strides in establishing and implementing a business practices program prior to this incident, the government merely stipulated that the company should bring its business practices program to fruition in a timely manner. The government acknowledged that this program would help the company prevent similar forms of corrupt behavior.

ABC's anticorruption program is part of the company's comprehensive global initiative to promote responsible business conduct throughout its operations and among its joint-venture partners. The company does not believe in having different business ethics programs for each region or creating a separate and distinct anticorruption program; it pursues a common set of best practices throughout the world.

The business practices officer at ABC notes, "A successful business practices program—including a company's efforts to combat corruption—boils down to three main issues: successfully communicating, monitoring, and enforcing its standards."

## Business Practices Guide

Since the late 1980s, the company has had a statement of its policies and standards. In the mid-1990s it developed and published its Business Practices Guide, which is available in 15 languages or language variations.[1]

Because almost all of ABC's business outside the United States depends on local or national governments, ABC runs the constant risk of coming into contact either directly or indirectly with corrupt behavior. Hence, the guide delivers a clear message to employees regarding corruption:

> ABC employees may not ever offer, give, or agree to pay—directly or indirectly—money or anything of value to influence the decision or action of another for the purpose of obtaining and/or retaining business. We never attempt to influence the decision or the action of a public official, political party, candidate for office or public organization to obtain or retain business.

The guide further stipulates that ABC employees are expected to abide by all local laws and standards, as well as the laws and standards of the United States. Yet it does indicate that the company observes local business practices and customs as long as they are both fair and legal.

Throughout, the guide emphasizes the importance of maintaining accurate books and records and of complying with standard accounting procedures. ABC believes that rigorous accounting procedures and policies can do much to ensure that the company avoids any form of corruption or detects possible forms of corruption.

ABC does permit facilitating payments under specific circumstances in some locations, but subject to stringent controls. Both the regional financial director and the regional legal director must be consulted before a facilitating payment can be made on behalf of the company.

## Implementation System

In the early 1990s ABC's Board of Directors mandated the establishment of the Office of Business Practices to take responsibility for assessing the company's business practice standards and monitoring its business practices. This decision was influenced by the company's core values study and the government investigation but also by such factors as market trends in business ethics and health care industry regulations and policy.

The company's business practices officer reports to the head of the Legal Department, but in matters relating to business practices she reports directly to the ABC Board of Directors. She meets with the Board of Directors twice a year to report on the activities of the Office of Business Practices and to communicate any issues pertinent to business practices within the company. If necessary, she can call an ad hoc meeting with the Board of Directors.

### Regional Business Ethics Panels

ABC holds its managers responsible for:

* Serving as role models for the company's values and standards
* Promoting responsible business practices
* Ensuring that employees feel comfortable talking openly about business practices issues
* Easing employee concerns about retaliation.

It is managers who are responsible for implementing initiatives or specific program elements originating from the Office of Business Practices or from regional business practices panels.

The practices panels were established in the mid-1990s to provide support for compliance at the regional level in this global and diverse company. The panels are responsible for implementing the business practices initiative and any business practices programs that fall within their purview. They are made up of senior management employees and of functional area employees (for example, representatives of the Human Resource Department or the Legal Department). The members are elected by the Office of Business Practices, which seeks a fair representation of countries within a geographic region. There are five regional panels: two in Asia and one each in Europe, Latin America, and North America. The chairperson for each regional panel reports directly to the Office of Business Practices, which in turn reports any substantive regional information directly to the Board of Directors.

According to the business practices officer,

> This communications network on business practices has been extremely effective for our company. Instead of having one office in North America responsible for the business practices program, we have multiple partners who help ensure that we remain on track with regard to how we conduct business. Information flows smoothly from each region directly to our Board.

## Communications and Training

In the early 1990s the Office of Business Practices developed an employee training program organized around vignettes on videotape that were used as a prelude to discussion. ABC managers were trained to deliver the program to employees. The program was made mandatory for all employees around the world, and management accepted the responsibility for tracking and recording employee participation in it. (As a control measure, the company made these records subject to audit.) New employees were required to receive the business practices training within the first three months of joining the company. The training program has been extremely successful in the United States, but non-U.S. employees, including those from the East Asia and Pacific region, have often found it "too American."

A new business practices training course for East Asia and Pacific relies heavily on discussion of typical situations that company employees experience. The design reflects contributions of company staff from the region, to make sure that regional needs and concerns are covered. Employees receive training in their own languages. The business practices officer noted,

> Not only should participants at a business practices workshop be able to understand what the facilitator is presenting; they must be able to engage actively in discussion of the key issues. We were asking our employees to participate in highly interactive training sessions, which had to be conducted in the participants' own languages.

Scenario questions are printed in the form of a deck of cards, color-coded by difficulty, to make for an effective and flexible teaching tool. By selecting different sets of scenario questions, the program can be made relevant for any group of participants or redelivered to the same group of participants. The cards can also be used in other ways: for example, managers can use one or two cards from the set in staff training sessions or incorporate them in a regional company newsletter.

Another element of the training program that was well received among Asian employees was the conversion of the statements in the Business Practices Guide into specific principles. In this way, a general statement about the company's policy on improper payments was reduced to simple principles such as "Never offer money to a government official." The business practices officer observed, "In rearticulating our standards with simplicity in mind, we were able to offer our EAP employees general statements about our policies and procedures that better addressed their expectations." She also noted, "It is important to communicate to employees that they are not expected to know all the answers. However, our employees must know who would be the best person to go to for guidance."

When the new training course for EAP was rolled out, the feedback from participants was overwhelmingly positive. In fact, the program was so well received by Asian employees that the company decided to use it in Europe and Latin America, where it has also gained acceptance.

The business practices officer observed,

> That our colleagues in Asia both noted the need for and participated largely in the process of creating a training program tailored to the region is significant. I think it demonstrates the level of commitment of our employees and indicates the ever-growing appreciation and importance of responsible business throughout the world.

Employees in certain EAP countries receive training annually; elsewhere, the cycle is somewhat longer.

## Employee Certification

Every ABC employee around the world receives a copy of the Business Practices Guide and its updates, and each is asked to sign an acknowledgment card stating that they have received the document and have read and understood it. Managers are responsible for tracking and recording this information, which is subject to corporate auditing as a means of guaranteeing that all employees are receiving and reading the guide.

Each year, the Office of Business Practices requires that approximately 10 percent of the company's management and sales force sign a disclosure asserting that they:

1. Have read the Business Practices Guide
2. Understand the Business Practices Guide
3. Are committed to the standards in their work lives
4. Are committed to promoting the standards among employees
5. Have not violated those standards in the past year
6. Have or have not encountered business practices issues.

ABC has found that having managers sign disclosure statements is an excellent method of reiterating the importance of the Business Practices Guide, the business practices program, and management's leadership role with respect to the overall initiative.

## Reporting and Warning Procedures

Since the late 1980s, ABC has maintained a telephone help line for employees on business practices issues. This is only of practical use for employees located within the United States.

ABC ensures that all of its employees in the EAP region are aware of the resources available to them for seeking guidance or raising a business practices concern. An employee may speak with any or all of the following:

- His or her direct managers
- A functional resource (human resources, legal, finance, and so on)
- A regional business practices panel
- The Office of Business Practices.

Every employee receives printed materials that list the relevant contact information for each of these corporate and local resources. Each of these resources is empowered to:

- Offer guidance on or interpret the company's policies and standards
- Gather additional information from other resources on behalf of an employee
- Initiate or conduct a business practices inquiry
- Resolve a business practices issue
- Ensure employee confidentiality
- Protect an employee from retaliation.

## Application to Partners

EAP employees who work for joint ventures in which ABC is a minor partner are not subject to the corporation's Business Practices Guide. ABC does, however, bring its business practices program to the table and tries to make it a priority. Some of its business partners have been keen to adopt the guide; others have opted to disregard it.

## Note

This section includes major contributions by the International Business Ethics Institute.

1. The company's business practices officer felt it imperative that the company not term its business practices document a code of conduct or a code of ethics. She felt that associating the guide with "conduct" or "ethics" might cause the company's diverse employee population to believe that ABC was attempting to influence the general conduct or ethical position of its employees. She also recognized that the word "ethics" can be extremely problematic, particularly when trying to translate the term accurately from one language into another, and she felt that even among U.S. employees, the term "ethics" might be found objectionable. Hence she recommended that the company portray the document as a business practices guide—a tool for conducting business responsibly.

# "NATCOM"

(*Note:* The real name of this corporation has been withheld to protect confidentiality; all the other facts reported in this case are unchanged.)

"NATCOM" is a global leader in the communications industry, providing telecommunications and Internet services. This North American company has been in business for more than a century and now has 60,000 employees worldwide, with operations in more than 72 countries. Its customer base includes local and multinational businesses, government institutions and agencies, and utility companies.

In 1975 the corporation began operations in East Asia and Pacific, and it now has more than 4,000 employees in the region, joint-venture projects included. The principal EAP sales offices are located in China, Hong Kong (China), Japan, and Singapore. Other important regional sales centers are in Indonesia, Korea, Malaysia, the Philippines, Taiwan (China), and Thailand. NATCOM operates a significant research and development facility in China, where it is also involved in five manufacturing joint ventures.

NATCOM was one of the first companies to make its code of business practices available to all its stakeholders—employees, customers, suppliers, stockholders, and the public—through its Internet site. The company felt that it was important to publicize what it stands for and how it goes about conducting business. An unexpected result is the feedback on the code from external sources—for example, from customers who have contacted the company to relate that they have perceived disparities between the company's policies and values and the behavior of the employees with whom they interact.

## Origins of the Ethics Program

NATCOM established a comprehensive anticorruption initiative in the mid-1990s, not in response to violations of law or of corporate policy but because of a proactive concern by the company's CEO about minimizing risks to the company and its operations. The company's senior executives assigned primary responsibility for establishing and implementing an anticorruption initiative to the Office of Security and Auditing, a unit of five full-time staff within the Legal Department.

## Code of Business Practices

NATCOM has had a Code of Business Practices for many years; the most recent version dates from 1995, with some revisions since then. The code articulates the company's values and vision and gives employees general directions for making ethical decisions on behalf of the company. The code uses deliberately simple language to make the corporation's policies and values easy to translate and to be understood by employees around the world.

On corruption issues, the code notes:

> Our policies account for the social and economic goals of each country where we do business. We abide by the national and local laws of the countries in which we operate.

The code clearly articulates the company's position on bribery and corruption:

> It is never acceptable to give, ask for, or take any form of bribe or inducement. This policy applies to every one of our employees in every country where we have operations around the world, even where bribery is considered customary and/or necessary to conduct business.

The code provides guidelines for dealing with such problems as offering or receiving gifts and entertainment (see box CS.11).

In preparing the code, the corporation sought feedback from employees. More than 1,100 employees made comments on a draft version through the intranet. According to the director of the Office of Security and Auditing, the breadth of the reaction conveyed the extent of employee interest in and support for the ethics program. The company also conducted focus groups on the draft code in several EAP countries, in regional languages where necessary.

## Implementation System

Noteworthy features of NATCOM's implementation programs include communications and training, and employee certification.

---

**Box CS.11.    Excerpt from NATCOM's Code of Business Practices: Gift and Entertainment Policy**

NATCOM's gift and entertainment policy is fixed and does not vary with such factors as the holiday seasons or special events. Forms of gifts and entertainment include—but are not limited to—meals and beverages, travel and lodging, tickets for sports or cultural events, cash, services, and merchandise.

NATCOM considers gifts and entertainment as business courtesies that can help us to build positive business relations. In some cultures, giving gifts and entertaining are an important part of conducting business. Gifts and entertainment can pose problems when they interfere or are believed to interfere with the business decisions we make and the business actions we take.

In light of this, NATCOM employees may only offer promotional items (pens, calendars, etc.) to customers or prospective customers. Entertaining clients should be restricted to modest and infrequent business meals or modest and infrequent sports or cultural entertainment. It should be noted that we may only offer our customers such tickets when we ourselves will accompany the customer.

This document cannot cover every instance that may arise with regard to appropriate forms of gifts and entertainment. Hence, if you are unsure about whether a gift or form of entertainment would be acceptable, you may wish to ask yourself:

- Is it of moderate value?
- Would I be comfortable giving or receiving this gift in front of my family or colleagues?
- Does giving this gift violate the law or the customer's own code of business practices?

Finally, remember that an authorized employee must approve all gifts and entertainment in advance and that the expenses incurred through giving gifts or entertaining must be accounted for accurately and appropriately.

---

## Communications and Training

All NATCOM employees received a copy of the code on its release, and every new employee receives one during orientation. When the company revises the code, it provides new versions to all employees. The code is issued in regional languages and in several language variations (for example, complex versus simple characters in Chinese) for all of the EAP countries in which NATCOM has operations. The code document is available on the NATCOM intranet site, where employees can download the text in any of the languages into which it has been translated.

To support the introduction of the code, a companywide training program in business ethics was developed by the Office of Security and Auditing with the help of the consultant on international business ethics. All employees at every level attend half-day training workshops on business ethics, which contain a strong anticorruption component. Country managers deliver the business ethics training to employees around specific functional areas so that employees with similar needs and concerns can benefit from group instruction and discussion. The training has been made as interactive as possible and includes case study and scenario exercises that are tailored to regional needs and the concerns of participants.

The training curriculum for all new employees and new managers includes an anticorruption and business ethics component.

## Certification by Employees

NATCOM employees must sign an annual disclosure statement indicating that they have received and read the code.

## Reporting and Warning Procedures

Employees who have questions on ethics issues or who wish to report unethical behavior have several channels open to them. They can talk to their managers, contact the Office of Security and Auditing directly, call the help line, or contact regional ethics officers.

## Help Line

The Office of Security and Auditing created a help line through which employees can articulate their concerns to the company 24 hours a day, seven days a week, in their own languages. As a telecommunications company, NATCOM was able to ensure that employees, no matter where located, would be able to contact the help line without technical difficulty. An external security organization manages the help line on behalf of the company, documenting all the calls it receives from employees and transmitting this information directly to the Office of Security and Auditing.

NATCOM's director of security and auditing explained that many employees in the EAP region have a culturally based apprehension about reporting violations—a sentiment that the company has also encountered in Western Europe. "When it came time to introduce the help-line resource to our folks in Asia/Pacific, we wanted to make certain that it was communicated as a way to seek guidance and support from the company, not as a means of reporting violations." Both in the Code of Business Practices and in the training program materials, the descriptions of the help line were drafted so as to make it acceptable to employees in the EAP region.

The help line receives about 2,000 calls a year from around the world. The proportion of calls from EAP employees is in line with the shares for the corporation's other regions, suggesting that the help line has become a viable resource in EAP. In 2000 the chief concerns of EAP callers were conflict of interest (45 percent of calls), gifts and entertainment (20 percent), and bribery or facilitation payments (15 percent).

## Regional Ethics Contact Persons

A network of regional business ethics contact persons was set up to offer employees an alternative channel for advice and reporting to ensure that employees know they can speak with someone in operations and can articulate their concerns in their own languages. These contact persons are NATCOM employees who, in addition to their routine responsibilities, are charged with being a source of guidance on business ethics issues. They each receive an initial two-day training course and refresher courses every two years from the Office of Security and Auditing. In EAP there are currently four such contact persons spread throughout the region, each of whom has done the job ever since the ethics program came into effect. Most often, they divide their time between ethics-related matters and employee relations, environmental concerns, and health and safety issues.

The director of security and auditing observes, "Issues have been brought to the forefront because of the existence of our safety valve [the help line and the network of ethics contact persons] and we are now in a much better position to address employees' concerns." The corporation has used the reporting channels as a way not only of becoming aware of and reacting to problems or potential problems but also of taking a more proactive stance.

## EAP Governance Committee

NATCOM has created a Governance Committee in the EAP region made up of representatives from the Financial Audit Department, the Office of Security and Auditing, the Legal Department, and the Sales and Marketing Division. The committee reviews any payment that may give the appearance of exceeding a facilitation payment. If an agent has questions about a payment that he or she has been asked to make on behalf of the company, the committee meets to review the case and determine whether the payment is acceptable.

## Bidding Reviews

The director of security and auditing explained that auditing requirements do not specify that facilitation payments be recorded separately from the complete cost of a project or service fee. But to understand better how funds get allocated to facilitation payments and bribes, and how they may erode its profit margins, NATCOM tightened its review of the bidding process, focusing its attention on the costs at each phase.

The new reviews have revealed that increased costs are associated with third-party agents and representatives. As a result, NATCOM has tightened its policy on hiring agents and representatives; all agents and representatives must now sign an agreement that they have read and will adhere to NATCOM's Code of Business Practices.

## Long-Term versus Short-Term Benefits

NATCOM believes that it has lost business in East Asia and Pacific as a consequence of taking an uncompromising position against engaging in any form of bribery. For example, one prospective client was an EAP government that was well known for its high level of corruption. The company tendered a contract bid and was intent on respecting its policies by not resorting to bribes to influence the decisionmaking process. Local executives strongly suspected that the reason NATCOM lost the contract to a competitor was because of its strong position against bribing public officials.

When the corrupt government fell, NATCOM was able to secure the new government as a client. In fact, the new government refused to do business with any of the companies that had worked for the old regime. Over the long term, NATCOM was able to establish business relations with this government while remaining true to its values and standards.

## Implementation Issues

As calls to NATCOM's help line show, judgments about the appropriate means of entertaining prospective clients, especially government clients, can be problematic (see box CS.12). EAP governments may provide extremely limited funds to their officials for business-related travel, and some government officials have even arrived at NATCOM facilities without any funds whatsoever. The director of security and auditing explains,

---

**Box CS.12.   Walking a Fine Line on Entertainment**

The following example does not contravene the U.S. Foreign Corrupt Practices Act, but it illustrates how entertainment practices might raise questions in the public eye about what is appropriate. Although NAT-COM has significant manufacturing operations and a research and development center in East Asia and Pacific, it has brought large groups of government officials from EAP to North America to view the company's product lines. Traditionally, the two-week itinerary includes only half a day of product demonstration. Some of the remaining time might be spent on trips to such locations as Las Vegas or Orlando. Because the officials often have limited travel funds of their own, NAT-COM not only covers their travel expenses but also provides about US$1,000 in spending money to each person. NATCOM's director of the Office of Client Relations, which oversees such matters, explains that the corporation provides spending money directly to guests of the company because allocating an employee to accompany them at all times to pay their expenses is neither feasible nor desirable.

---

We scrutinize each instance where we entertain government clients. Often, it is not cut-and-dried bribery that is at issue. It is the perception that something corrupt is taking place. NATCOM's name is well respected the world over, and we want to keep it that way.

Facilitation payments, too, can be a source of confusion for NATCOM employees. NATCOM's Code of Business Practices states that facilitation payments are permissible in certain instances provided that they are for the purpose of obtaining routine business services and that they are accurately documented as business expenses. The code also states that facilitation payments are not allowed in countries where they are illegal. Hence, employees assume direct responsibility for determining the legality of a facilitation payment, which they must do by contacting corporate resources such as the Legal Department or the Office of Security and Auditing.

## Looking Ahead

Some NATCOM officials have been somewhat indifferent about the U.S. Foreign Corrupt Practices Act because NATCOM does not have its headquarters in the United States. Other reasons will be needed to compel them to take the antibribery initiative seriously. The worldwide trend toward deregulation of the telecommunications industry has reduced the incentives to pay government bribes. The OECD Anti-Bribery Convention, for its part, is only as effective as the supporting legislation in NATCOM's home country, Canada, which sets as penalties a fine of no more than US$25,000, a prison sentence of no more than five years, or both. Furthermore, enforcing the OECD Convention is extremely difficult. In view of the profits that can be reaped from corrupt behavior, the convention does not provide a definitive incentive for companies to root out all corruption within their ranks.

This section includes major contributions by the International Business Ethics Institute.

# ABB Group

The 1988 merger of Swedish-based Asea and Swiss-based Brown Boveri gave birth to the global engineering corporation now named ABB. Headquartered in Switzerland, the ABB Group serves customers in power transmission and distribution; oil, gas, and petrochemicals; building technologies; and financial services. ABB employs about 160,000 people in more than 100 countries. The East Asia and Pacific region accounts for 11 percent of ABB's employees and for 12 percent of its revenues.

ABB owns 100 percent of its component companies in the region except in Indonesia and China. In China it owns or partly owns 25 companies, most of which are joint ventures owned on a 50/50 basis. Altogether, these companies employ about 6,000 people. Asia representatives are located in Australia, China (including Hong Kong), India, Japan, Korea, Malaysia, New Zealand, the Philippines, Singapore, Taiwan (China), Thailand, and Vietnam.

Over more than a decade, ABB has been able to count on the commitment of high-level management to its corporate ethics policy. The board and a succession of charismatic CEOs have visibly involved themselves in building a corporate culture and a compliance program. Throughout, the messages have been consistent.

## Origins of the Ethics Program

ABB first introduced a code of ethics in 1988 at the instigation of the CEO, Percy Barnevik, as part of a broader effort to make clear the company's overall mission and values. Progressively more forceful ethics statements have since been introduced, as the company has developed a culture of compliance. ABB management's concern with business ethics has been a preemptive one rather than a response to violations of law or of company policy.

The group's then-CEO, Jörgen Centerman, wrote in the foreword of the company's "Business Ethics" booklet:

ABB's reputation is our most valuable asset, and it is determined by how we act. Our customers and other stakeholders expect us to maintain the highest ethical standards, to fulfill our commitment and to act with complete integrity. . . . Every ABB company and all ABB employees must conform to our business ethics standards. All ABB managers should take an active role in their implementation and ensure that they are communicated and kept alive. . . . We should be honest in every situation and ethical in all our business practices. Our reputation is determined by the smallest infraction.

The chief legal counsel, Kurt Hermann, said in an interview,

We believe that ethical and economic values are interdependent and that the business community must always strive to operate within the accepted norms established by national and international authorities.

Like other global firms in a changing world, ABB has had to implement universal ethical business standards in order to preserve its global reputation. Being global means that ABB now has a much more diverse body of employees; it recruits and trains engineers and technicians from all over the world. ABB considers it important to give its component companies a high degree of autonomy in the countries in which it operates. As Hermann remarked, "to obtain better business practices in a changing world, ABB has changed a lot; the very special culture of ABB is multiculture." In these circumstances the formulation and implementation of ethical business procedures is a challenge because, on the one hand, international ethical standards are not adaptable country by country and, on the other hand, ABB recognizes and respects cultural differences. The company requires all ABB employees to comply with its own business principles and at the same time to conform to the relevant laws and obligations of the countries in which they operate. Hermann notes, "It is not easy to change traditions in business; it takes time, but the direction is very positive and very clear."

## Ethics Standards and Code of Practice

ABB subscribes to the basic principles in the International Chamber of Commerce (ICC) Rules of Conduct (1999), the OECD Anti-Bribery

Convention (1997), and the U.S. Foreign Corrupt Practices Act (1997). The corporation's internal publication "Compliance 2000" gives a detailed description of appropriate business behaviors. ABB Business Ethics Standards cover:

- Conflict of interest
- Confidentiality and protection of assets
- Insider trading
- Bribery and corruption
- Intermediaries
- Political contributions
- Antitrust compliance
- Disclosure and records
- Violations of corporate policies
- Responsibility and implementation.

Employees are instructed to:

- Apply "zero tolerance" in ensuring strict adherence to local and international laws and regulations
- Ensure that all ABB business transactions are fully and fairly recorded according to the company's accounting principles
- Regularly monitor ethical conduct and ensure that accessible systems are in place for employees to report potential violations.

The company's policies on bribery and corruption, intermediaries, and political contributions are summarized in box CS.13.

## Implementation System

In 1998 then-CEO Goran Lindhal asked Chief Legal Counsel Hermann to develop a network that would promote compliance with ABB ethics standards throughout the group. Hermann was assisted by a task force made up of the head of internal communications, the general counsel, the compliance director for Asia, the head auditor for Asia, and the general counsel and chief auditor for ABB in the United States. The task force decided that each country and region should have a compliance counsel and that each region should have a regional coordinator. The compliance system was designed to include auditing and monitoring procedures that would encourage employees to report potential violations. Provisions were made for employee communications and for an ethics training program.

**Box CS.13.  Excerpts from ABB's Ethics Standards**

**Bribery and corruption**

The code reads: "No ABB company or employees shall offer or provide an undue monetary or other advantage to any person or persons, including public officials or customer employees, in violation of laws and the officials' or employees' legal duties, in order to obtain or retain business." There are no exceptions, and there is no local adaptation of bribery and corruption policies.

For gifts, entertainment, and traveling expenses, ABB Group standards are as follows:

- ABB companies or ABB employees will only give or accept entertainment or gifts that are for business purposes and are not substantial.
- The limits given are the maximum limits in accordance with ABB ethical standards. The region and the country presidents will put in place their own local rules.
- The limits are US$100 for gifts and US$250 for entertainment; any larger amount must be approved by the superior and is open to audit.
- Traveling expenses for customers, government officials, and so on are dealt with case by case, are to be approved by the superior, and are open to audit.

As regards facilitation payments, ABB's preference at all times is not to make such payments. Where such payments are needed, the following guideline is mandatory:

- Depending on the amount, for a contract of approximately US$1 million, the facilitating fee is limited to approximately US$10,000.
- For a contract of US$100 million, the facilitating fee is limited to approximately US$20,000; the limit for large contracts is US$50,000.

The company has an internal approval procedure for facilitation payments.

**Intermediaries**

The code reads: "Agreements with consultants, brokers, sponsors, agents, or other intermediaries shall not be used to channel payments to any person or persons, including public officials or customer employees, and thereby circumvent ABB policies regarding bribery

and corruption. These agreements are strictly subject to the requirements set forth in the corresponding Group Directive."

Some basic rules are to be followed: payments shall represent no
more than the appropriate remuneration for services rendered; services shall be professional and substantial in relation to the project or
business transaction; and only individuals or entities conducting a
commercial activity shall act as intermediaries. Before any commitment to an intermediary is made, it must be approved, and two signa-
tures are required. Proper records are to be maintained of all payments
to intermediaries.

**Political contributions**
"Contributions to political parties or committees, or to individual politicians, should not in principle be given." Any exceptions are to be cleared
in advance; they are possible in countries where payments are permitted
by the applicable legislation. ABB must ensure that such payments are
properly recorded and are disclosed openly. Laws and regulations on
political contributions differ from country to country, and each ABB unit
is responsible for knowledge of the respective national laws.

*Source:* ABB, "Compliance 2000."

## Compliance Network

Today the decentralized compliance structure comprises:

- The Central Compliance Unit, managed by Hermann and the senior
  vice president and senior adviser, Corporate Communications
- The Legal Group–Compliance, based in Zurich
- Forty-six senior compliance officers for the 6 geographic zones, includ-
  ing 10 for Asia and Pacific
- A legal compliance counsel for each major country.

Regional information is managed at the regional level. For East Asia
and Pacific, the chief legal compliance counsel for Asia, Peter Kinsey
(based in Australia), provides a central help desk, support for education
and information, and compliance follow-ups and audits for the region.
Country compliance officers report directly to him.

The compliance network in each region has its own two-day regional
meeting each year. Compliance counsels have access to the company's
Website, which is actively used for compliance discussions and questions
not just by the counsels but also by employees at large. With support from

the Central Compliance Unit, educational materials, letters, and help-desk information are immediately available on the Web. Any question can be asked, and the database is full of exchanges of views and answers from employees at different levels worldwide on ways to conduct business and follow rules of conduct.

The Central Compliance Unit receives some questions that must be dealt with case by case, with consideration for country characteristics. For East Asia and Pacific, for example, question topics have included sponsorship for a hospital and payment for a state funeral.

## Communications and Training

Staff publications give precise descriptions of corrupt practices and explanations of how they can undermine company business.

The training program includes an "Ethical Road Show" that presents the ABB Business Ethics Guidelines and ABB Business Ethics Standards. Separate presentations have been developed for senior management, salespeople in contact with customers, clerical workers, and factory workers. The training sessions provide for group discussions on business ethics issues.

In Asia and Pacific Kinsey started with a compliance seminar to "train the trainers" at the regional level, with recommendations regarding what to do within each country. The content of the presentation is not altered for local audiences.

The ethics training is a continuing process, since there are always new people to be trained. The feedback received in Zurich on the business ethics training program is very positive: "People like it!"

## Employee Certification

ABB has in place a process of certification of staff in the program, followed by a compliance action plan and program review.

## Reporting and Warning Procedures

Because of the company's decentralized structure, it was decided that each country or region should set up its own hotline system. The success of this initiative varies across regions; in Europe, the hotline is less used than in other regions. In addition, it is made unequivocally clear that for specific questions, any employee can use the 24-hour hotline based in Zurich to get advice or report irregularities.

ABB believes that it has lost contracts in Indonesia and Thailand after refusing any form of bribery regarding calls for tenders. "ABB does not bribe," says Hermann. "We are not naïve—we know that corruption exists in Asia and everywhere in the world. . . . But we must resist corruption because we want to compete on equal terms."

## New Corporate Social Policy

The way ABB justifies the need for an anticorruption stance and program may be changing. The group's *Sustainability Report 2000* outlined a new corporate social policy with a strong commitment to sustainability. It stated, "Along with our ambition to make a positive contribution economically and environmentally, we see social performance as the third dimension of sustainability. . . . We strive to balance economic, environmental, and social priorities to create value for our stakeholders." The company's business ethics principles are part of its social policy and are hence an aspect of its sustainability management program. (The social policy defines ABB's stance in such areas as human rights, employee working rights and consultation, community involvement, and business ethics; see box CS.14.) There is coherence and consistency in ABB's efforts. A commitment to sustainability is probably the best way to demonstrate integrity against corruption.

---

**Box CS.14.    Chinese Firms Featured in ABB's Study of Its Social Responsibility Policy in Asia**

ABB recognizes that social responsibility is a prerequisite for maintaining a license to operate. A rigorous policy on human rights and business ethics, with adaptation to country-specific needs, can be a preemptive stance and a source of competitive advantage.

To evaluate its policy on social responsibility, ABB studied the social contributions arising from long-term activities at ABB factories in China and six other countries. The framework for these studies was benchmarked against the OECD's proposed Guidelines for Multinational Enterprises, the Social Accountability 8000 standard, and the United Nations Global Compact.

In China two ABB companies based in Xiamen were studied: ABB Xiamen Switchgear Co. Ltd., established in 1993, and ABB Xiamen Low Voltage Equipment Co. Ltd., established in 1994. ABB is one of the most prominent international companies in China and one of the top taxpayers in Xiamen. Its local purchases in the Xiamen region are more than US$20 million a year, generating significant benefits for area companies.

In 1998 John Yung, general manager of ABB Xiamen Switchgear, received the Friendship Award, which is given to foreigners who have made an outstanding contribution to China's economic and social development. Yung was among 46 recipients of the award, selected from 2,000 nominees.

The ABB Group has made several long-term investments in training and education in China. In 1995 it launched a scholarship program at several Chinese universities. In 1996 it established a training center and a management localization program in Xiamen. And in 2000, in cooperation with the Electrical Engineering Department of Xian Jiaotong University, it set up a training center for the sales and engineering of low-voltage electrical products and systems.

## Application to Partners

Joint ventures are not bound by ABB's policies, but the company clearly states that where ABB has a share of business, regardless of what percentage is controlled, it requires compliance with its code of ethics. "We have never had a problem with this policy in East Asia/Pacific," notes Kinsey, the legal compliance counsel for Asia.

Although ABB has no statement on joint-venture partner status with regard to anticorruption policy, the statement on sustainability comes close: "Incentivize suppliers who have sustainability policies and systems similar to our own." The social policy includes a point on suppliers: "To establish and maintain appropriate procedures to evaluate and select major suppliers and subcontractors on their ability to meet the requirements of ABB's social policy and principles and to maintain reasonable evidence that these requirements are continuing to be met."

This section includes major contributions by Mr. Jacques Carbou.

# Royal Dutch/Shell Group

The companies of the Royal Dutch/Shell Group are engaged in petroleum exploration and production and in production of downstream electric power, oil products, chemicals, and renewable energy, as well as other activities. In 2001 *Fortune* magazine ranked Shell, valued at US$149 billion, as the sixth-largest corporation in the world and the second-largest in Europe. The corporation has 96,000 employees and is active in more than 135 countries. Shell companies have operations throughout Asia, particularly in oil and gas exploration and production, chemicals, and research and technical services.

Shell took a deliberate interest in corporate governance concerns from a relatively early date. Part of the reason is the corporation's unusual structure. Its two parent companies, Royal Dutch and Shell Transport, merged their interests in 1907 but retained their separate identities and equity trading. The two are public companies but are not themselves part of the Royal Dutch/Shell Group and do not directly engage in operational activities. They hold, directly or indirectly, all group interests in the service companies and the operating companies.

## Origins of the Corporate Governance and Ethics Program

Shell first published a Statement of General Business Principles in 1976. Fifteen years later, however, the environmental outcry over the fate of the floating structure *Brent Spar* showed that the company had misjudged the public mood. Shell had used *Brent Spar* as a loading buoy and storage tank. When, in 1991, it was learned that Shell was planning to sink the structure in the Atlantic Ocean, the reaction was a boycott of Shell products that cost the company millions of dollars. In response, the corporation streamlined its organization to improve its financial performance. It also organized roundtable discussions in 15 countries and conducted opinion research. The results showed management that Shell needed to clearly articulate its values and to make sure they were reflected in its behavior.

The new Business Principles that were introduced across the corporation in 1997 express core values of honesty, integrity, and respect for people (see box CS.15). The introduction states:

Upholding the Shell reputation is paramount. We are judged by how we act. Our reputation will be upheld if we act with honesty and integrity in all our dealings and we do what we think is right at all times within the legitimate role of business.

In 1999 the corporation published and distributed to all its employees a 56-page primer, "Dealing with Bribery and Corruption." The primer describes some of the forms of corruption that can undermine Shell businesses, illustrates them with examples based on actual experiences of employees, and outlines good practices. It points out that:

Managers should be aware that staying honest can require time and effort and may involve extra expenditure or loss of business opportunity. Employees should not be criticized, nor should they feel they have to compromise their organization, if it turns out that the best honest solution involves extra cost or loss of business.

## Implementation System

The policy on business integrity is supported by structures and procedures developed at different levels within the group:

- Senior management commitment and involvement
- Written policies and guidelines
- Internal controls and record keeping
- Auditing
- Communication channels
- Accountability
- Training and awareness raising (extra training is provided for "high risk" employees such as those involved in contracting and procurement activities)
- Third-party checks
- Investigations.

The Group Audit Committee, set up in 1976, deals with financial and internal control matters. The Social Responsibility Committee, which was established in 1997, reviews the policies and conduct of Shell companies with respect to the Business Principles. The Group Internal Audit assesses the group's control framework and makes recommendations for improving

**Box CS.15.    Shell General Business Principles**

Among the nine Shell Business Principles, three are of particular relevance for this study.

**Responsibilities**
Shell companies recognize five areas of responsibility: to shareholders, customers, employees, those with whom the companies do business, and society. The responsibility toward employees is to respect their human rights. The responsibility toward contractors, suppliers, and joint-venture partners is to promote the application of these principles to seek mutually beneficial relationships. "The ability to promote these principles effectively will be an important factor in the decision to enter into or remain in such relationships." The responsibility to society is "to observe the laws of the countries in which [Shell companies] operate, to express support for fundamental human rights in line with the legitimate role of business." This principle also clearly states that integrity and fighting bribery and corruption are responsibilities that extend to Shell's business partners.

**Business integrity**
"Shell companies insist on honesty, integrity, and fairness in all aspects of their business and expect the same in their relationships with all those with whom they do business. The direct or indirect offer, payment, soliciting, and acceptance of bribes in any form are unacceptable practices. Employees must avoid conflicts of interests between their private financial activities and their part in the conduct of company business. All business transactions on behalf of a Shell company must be reflected accurately and fairly in the accounts of the company in accordance with established procedures and be subject to audit."

**Political activities**
"Shell companies act in a socially responsible manner within the laws of the countries in which they operate in pursuit of their legitimate commercial objectives.

"Shell companies do not make payments to political parties, organizations, or their representatives or take any part in party politics. However, when dealing with governments, Shell companies have the right and the responsibility to make their position known on any matter which affects themselves, their employees, their customers, or their shareholders. They also have the right to make their position known on matters affecting the community, where they have a contribution to make."

management systems. The internal audit committees of individual Shell companies and businesses periodically review the business controls in place, provide support to line management, and decide, among other things, whether and how an investigation is to be conducted. The investigation process would include disseminating lessons learned from the incident.

## Compliance Procedures

The procedures for maintaining business integrity are as follows:

- The letter of representation. Each country manager signs a regular letter of representation to corporate headquarters to the effect that his or her branch or subsidiary has complied with the Shell Business Principles. Any instances of bribery must be reported to the highest levels in the group by means of these letters. "All cases are investigated and employees who take, pay or solicit bribes will be dismissed and, if possible, prosecuted," says the primer on "Dealing with Bribery and Corruption."
- Business control incident reports.
- The business principles assurance process, which monitors and assesses progress.

"Tell Shell" is now firmly established as a key feature of Shell's corporate ethics program. This forum was created to encourage Shell employees to dialogue on issues and is much used for a wide range of comment, queries, and debate. Around 90 messages are received every month; only 7 percent are anonymous. Messages are received from all over the world by mail (28 percent), by e-mail (64 percent), and directly on Shell's Web forum (8 percent). EAP accounts for 13 percent of the overall Tell Shell response. Senior executives read and discuss the comments, which provide an important indicator of people's feelings on issues of concern to Shell.

Every year, each Shell country chairman meets with the group managing director responsible for that region to discuss progress and problems in the implementation of the Shell Business Principles in the country. The subject of business principles is also an important agenda item for the conference of country chairmen.

## Public Reporting

Shell is unusual in that it documents key aspects of its compliance efforts for the public in its annual report. As Mark Moody-Stuart, the former Shell chairman, put it, "In today's transparent world it is not enough simply to handle such problems (bribery and corruption) justly, correctly, and efficiently. Information about what has been done, and why, must be provided to a wide range of interest groups."

In 2000, according to the Shell annual report, *People, Planet and Profits*, 106 contracts were terminated and 2 joint ventures were divested for incompatibility with Shell's Business Principles. Four incidents of bribery were identified, resulting in seven dismissals.[1]

## Application to Partners

Shell's business partners are clearly expected to adhere to the anticorruption guidelines (see box CS.16). In the introduction to the primer, Moody-Stuart wrote, "We need to ensure not only that our policies are effectively and consistently applied, but also that they are understood by our current and potential business partners." And the appendix to the primer notes,

> The rules of engagement state that joint venture companies in which Shell companies have a controlling interest are generally expected to adopt the Shell Group Business Principles without change. Minor amendments or additions to reflect local conditions or sensitivities are acceptable providing they do not undermine the Shell Group Business Principles in any material way.

## Experience with the Ethics Program in East Asia and Pacific

"East Asia-Pacific is a challenging area," says John Withrington, head of Shell's International Directorate, and former Shell CEO in Thailand. "On the bribery-corruption side, it is a major problem."

In Shell's North East Asia cluster of companies, corporationwide directives on ethics are supplemented with regional materials. A first booklet for Asia was published in November 1996, and a new version, "Business Standards: Shell's Guide to Good Business Practice," was published in August 1999 in English, Chinese, and Korean. A personal message from Brian Anderson, chairman of Shell Companies in North East Asia, explained that the booklet's aim was "to help our staff—especially those in close contact with customers, suppliers, and other third parties—be clear about what is and what is not acceptable behavior in such areas as the giving and receiving of gifts and business entertaining." In a note to all employees of Shell in North East Asia, Anderson emphasized, "We will *always* investigate fully and take whatever action is appropriate, including if necessary alerting the authorities. . . . *every* member of staff has a duty to tell management about *any* suspected breaches of our principles."

---

**Box CS.16.   Ethics Experience in Shell Joint Ventures in the Philippines**

Shell's corporate presence in the Philippines dates from 1914. Oscar Reyes, country manager of Shell Philippines, observes that the level of commitment to the principles is highest within Shell itself. In activities where Shell owns 100 percent of the company, corporate business principles and policies are clearly communicated and well understood.

In all joint ventures, "the Shell General Business Principles are shared with [the partner], and the country manager's responsibilities are to make sure that these values are shared." The critical distinction that affects adherence to the principles, says Reyes, is not the percentage of the joint venture owned by Shell but whether Shell is the operator. A joint venture operated by Shell is easy to manage according to the Shell General Business Principles. Where joint-venture managers do not agree with the Shell General Business Principles, Shell achieves results through its representation on the joint-venture board. If concerns arise, Shell will suggest more aggressively that it wants documentation.

In joint ventures where Shell is not the operator, it is more difficult to secure adherence to the principles, but there are still possibilities for fighting corruption by checking and auditing the activity.

Reyes notes that where Shell owns a minority share in a joint venture—40 percent, for instance—it is possible to control partner selection and governance through periodic communication, information sharing, and audits, with the choice of an external auditor acceptable to Shell.

Regarding procurement, there is a contract coordinating committee for each Shell contract. In joint ventures in which Shell is the operator, all procurement of goods or services above a set amount goes through the committee. The rules are clear.

The whistle-blowing system is also understood and used by employees, says Reyes. For example, a report came in from an employee in the lubricant business saying that the warehouse where he worked had been stocked with more cartons than were listed and that the excess was to be sold off.

---

Shell's efforts on business principles are firmly in line with national priorities in several countries, notably in China, where the anticorruption drive is a highly publicized part of the government's agenda (see box CS.17); in Hong Kong (China), with its Independent Commission Against Corruption (ICAC); and in Korea, which is promoting ethical business practices.

---

**Box CS.17.   Implementing the Shell Business Principles in China**

Shell has been active in China for more than a century. (Both Shell parent companies Royal Dutch and Shell Transport began operations in Hong Kong and Shanghai separately in 1894. In 1903 they agreed to establish joint operations in the region through the Asiatic Petroleum Corporation, even before merging into Royal Dutch/Shell in 1907.) The company now operates five core businesses in China: exploration, oil products, chemicals, gas and power, and renewables. Shell China has 1,100 staff in more than 20 cities and has concluded 20 joint ventures.

Corruption may be a challenging issue, especially at the provincial level. Business practices are shaped by guangxi traditions and take advantage of unclear rules and regulations. Shell responds to this situation with communication, intensive ethics training, and an annual letter of compliance process.

*Communication* involves the chairman's regular message to staff; distribution in Chinese of the Shell General Business Principles and the Business Standards booklet; and communication to employees and main contractors and suppliers about any breach of ethics standards.

*Intensive ethics training* is conducted for all employees; 1,200 people received this training in 1998, 450 in 1999, and 600 in 2000. Holders of sensitive positions receive additional training (400 were trained in 1998). "Each of Shell's five businesses has its own risk profile," says Tan Ek Kia, country chairman for China. "A key feature of the downstream businesses is that most of the staff is young and inexperienced."

The managers of each of Shell's five businesses in China send *letters of representation* to the country manager. Staff members also complete questionnaires that provide input for the country manager's letter of representation to corporate headquarters.

Shell has never had to modify a management compliance letter and statement of irregularities in China, even in joint-venture operations where Shell is not the operator. With joint-venture partners, Shell includes the Business Principles as part of the articles of association. Shell has operational control in all but one of its 20 joint ventures in China. For example, Tan Ek Kia explains, the Nanhai joint venture, which can be considered a model, has included the principles as part of its articles of association, and Shell has preserved audit rights as a matter of contract. The internal audit program looks at all business processes, including implementation of the Business Principles.

# Note

This section includes major contributions by Mr. Jacques Carbou.

1. Lynn Sharp Paine of the Harvard Business School has commented, "Today's leading companies are being held to a higher standard of performance all around the globe. Increasingly, they will need reports like this *People, Planet and Profits* not only to assure the world they are living up to the new standard, but also to help their own managers do their jobs. Hats off to Shell for tackling this complex area of measurement and reporting." Commenting on the reported figures for 1998–99, however, *The Economist* (2002) notes, "The extraordinary low numbers in the chart have been questioned by several people who have worked with or for Shell in Nigeria. Either the company's internal investigation and reporting systems are inadequate, they allege, or the figures are being economical with the truth." For the complete text of the 2000 Shell bribery statement, see Berenbeim (2000: 31).

# Société Générale de Surveillance

Société Générale de Surveillance (the SGS Group) is the world's largest organization for verification, testing, and certification. Founded in 1878 in France to inspect and certify grain shipments, SGS moved its headquarters to Geneva in 1919. SGS operates more than 1,200 offices and laboratories in 140 countries and has more than 30,000 employees. The group's activities cover verification and monitoring for international trade in agricultural, mineral, petroleum, and consumer products, as well as certification and services for governments and international institutions. SGS has eight business segments: Agricultural Services, Minerals Services, Redwood Services, Consumer Products Services, International Certification Services, Global Trade Solutions, Industrial Services, and Other Services. East Asia and Pacific is an important area for the group: it accounts for 17 percent of total revenues, 29 percent of operating profit, and one in four employees.

For SGS, whose business is verification and certification, a commitment to integrity is the cornerstone of its reputation. Since the late 1990s, the company has been making integrated efforts to build an internal culture of integrity, placing "a concern for ethics at the core of all activities."

## Origins of the Ethics Program

SGS began work on an anticorruption program after its reputation was damaged when Benazir Bhutto, then prime minister of Pakistan, was forced to resign in 1990 and was sent to court for corruption. SGS had contracted with a consultant acting on behalf of Bhutto and her husband.

To improve business integrity, CEO Anthony Czura established an Ethics Committee consisting of the chairman of the board, the CEO, the chief compliance officer, and an external member. The head of Internal Audit attends the meetings. Members of the SGS Executive Board who confront specific issues with ethical dimensions also take part in the committee's work.

The committee now oversees implementation of the SGS Group's Code of Ethics. It reviews all agreements for procuring and developing business opportunities with agents, consultants, advisers, lobbyists, and other third parties in order to identify possible conflicts of interest concerning SGS employees; it considers and acts on the results of investigations into violations of the code; and it issues guidelines on employee training in ethical issues. Four times a year it considers reports on compliance prepared by the chief compliance officer.

## Corporate Code of Ethics

SGS adopted its first Code of Ethics in 1997. A new code, with reinforced procedures for implementation, was issued in August 1999. The code opens with a statement of integrity, signed by the chairman of the board and the CEO:

- Be honest and transparent in all SGS activities.
- Avoid conflicts of interest.
- Comply with all applicable laws and regulations.
- Maintain a culture where ethical conduct is recognized and valued.

The statement adds, "Follow these principles strictly, not only their rules but their spirit."

The code focuses mainly on rules and principles for preventing corruption. It emphasizes the importance of accurate and transparent financial records, with no room for practices that would not withstand public scrutiny. It states emphatically that no funds or assets are to be used to obtain privileges or special benefits from public officials or to influence their decisions. SGS employees, in turn, must avoid conflicts of interest and must not solicit or accept any favor or office that could lead to such a situation.

Under the title "Improper Payment," the code states: "No payment shall be made, and no advantage shall be granted, by any employee, directly or indirectly, to any official or civil servant or any government for the purpose of influencing any act or decision of that government."

## Implementation System

The company recognizes that the overall issue is to change employees' attitudes and behavior regarding corruption. Employee communication, training, and monitoring of compliance, are designed to reinforce each other to promote an ethical work environment within the group.

---

**Box CS.18.  Developing the SGS Ethics Training Program**

An Ethics Task Force Committee representative of SGS employees worldwide was established in October 1999 to oversee the development of the group's training program. To gather information that would help match the program to local needs, the company sent a detailed questionnaire to its offices in 118 countries and organized focus groups of managers in Cameroon, Côte d'Ivoire, and Kenya, as well as in Geneva, with the help of the International Business Ethics Institute.

The management training program was developed during February–April 2000 and was revised and finalized during May–September of the same year. Tests were carried out in April 2000 in Hungary, Kenya, and Taiwan (China). Regional "Train the Trainer" workshops were organized in Cameroon, Dubai, Russia, Switzerland, Thailand, and the United States in September–October. Subsequently, the 60 new ethics trainers immediately began to deliver courses for senior and middle managers.

---

## Communications and Training

The revised code has been published in more than 20 languages and distributed to all employees. It is also available on the SGS Internet site, as well as on the company intranet. An ethics poster is displayed in all SGS offices worldwide.

Jean-Pierre Méan, chief compliance officer, notes that according to comments and reports from various countries, the great majority of employees recognize and appreciate the commitment of top management to building an ethical culture.

The SGS training program plays an essential role in building a worldwide ethical culture. Training for managers was developed and implemented first, starting in 2000 (see box CS.18), and all 2,300 managers have now undergone a one-day ethics training session. Training for employees throughout the organization is under way. The training is closely tailored to regional characteristics and needs.

The goals of the training program are to:

- Enhance understanding of SGS's commitment to business ethics
- Familiarize trainees with business ethics resources
- Enhance management skills that foster an ethical workplace environment
- Improve ability to apply standards to business situations.

The training is made as interactive as possible. It includes discussion of the Code of Ethics and case studies, and it places a strong emphasis on the discussion of real situations that have arisen. Box CS.19 provides an example.

## Employee Certification

Each SGS employee is required to sign a statement acknowledging receipt of the code and agreeing to abide by its provisions. The code is distributed to each new employee and is part of the employment contract. Compliance with the code is assessed as part of each employee's performance review.

Since 2000, senior managers have been required to monitor and report on compliance with the code.

## Compliance Systems

Because rigorous security measures and internal audits are key to preserving SGS's reputation, no one person may do an entire job alone. All work is checked by the Internal Audit Department, whose work is in turn subject to random checks by the manager of auditors. Every prospective auditor is screened for criminal record and potential conflict of interest.

An ethics help line/hotline manned by the Security and Audit Departments was established in July 1999. In Geneva the chief compliance officer uses the reporting system to become aware of actual or potential problems but also as a way of ensuring that employees understand the company's position and policies. At the time of writing, the help line was still relatively little used. In China Aloysius Tan of the SGS Audit Department, based in Shanghai, says, "We have a reasonable utilization of the whistle-blowing system in this country. Roughly 40 percent of informants identify themselves, 60 percent don't." He adds that "the volume of complaints may not be as high as in the United States, but we do get them."

## Issues

Conversations with company officers suggest that SGS has proportionately more compliance problems with employees in Asia than elsewhere. In particular, the concept of "appearance of conflict of interest" is not well understood in Asia. The Code of Ethics gives a detailed explanation of conflict of interest, and the training program sums it up as

---

**Box CS.19.   Sample Case Study from the SGS Training Program**

Machine Technology Certifications (MTC) is an international testing and inspection company. It is the end of the year and the Minerals Department of MTC-Asia has been working at capacity for the past month. The aggressive business practices of MTC's competitors in the Asian market are making it exceedingly difficult for the company to maintain or increase its share of the market.

Rick is the senior manager of MTC-Asia. He receives an unexpected visit from Sue Lynn, a longtime friend and a representative of APF, a consulting agency in the metal industry. Because it is the holiday season, Sue Lynn has brought with her several gifts for Rick's children and a small piece of jewelry for his wife, which Rick accepts. After some talk, Sue Lynn indicates that she has an important inspection to be performed immediately.

Sue Lynn explains that the inspection APF is requesting involves a shipment of ore at the local port that needs to be inspected and shipped as soon as possible. APF is eager to ship the refined ore to its most important client for use in manufacturing processes. Sue Lynn assures Rick that this first job will very likely bring about additional and continued revenues from APF, a company that MTC has been trying to obtain work from for the past two years.

Rick recognizes the potential importance of this single job for MTC, and when Sue Lynn requests a "brokerage fee" in order to recommend MTC to her client, Rick agrees. Although he might prefer to run his decision by the head office, he realizes that if he does so, the approval might not come until too late. Rick determines that he can submit the expenses legitimately as a payment to a third party who has provided competitive intelligence on behalf of the company.

As soon as Sue Lynn leaves, Rick realizes that he is going to have difficulty locating a qualified employee to perform the inspection. The only qualified inspector is Harry, who is already overscheduled for the next two months. Because of the potential importance of the client to MTC, Rick believes that the best course of action would be to pull Harry off several "lesser" accounts, even though doing so might cause some delays in previously scheduled inspections.

Harry appears at Rick's door. Rick asks, "How did the inspection go?" Harry responds, "Well, it didn't. Because this is a new contract and not the type of inspection that MTC normally performs, the port authorities stopped me before I could take the necessary samples. A mid-ranking official told me that we have to pay a special licensing fee of US$1,000 in cash before I can gain access to the shipment." Harry goes on to explain that he knows a consultant who could facilitate this transaction for far less money so that the samples could be taken in a few hours.

Rick says, "Contact the consultant and make the necessary arrangements. Mr. Chen, the president of APF, is really impatient to receive the results of our inspection. This is a vital contract for MTC—in fact, this contract may well decide our future in this region."

Rick is at his desk when he receives a call from Mr. Chen, who wishes to discuss a couple of figures that appear on the inspection report. Mr. Chen requests Rick to round up the percentage of the ore's purity from 91.45 to 93 percent. Rick indicates that this likely falls outside of acceptable tolerances.

Mr. Chen continues the conversation by saying, "I'm quite pleased with how quickly MTC was able to perform this inspection for us. We've got a couple of other shipments that we will need to have inspected before the end of the month. Call me once you've faxed the new report to me and we can arrange a dinner meeting next week to discuss future business."

Situations where personal interests become more important than the Company's best interests, such as:

- Personal relationships
- Business relationships
- Position outside the company.

This section includes major contributions by Mr. Jacques Carbou.

# Suez Group

The Suez Group, a Fortune 500 global utilities company based in France, is the result of the 1996 merger of two groups that have operated since the middle of the 19th century. The first, La Lyonnaise des Eaux et de l'Eclairage, has been one of the major water utilities worldwide, while the diversified Suez Company originated in the Suez Canal operations. Today, the Suez Group is a US$32 billion company with 180,000 employees in more than 120 countries. It primarily operates four business segments—energy, water, waste services, and communications—but also has businesses in construction and financial services. The business segments are managed separately because they develop, manufacture, and sell distinct products and services.

Suez began operations in East Asia and Pacific in the 1980s and today employs 6,350 people there, providing water, electricity, and waste services in cities across the region. EAP represented 5 percent of the total revenues of Suez for 2000.

## Origins of the Ethics Program

Not until after the merger of Suez with Lyonnaise was a cohesive effort made to develop a corporate ethics program. For the combined company, international operations were key to the strategy for growth, and CEO Jérôme Monod saw that it was urgent to develop a set of core principles for ethical business that the company could apply worldwide. As Philippe de Margerie, general counsel, notes:

> Becoming worldwide in scope means becoming multicultural, which in turn means learning and growing from other cultures, and seeking new management modes. . . . Ethical values are precisely where men and women come together, whatever their national backgrounds or other differences. The mutual understanding that comes from shared values is essential to confidence, which is at the heart of any business relationship.

Reducing reputational risks was another major consideration. Mindful of the scandal of 1990 in France, in which some executives of Lyonnaise des Eaux had been jailed for making political contributions on behalf of the company, management sought to minimize the risks of further unethical behavior as the company's operations expanded. Gérard Mestrallet, who became president of the Executive Board of Suez in June 1997, has said:

> We are a Group with worldwide interests and ambitions, which means our image is global too. That is potentially a source of weakness, in the sense that in today's world of global, instantaneously transmitted news, a reputation that took years to build can be shattered in minutes. . . . I am convinced that the greatest threat to our Group is not so much a financial or a political crisis, as a crisis in our image.

A third key consideration was commitment to transparency. Then-CEO Monod wrote:

> Mindful of its commitments in terms of corporate governance and of its obligations towards its shareholders, employees, and the financial market authorities, Suez-Lyonnaise des Eaux places particular importance on ensuring full and clear disclosure in every aspect of its financial reporting.

Suez has developed an ambitious ethics program that extends to its subsidiary organizations. In the elaboration of the program, a concern for corporate governance, the codification of ethical standards, and the development of a compliance culture have been closely related from the beginning.

Work on the ethics program began in 1997 when the Supervisory Board of Suez created the Ethics Committee, involved itself in the formulation of a code of ethics, and appointed an ethics officer to work closely with the general counsel.

## Basic Documents

The Suez Group's ethical vision is laid out in a series of documents:

- Corporate Values and Ethics Charter (December 1998)
- Rules for the Organization and Conduct of Group Companies (December 1998)
- Group Values (April 1999)
- International Social Charter (December 1999)
- Environmental Charter (February 2000).

These documents, gathered in a single folder, have been widely distributed to the management of group companies. They are also published on the Suez Website.

The Ethics Charter defines a specific set of ethical practices that are designed to ensure

- Compliance with corporate governance principles
- Accuracy in financial reporting
- Building of long-term relationships with suppliers based on transparency and fairness
- Maintenance of transparent and balanced relations with and between the group's subsidiaries
- Safeguarding of the host community in which the group operates by strictly prohibiting political contributions
- Avoidance of corruption in all its forms.

Subdivisions of Suez have issued supplementary ethics resources that give specific guidance for their own sectors. The Water Division (Ondeo), for example, has issued procedures for choosing investor-partners and for selecting and monitoring the division's business agents. The procedures clearly state that Ondeo Services

> regards international corruption as an obstacle to global economic growth and as a source of economic and social distortions. Ondeo Services is committed to growth with partners who share its way of thinking. It also seeks to avoid having the selection of an inappropriate partner lead to behavior contrary to its policy or its ethical values, thereby compromising its reputation and future.

## Implementation System

Suez Group's ethics program depends on four elements:

- An Ethics Committee
- A network of ethics officers
- Communications and training
- Personnel evaluation programs.

### Ethics Committee

The Ethics Committee has four members: two members of the Suez Board of Directors (one of whom is an independent board member), and two executives of the Suez Group. The committee coordinates the procedures required in implementing the Ethics Charter with respect to providing training, circulating the document, overseeing compliance, and updating the charter. The committee meets several times a year, and the minutes of each meeting are communicated to the board's Audit Committee, as well as to the other members of the Supervisory Board and the president of the Executive Board. The committee's recommendations and opinions are reviewed and approved by the Supervisory Board.

Since the Suez Group's constituent companies are required to establish structures and procedures that ensure compliance with the common code of ethical values, ethics committees have now been established by the boards of directors of all the main subsidiaries of Suez.

In July 1999 Suez broadened the mandate of the Ethics Committee to cover environmental issues, and the name was changed to the Ethics and Environment Committee. This move was clearly designed to extend the company's ethical responsibilities to environmental protection and promotion of sustainable development.

## Network of Ethics Officers

Suez has developed a network of some 50 ethics officers within the group and its major subdivisions. The creation of this network of officers is proving an important step in spreading awareness of the company's ethics requirements within its subsidiaries. The role of the ethics officers is twofold: they are the main actors responsible for making company ethics known among all employees, in collaboration with the Human Resources and Communications Departments, and they are responsible for monitoring compliance. All employees have easy access to the ethics officer for their particular business area in order to seek guidance and counsel, or even to draw attention to difficulties with or violations of the charter's tenets.

The officers ensure that group companies observe their codes of conduct in keeping with the legal and regulatory framework of the countries in which they operate, and they recommend improvements or adjustments where needed.

Ethics officers are selected from company executive management. Special care is taken to ensure their independence, as well as their ability to relate to their peers and to company employees in general. They are assisted by the Legal Department and by the risk manager, where there is one. They receive reliable information through close, cooperative relations with the Internal Audit Department and, more generally, with accounting departments.

The network of ethics managers continues to expand within the subsidiaries. To help coordinate their actions, Suez holds an annual conference of ethics managers, which is attended by the president of the Executive Board.

## Communications and Training

The Suez Group's human resources departments are required to furnish each employee with a code of conduct reflecting the group's ethics and the particular sector's respective business ethics statement. They are also required to provide information and organize training and awareness programs to familiarize employees with these standards of conduct.

Training was key to the creation of the network of ethics officers. Suez employed the professional services of a consulting organization in the field of international business ethics to assist with the training.

Training is also an important part of building a culture of compliance. About a thousand executives of group companies and subsidiaries receive ethics and values training each year, and the annual welcome seminar that brings together hundreds of young managers from around the globe now includes a session on group ethics and values. The chief compliance officer, Henry-Benoît Loosdregt, participates in the training sessions for new managers.

## Personnel Evaluations

Annual performance reviews take into account each employee's performance with regard to the Ethics Charter.

## Compliance Procedures

The group's internal procedures with regard to investments examine three subjects: legal issues financial issues, and coinvestors' background (the last, for joint-venture agreements). The results for each are reported in a presentation to the Investment Committee. All fees and commissions must be explained and justified to the Investment Committee, to eliminate anything that would be an illegal commission or a bribe.

Every year, the chairmen of the main companies in the group must send letters of compliance to the chairman of the Executive Board stating that their businesses are in compliance with the company Code of Conduct. This requirement is gradually spreading within the group's subsidiaries.

## Application to Subsidiaries and Affiliates

The Ethics Charter applies not only to the directly controlled subsidiaries of Suez but also to their own subsidiaries and to affiliates of the subsidiaries. Representatives strongly encourage companies in which they have minority interests to adopt the tenets contained in the Ethics Charter in drafting their own rules of conduct.

---

**Box CS.20. "Going for Small Things" in China**

Jacques Letondot, Suez manager for China, Hong Kong (China), and Macao (China), where Suez provides urban water services through joint ventures, says that in his seven years Suez has never had a situation where "we had to offer a bribe nor to deal with an unethical demand." In the water sector, according to Letondot, Suez has two advantages in avoiding corruption:

- Suez provides water to local populations, and countries are very sensitive on this issue involving national pride. So there is a need for efficiency and capability.
- There is a minimum technical threshold for water to be good. To achieve this, the operator has to be a well-known company.

In China the central government is aware of the risks and inefficiencies of corruption, but this awareness has not always filtered down to local municipal governments—the entities that Suez deals with. In such circumstances, Letondot says, the best strategy for preventing corruption is to avoid big, high-profile projects and to make many small, low-profile investments (US$15 million–US$25 million). "If it is a small project you can't ask for a big bribe. All you can afford is a good dinner in a nice restaurant. . . . Going for small things is a good way to protect yourself."

---

## Experience with the Ethics Program in East Asia and Pacific

In East Asia and Pacific major efforts are being made to implement the ethics program. Suez companies and subsidiaries have different experiences from country to country, but results are already visible (see boxes CS.20 and CS.21).

---

**Box CS.21. New Rules for Water Supply in Jakarta**

Christian Michelon, the Suez regional director for water, had been warned about corruption in Indonesia but found the reality much worse than expected. In partnership with the Salim Group of Indonesia, Suez negotiated a 25-year concession contract with Pam Jaya, the local public water company, to supply water services to half the population of Jakarta.

At Pam Jaya, illicit dealings were customary. From 20 to 25 percent of Pam Jaya's expenses went to high-ranking government and city council officials. The utility commonly made extra money on its customers by charging them for unnecessary meter readings, illegally establishing new connections, rigging the bill payment system, or pocketing the salaries of nonexistent "daily workers." Corruption allowed employees at all levels to triple or quadruple their salaries.

The concession contract involved a major reform program: the goal within the next five years was to reduce water losses from 60 percent of overall business to 35 percent and to increase the volume of water sold by 40 percent. The work implied heavy investments and cooperation between Pam Jaya's teams and those of the Suez-Salim joint-venture company.

Despite the expertise of Suez's local partner Salim in legal, financial, fiscal, and labor-related issues, and its significant lobbying capacities, the agreement with Pam Jaya was preceded by seemingly endless negotiations. On receiving government approval, Suez had to engage in feasibility studies that lasted a year. The subsequent negotiations lasted two years and were followed by an official agreement in 1997. The resulting contract, which spanned 1,500 pages, came into effect in 1998, just as President Suharto resigned.

During the political troubles, Pam Jaya attempted to terminate its contract with Suez by encouraging frequent strikes and threatening personnel. When Suez offered to extend a 20 percent pay raise to all Pam Jaya employees, local workers were not at all interested—to them, Suez was in fact offering an 80 percent reduction! When expatriates were evacuated from Jakarta, Pam Jaya took over the Suez-Salim joint-venture company and requested that the contract with Suez be terminated immediately. But Suez fought for its contract and was able to prove to the new government that it did not engage in corrupt activities. After agreeing to change the name of the joint-venture company and to give 10 percent of its shares to the government, Suez was able to resume business in June 1998.

Throughout the negotiation process, Suez had been careful to avoid any hint of corruption. It had clearly explained its ethics and values policy to Salim, specifying that it was opposed to any form of bribery. To ensure the utmost transparency, it had brought World Bank consultants and international lawyers and bankers into the process. In order to reduce the opportunities for corruption, it was decided that all future calls for tender should be made official and published in the media. When dealing with larger contracts, it was suggested that the official bid opening be held in the presence of government representatives. It was decided that all tenders should include provisions on transparency.

Within the business, additional measures have been taken: all functions and tasks are separated, and half of the sales office chiefs are replaced every two years. Payments are controlled using barcodes, and random controls have been implemented throughout the organization. The official cost of connections is regularly published in the media. All major contracts are managed separately, and all new connections are registered automatically, using specific software. Daily workers are paid directly, and Suez expatriates are always on site to validate operating expenses and payrolls. These specially chosen employees sign agreements stating that they will act in an upright manner and that they accept that they can be fired on the spot for any wrongdoing. Even so, Michelon personally signs all of the checks issued by the company, as the safest way of preventing problems.

This section includes major contributions by Mr. Jacques Carbou.

# Appendix A
# Vulnerability of Firms to Extortion: An Econometric Analysis

The World Business Environment Survey (WBES) uses two major measures of corruption:

- The perception of corruption as an obstacle to business, on a scale of 1 (best) to 4 (worst)
- Bribes as a percentage of the company's volume of sales, classified in seven intervals, as shown in the table.

| Interval | 1 | 2 | 3 | 4 | 5 | 6 | 7 |
|---|---|---|---|---|---|---|---|
| Bribes as a percentage of sales | 0 | 0–1 | 1–2 | 2–10 | 10–12 | 12–25 | > 25 |

Whereas the first variable is a perceptions index comparable to those provided by other surveys, the second is a direct measure of the outcome.

Both indicators are available for more than 5,000 corporations in 80 countries. Either might be influenced by, at least, firm size, foreign ownership, performance, and country-specific variables. Such dependence translates into a functional relationship in the form:

Corruption indicator = F(size of the corporation, foreign ownership, performance, country variable)

with the functional coefficients to be estimated econometrically.

## Cross-Country Analysis

An adequate econometric technique for regressing an ordinal discrete dependent variable such as the perception ratings provided by the WBES is the ordered probit or logit model.[1] Clarke and Xu (2002) have recently applied a probit model to the same data set, using slightly different variables. The technique allows a direct comparison of the impacts of the independent variables on the two indicators, although the ordinal scales differ between those two indicators (in this case, 1–4 versus 1–7). The results of the regressions are given in tables A.1 and A.2.

- Looking at the size of the bribe paid in relation to company sales volume, company size, and ownership matter significantly. Large corporations and foreign-owned corporations pay significantly less in bribes. Being foreign owned reduces a firm's vulnerability to extortion by an amount equivalent to a 1-point improvement on Transparency International's 10-point Corruption Perceptions Index (CPI). The difference in vulnerability between small corporations (with fewer than 50 employees) and large corporations (with more than 500 employees) is equivalent to 2 points on the CPI (regressions 3 and 4 in table A.2).
- As to the perception of corruption as an obstacle to business, the impact of foreign ownership is not significant. And although smaller firms tend to be more worried about corruption, this difference is less than their increase in vulnerability to corruption (measured again in terms of amount of bribes as a percentage of sales volume). Typically, the difference in perception of corruption between small and large corporations is equivalent to only 0.4 point on the CPI (regression 2 in table A.1).
- The impact of performance (measured by a dummy variable) is also significant, with performing companies being less vulnerable than

### Table A.1. Probit Regression: Dependent Variable, Corruption as an Obstacle to Business

|  | 1 | 2 |
|---|---|---|
| Size variable[a] | –0.106 | –0.056 |
|  | (4.1)** | (2.11)** |
| Foreign ownership | 0.08 | 0.056 |
| dummy[b] | (1.73)* | (1.1) |
| Country dummy | Yes | No |
| CPI | No | –0.27 |
|  |  | (29.6)** |

* Significant at the 10 percent level.
** Significant at the 5 percent level.
Note: CPI, Transparency International Corruption Perceptions Index. A positive coefficient implies an increase in vulnerability. Numbers in parentheses are $t$-statistics.
a. 0, < 50 employees; 1, from 50 to 500 employees; 2, > 500 employees.
b. 0, yes; 1, no.

## Table A.2. Probit Regression: Dependent Variable, Bribe as Percentage of Sales (on a Discrete Scale of 1 to 7)

|                          | 3        | 4         | 5        |
|--------------------------|----------|-----------|----------|
| Size variable[a]         | –0.16    | –0.267    | –0.15    |
|                          | (6.06)** | (9.91)**  | (5.2)**  |
| Foreign ownership        | 0.18     | 0.25      | 0.19     |
| dummy[b]                 | (3.64)** | (4.8)**   | (3.4)**  |
| Performance dummy[c]     |          |           | 0.19     |
|                          |          |           | (4.4)**  |
| Country dummy            | Yes      | No        | Yes      |
| CPI                      | No       | –0.30     | No       |
|                          |          | (29.4)**  |          |

\* Significant at the 10 percent level.
\*\* Significant at the 5 percent level.
Note: CPI, Transparency International Corruption Perceptions Index. A positive coefficient implies an increase in vulnerability. Numbers in parentheses are t-statistics.
a. 0, < 50 employees; 1, from 50 to 500 employees; 2, > 500 employees.
b. 0, yes; 1, no.
c. 0, performing; 1, nonperforming; measured by sales growth over the past two years.

nonperformers, as measured by sales growth over the preceding two years. The magnitude of the effect is comparable to that of foreign ownership (regression 5 in table A.2).

## How Corruption Compares with Other Business Constraints: A Within-Country Analysis (Indonesia)

Large country-based surveys permit examination of how corruption compares with other constraints in the business environment and how different measures of corruption at the firm level compare among themselves. A private survey by the Partnership for Governance Reform in Indonesia (2001) provides an adequate database for 400 firms. Fifteen constraints are gauged on a scale of 1 ("not a problem") to 5 ("serious problem"). The actual outcome of corruption is measured in percentage of sales (table A.3).

• There is a wide dispersion in firms' perceptions, as witnessed by the standard deviation in the perception.
• Quite naturally, the perception of the impact of corruption is strongly correlated with the prevalence of fraud in the private sector and the ineffectiveness of the judiciary.

## Table A.3. Constraints on Business Activity in Indonesia, on a Scale of 1 to 5

| | | | Correlation coefficient | | |
|---|---|---|---|---|---|
| Constraint | Mean (5 = most severe impact) | Standard deviation | Corruption in the public sector | Corruption in the private sector | Level of additional payment (percentage of sales) |
| Financing | 3.6 | 1.0 | –0.03 | 0.02 | 0.01 |
| Infrastructure | 3.2 | 1.0 | 0.03 | 0.06 | –0.07 |
| Availability and price of inputs | 3.3 | 1.0 | 0.03 | 0.01 | 0.02 |
| Availability and price of skilled labor | 3.0 | 0.8 | 0.09* | 0.10* | –0.04 |
| Cost of labor | 3.2 | 0.9 | 0.06 | 0.05 | –0.08 |
| Insufficient or unstable demand | 3.2 | 0.9 | 0.03 | 0.10* | 0.01 |
| High taxes | 3.5 | 1.0 | 0.14* | 0.23* | 0.13* |
| Complex regulations | 3.2 | 0.9 | 0.12* | 0.14* | 0.06 |
| Political uncertainty or instability | 3.5 | 1.0 | 0.15* | 0.13* | 0.01 |
| Inflation | 3.4 | 0.9 | 0.17* | 0.13* | 0.08 |
| Unstable exchange rate | 3.7 | 0.9 | 0.17* | 0.10* | 0.06 |
| Ineffective courts | 2.9 | 1.0 | 0.62* | 0.42* | 0.06 |
| Corruption in the public sector | 3.2 | 1.1 | 1.00* | 0.59* | 0.09* |
| Corruption in the private sector | 2.8 | 0.9 | 0.59* | 1.00* | 0.19* |
| Crime, theft, disorder | 3.2 | 1.1 | 0.28* | 0.33* | 0.17* |

* Significant at the 10 percent level.
*Source:* Partnership for Governance Reform in Indonesia (2001).

- The perception of corruption is only weakly correlated with the outcome, which suggests that the individual firm's attitude toward corruption is largely determined by management values and perceptions of priorities.

The qualitative connections between constraints are well illustrated in figure A.1. The hierarchy in the cluster graph is hardly surprising.

## Figure A.1. Cluster Graph of the Relationships between Constraints on Business Activity in Indonesia

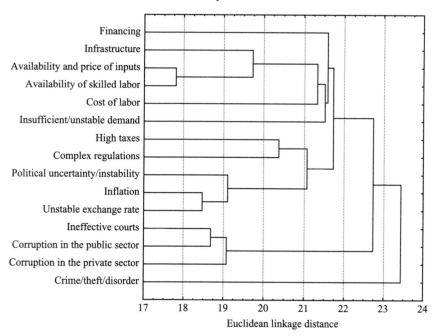

Euclidean linkage distance

## Note

1. For a detailed description of the procedure and the interpretation of the regression coefficients, see, for example, Greene (2000): ch. 19.

# Appendix B
# Alternative Interpretations of the Bribe Payers Index

Transparency International's Bribe Payers Index (BPI) for 2002 is based on a survey of 835 business executives (including representatives of international firms) in 15 emerging economies.[1] Respondents were asked to give their perceptions of corrupt practices in their countries by multinational corporations exporting from 21 developed or emerging countries (including Russia and major exporters from East Asia).[2] The exporting countries are ranked on a scale of 1 (worst practices) to 10 (best practices).

How may the BPI be explained by other variables? The correlations between the BPI and the size of the exporter or the level of perceived corruption in the exporting countries (as measured by Transparency International's Corruption Perceptions Index) are very clear (see figures B.1 and B.2). The correlation between corruption at home and propensity to bribe points to a plausible connection: corrupt practices at home are likely to be reflected in business practices abroad.

Since those surveyed are not the bribe *takers,* the BPI is not a direct measurement of corrupt practices. A bias in this measure may stem from the fact that a respondent will have heard more about corrupt practices by exporters with larger market shares. Indeed, analysis confirms that there are systematic increases in score between a large exporter and its smaller neighbor—for example, between the United States (5.3) and Canada (8.1); France (5.5) and Belgium (7.8); and Germany (6.3) and Austria (8.2). Given the economic integration of those pairs of countries and the closeness of their business cultures, languages, and ethical values in general, there is no obvious explanation for the large difference in BPI between the small and the large country in each pair, other than a systematic size bias in the survey.

Furthermore, the six major exporting OECD countries are in the same range of the BPI (the United Kingdom being slightly higher and Italy slightly lower). Therefore after correcting for the possible country size bias introduced by the survey, the BPI may no longer indicate to

## Figure B.1.  Propensity to Bribe and Corruption at Home

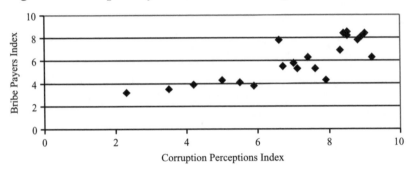

## Figure B.2.  Propensity to Bribe and Country Size (Developed Countries Only)

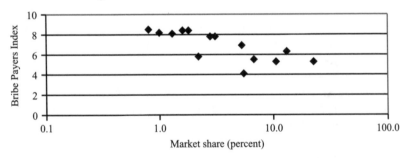

*Note:* Emerging countries in Asia and the former Soviet Union are not represented.

## Table B.1. Regression of the Transparency International Bribe Payers Index against the Corruption Perceptions Index and Other Characteristics of the Exporter

|  | 1 | 2 | 3 | 4 | 5 |
|---|---|---|---|---|---|
| Ln(market share) | None | −0.61 | −0.53 | −0.65 | −0.80 |
|  |  | (2.4) | (2.6) | (3.4) | (4.2) |
| CPI | 0.77 | 0.76 | 0.66 | 0.69 | 0.57 |
|  | (5.8) | (6.3) | (6.6) | (7.7) | (6.0) |
| East Asia and Pacific dummy | None | None | −1.31 (3.3) | None | None |
| Guanxi dummy | None | None | None | −1.52 (3.8) | None |
| OECD Convention dummy | None | None | None | None | +1.72 (4.3) |
| $R^2$ | 0.64 | 0.73 | 0.83 | 0.85 | 0.87 |
| d.f. | 19 | 18 | 17 | 17 | 17 |
| F | 34 | 24 | 28 | 32 | 36 |

Note: Numbers in parentheses are t-statistics.

substantial differences among the OECD exporting countries in their propensity to bribe.

Regression of the BPI on country size, the Corruption Perceptions Index (CPI), and a regional variable shows that the best fit is obtained by introducing a dummy variable to reflect country adherence (or otherwise) to the OECD Anti-Bribery Convention (see the last column in table B.1).[3] Other things being equal, a country that has signed the convention is perceived as having a better CPI, by a substantial amount (1.8). This may explain the difference in propensity to bribe between, for example, Singapore and Hong Kong (China), on the one hand, and Switzerland and Sweden, on the other hand. This finding is consistent with the observation made in chapter 3 that the OECD Convention regime is catalyzing the implementation of compliance techniques.

Thus on close inspection, the Transparency International survey data shows that home-country prohibition of bribery is effective, although a first reading of the results might suggest the opposite.

Table B.1 show the results of regressions of the BPI versus the CPI and the market share of the exporter. Dummy variables are included to test the impact of various factors such as location in East Asia (3), the influence of the guanxi culture (4), and location in the EAP region and participation in the OECD Convention (5). Table B.2 presents the raw

## Table B.2.  CPI, BPI, and Trade Data for the Economies in the Sample

| Exporter | CPI 2001 | BPI 2002 | Market share (percent)[a] | OECD dummy |
|---|---|---|---|---|
| Australia | 8.5 | 8.5 | 0.8 | Yes |
| Austria | 7.8 | 8.2 | 1.0 | Yes |
| Belgium | 6.6 | 7.8 | 2.8 | Yes |
| Canada | 8.9 | 8.1 | 1.3 | Yes |
| China | 3.5 | 3.5 | 6.7 | |
| France | 6.7 | 5.5 | 6.8 | Yes |
| Hong Kong (China) | 7.9 | 4.3 | 2.9 | |
| Germany | 7.4 | 6.3 | 13.1 | Yes |
| Italy | 5.5 | 4.1 | 5.5 | Yes |
| Japan | 7.1 | 5.3 | 10.6 | Yes |
| Korea, Rep. of | 4.2 | 3.9 | 4.2 | Yes |
| Malaysia | 5.0 | 4.3 | 1.5 | |
| Netherlands | 8.8 | 7.8 | 3.1 | Yes |
| Russian Federation | 2.3 | 3.2 | 0.9 | |
| Singapore | 9.2 | 6.3 | 2.5 | |
| Spain | 7.0 | 5.8 | 2.2 | Yes |
| Sweden | 9.0 | 8.4 | 1.8 | Yes |
| Switzerland | 8.4 | 8.4 | 1.6 | Yes |
| Taiwan (China) | 5.9 | 3.8 | 2.8 | |
| United Kingdom | 8.3 | 6.9 | 5.3 | Yes |
| United States | 7.6 | 5.3 | 22.4 | Yes |
| Local corporations | | 1.9 | | |

*Note:* BPI, Transparency International Bribe Payers Index; CPI, Transparency International Corruption Perceptions Index. The CPI and BPI are on a scale of 1 (worst) to 10 (corruption free).
a. The market share is the geometric average of the market shares of exporting countries in the 15 individual destination markets surveyed by Transparency International.
*Source:* Transparency International (2002a); IMF, *Direction of Trade Statistics;* authors' calculations.

data for the 21 exporting countries in Transparency International's sample.

# Notes

1.  The economies included in the survey are Argentina, Brazil, Colombia, Hungary, India, Indonesia, Korea, Mexico, Morocco, Nigeria, the Philippines, Poland, Russia, South Africa, and Thailand.

2.  India and the Latin American and Caribbean countries are not included in the panel.

3. The logarithm of the market share of the exporter is taken as the independent size variable. The logarithmic dependence is a natural hypothesis: since the BPI is a perception, it is expected to follow a Weber-Fechner law. The perception of the intensity of the phenomenon is proportional to the logarithm of the intensity or frequency of the cause of the phenomenon. Here the BPI measures the intensity of bribery and is therefore proportional to the logarithm of the number of instances of bribery, which is itself proportional to the market share of the exporter.

# Appendix C
# Methodology for the Case Studies

The series of case studies was conducted with companies known to have implemented some procedure for addressing ethical issues in the context of their home-country or international operations. This information was obtained through Conference Board research or by collaborators in the project such as Reitaku University in Japan.

The case studies relied on interviews of executives with responsibility for business conduct policies. For some international corporations, managers posted in the East Asia and Pacific region were also visited.

Because the interviews needed to address sensitive topics with some cultural content, they required the help of experts who had the right access and were culturally close to the interviewees. Under World Bank and Conference Board supervision, many interviews were undertaken by locally based consultants who were fellow citizens of those being interviewed or at least spoke the same language.

To insure consistency in the research, the experts and the supervision team used, as much as possible, the instrument for the interviews that is replicated below.

## Case Study Interview Procedures

### Company information

Each case study will begin with a concise description of the company (nationality, products, services, etc.). This section should also include a history of the company's business in EAP. Although such information will not be included in the case study, we also need names, addresses, telephone numbers, faxes, and e-mail addresses for contacts in important EAP branches, divisions, or subsidiaries. In brief, here is what the company information section needs:

- Description of the company
- History of EAP operations

- 2000 FY company revenues
- 2000 FY EAP revenues
- Percentage of revenues from EAP
- Major EAP branches, divisions, subsidiaries
  - Business description of each
  - Revenues/each
  - EAP ownership structure/each—e.g., division/branch, wholly owned subsidiary, majority ownership subsidiary, minority ownership subsidiary, joint venture—company is equal partner, joint venture—company is dominant partner, joint venture—company is minority partner

## General issues

In addition to the specific elements of individual company programs, questions of general applicability need to be discussed. These concerns should be brought up at appropriate times during the interviews. They include:

- Awareness and acceptance of 1997 OECD Anti-Bribery Convention
- Dissemination of OECD Guidelines by local government agencies
- Impact of 1997 Asian financial crisis
- Comparison of EAP anticorruption program to U.S. model/practices
- Cultural adaptation required for anticorruption program implementation/management
- Company size/industry as factors in anticorruption program implementation/management

## Questions presented

Remember to ask for supporting evidence in the form of a policy document/statement or description of a detailed incident. An evidentiary peg may be needed to repeat the statement or assertion made. Information to obtain:

### Basic information

- Contacts (HQ and EAP)
- Clearance sources for permission to include quotations, documents in the report

### Management of ethical issues (general)

- Top management commitment
- Statements (codes, charters)

- Procedures for program formulation, implementation, monitoring for effectiveness
- Management template (decentralized, centralized, business unit, etc.)
- Is anticorruption an independent program or part of a broader effort?
- Cost of anticorruption program
- From what department(s) budget(s) is the money allocated?
- To what department(s) do anticorruption program employees report?
- What departments participate in the anticorruption program, and how are they involved?

## Implementation history

- Origins (e.g., specific incident, CEO initiative)
- External assistance (e.g., consultants, law firms, other companies)
- Relevance of external guidelines to specific problems (e.g., ICC, TI, OECD)
- Internal difficulties/obstacles (cultural barriers)
- Union cooperation/resistance

## Practical issues

- Management ethical framework (e.g., codes, contracts, policies)
- Compliance organization/procedures
- Does company distinguish between bribes and facilitation payments? If so, how?
- Does company have an agent who secures necessary government permits/approvals?
- If the company has such an agent, what are the limits on his/her activities?
- Is there a uniform policy for dealing with employees who bribe local officials?
- Description of training programs
- Who is involved in training programs (e.g., employees, joint-venture partners)?
- Subsidiary company relations (e.g., management practices, reporting, control)
- Is there third-party program appraisal/involvement? Discuss.

## Assessment of program

- Employee/union participation, support
- Third-party response (agents, subcontractors)
- Fallout (e.g., employee dismissal, lost contracts, cancellation of agreements)

- In which countries are programs most/least effective?
- Specific instances where program implementation has been difficult

## Limits to effectiveness of company-based programs

- Loss of contracts/business to less ethical competitors
- Exposure to risk from third-party behavior (e.g., contractor, joint-venture partner)
- Limits to effectiveness of self-regulation (country comparisons)
- Anticorruption environment (public sector initiatives/policies)
- Is there an effective role for international institutions (e.g., UN)?

## Company interest in participating in World Bank dissemination activities

- Is there a local company cooperative initiative (e.g., integrity pacts)?
- Would company anticorruption technical assistance programs be effective?
- Is this company willing to participate in such a program?
- Which countries are the best candidates for such a program?
- How would such a program operate in practice?

# Appendix D
# Resources and References
# Available on the Internet

## Global links

### *International organizations*

Organisation for Economic Co-operation and Development, Anti-Corruption Ring Online
<http://www1.oecd.org/daf/nocorruptionweb/>
World Bank Institute, Corporate Social Responsibility Program
<http://www.csrwbi.org>
World Bank Anticorruption Home Page
<http://www1.worldbank.org/publicsector/anticorrupt/partners.htm>
Asian Development Bank Anticorruption Home Page
<http://www.adb.org/Anticorruption/default.asp>

### *Major business and research networks active in the area*

The Conference Board, Global Council on Business Conduct
<http://www.conference-board.org/memberservices/councilsDe-tailUS.cfm?Council_ID=40>
Ethics Officer Association (United States)
<http://www.eoa.org>
European Business Ethics Network
<http://www.eben.org/>
International Society of Business, Economics, and Ethics (ISBEE)
<http://www.isbee.org>
Business Ethics Research Center (Japan)
<http://www.berc.gr.jp/english.htm>

## NGOs (global)

Transparency International
<http://www.transparency.org>

Social Accountability International.
<http://www.cepaa.org/>

## Guidelines and standards

Transparency International/Social Accountability International, Business Principles for Countering Bribery
http://www.sa-intl.org/Document%20Center/AntiBribery.htm>
OECD Guidelines for Multinational Enterprises
<http://www.oecd.org/EN/home/0,,EN-home-93-nodirectorate-no-no-no-7,00.html>
International Chamber of Commerce, Anti-Corruption
<http://www.iccwbo.org/home/menu_extortion_bribery.asp>
Caux Round Table Principles for Business
<http://www.cauxroundtable.org/>
Ethics Compliance Standard (ECS) 2000 (Reitaku University, Japan)
<http://ecs2000.reitaku-u.ac.jp/e-index/e-index.html>

### Major thematic initiatives

Transparent Agents and Contracting Entities (TRACE)
<http://www.traceinternational.org/>
International Federation of Consulting Engineers (Fédération Internationale des Ingénieurs-Conseils), Integrity Management Clearing House
<http://www1.fidic.org/resources/integrity/>
Defense Industry Initiative
<http://www.dii.org>

### Resources on related topics (internal control, corporate governance)

U.S. Foreign Corrupt Practices Act
<http://www.usdoj.gov/criminal/fraud/fcpa.html>
U.S. Sentencing Guidelines
<http://www.ussc.gov/orgguide.HTM>
International Federation of Accountants
<http://www.ifac.org/>
Committee of Sponsoring Organizations of the Treadway Commission (COSO)
<http://www.coso.org/>
Report on the Observance of Standards and Codes: country reports on accounting and auditing standards or corporate governance
<http://www.worldbank.org/ifa/rosc.html>

Global Corporate Governance Forum
<http://www.gcgf.org/>

# Regional and local resources

## *Regional resource centers and networks on ethics and compliance*

Business Ethics and Compliance Research Center (R-BEC), Reitaku University, Japan
<http://ecs2000.reitaku-u.ac.jp/e-index/e-index.html>
Hong Kong Ethics Development Centre
<http://www.icac.org.hk/hkedc/>
Federation of Korean Industries
<http://www.fki.or.kr/english/user/main/fki_up.html>

## Regional initiatives

Papers from the roundtable "The Role of the Private Sector in Fighting Corruption: An Implementation Agenda," Singapore, July 2002, sponsored by the Institute for Policy Studies, the World Bank, and Transparency International
<http://lnweb18.worldbank.org/eap/eap.nsf>
World Bank EAP region: private sector and anti-corruption (including some material from the roundtable "The Role of the Private Sector in Fighting Corruption: An Implementation Agenda," Singapore, July 2002)
<http://lnweb18.worldbank.org/eap/eap.nsf/Sectors/Governance+&+Anti+Corruption/CC132B802216D34A85256C3A00731A9D?OpenDocument>
Institute for Policy Studies (Singapore)
<http://www.ips.org.sg/>
ADB-OECD Anti-Corruption Action Plan
<http://www1.oecd.org/daf/ASIAcom/ActionPlan.htm>
Pacific Economic Cooperation Council: Guidelines for Good Corporate Governance
<http://www.pecc.net/resources/publications/corporate_governance.htm>

## *Country-based organizations with involvement in related areas*

Indonesia: Partnership for Governance Reform in Indonesia
<http://www.partnership.or.id/>

Korea: Center for Good Corporate Governance
<http://cgcg.or.kr/cgcg/cgcgmain/html_en/index.htm>
Philippine Institute of Certified Public Accountants
<http://www.picpa.com.ph/>
Philippines: Institute of Corporate Directors
<http://www.icd.ph/>
Thailand: Institute of Certified Accountants and Auditors of Thailand
<http://www.icaat.or.th/instruct/index.html>
Thailand Institute of Directors
<http://www.thai-iod.com/en/index.asp>

### Academic groups and business schools with programs on ethics or corporate social responsibility

Asian Institute of Management
<http://www.aim.edu.ph/>
Hong Kong Baptist University, School of Business, Focused Research Area on Business and Economic Ethics (FRABEE)
<http://www.hkbu.edu.hk/~beethics/>

### Anticorruption agencies

Independent Agency Against Corruption (Hong Kong, China)
<http://www.icac.org.hk>
Korean Independent Commission Against Corruption
<http://www.kicac.go.kr/PORTAL/Eng/index.jsp>
Corrupt Practices Investigation Bureau, Singapore
<http://www.cpib.gov.sg/>

## Other resources

### Nonprofit groups with extensive involvement in training and dissemination in emerging economies

Center for International Private Enterprise
<http://www.cipe.org>
Ethics Resources Center
<http://www.ethics.org>
The Prince of Wales International Business Leaders Forum, Corporate Social Responsibility Forum
<http://www.iblf.org/csr/csrwebassist.nsf/content/f1c2a3u4.html>

## Nonprofit organizations providing expertise to corporate members

International Business Ethics Institute
<http://www.business-ethics.org>
Business for Social Responsibility
<http://www.bsr.org/>
Institute of Business Ethics
<http://www.ibe.org.uk>

## Corporate Websites of participating companies with extensive information on ethics and compliance

SGS (Société Générale de Surveillance) Code of Ethics
<http://www.sgs.com/sgsgroup.nsf/pages/coeinteg.html>
Shell Business Principles
<http://www.shell.com/sgbp>

## Socially responsible investing

IntegreX (Japan)
<http://www.integrex.jp/>
Social Investment Forum
<http://www.socialinvest.org>
GreenMoney Journal
<http://www.greenmoneyjournal.com>

## Journals, magazines, and book reviews

*Journal of Business Ethics*
<http://www.kluweronline.com/issn/0167-4544/contents>
Ethics Web Bookstore
<http://www.ethicsweb.ca/books/index-business.htm>
*Ethikos: Examining Ethical Issues in Business*
<http://www.singerpubs.com/ethikos>

## Research and educational organizations

Business Ethics: Corporate Social Responsibility Report
<http://www.business-ethics.com>
Center for Business Ethics
<http://ecampus.bentley.edu/dept/cbe>

Center for Ethics, University of Tampa
<http://www.utampa.edu/academics/business/centers/ethics.html>
Center for the Study of Ethics in the Professions, Illinois Institute of
Technology
<http://www.iit.edu/departments/csep/>
Creating a Code of Ethics for Your Organization
<http://www.ethicsweb.ca/codes/>
Institute for Global Ethics
<http://www.globalethics.org>
Institute for Ethical Business Worldwide, University of Notre Dame
<http://www.ethicalbusiness.nd.edu>
Interfaith Center on Corporate Responsibility
<http://www.iccr.org/>
International Business Ethics Institute
<http://www.business-ethics.org>
Center for Ethics and Social Justice, Loyola University Chicago
<http://www.luc.edu/depts/ethics>
Society for Business Ethics
<http://www.luc.edu/depts/business/sbe/index.html>
Walker Information
<http://www.walkerinfo.com/resources/benchmark/#ethics>
The Carol and Lawrence Zicklin Center for Business Ethics Research,
Wharton School, University of Pennsylvania
<http://www.zicklincenter.org>

## Other resources, Pacific area

Australian Association for Professional and Applied Ethics
<http://www.arts.unsw.edu.au/aapae/>
Australian Business Ethics Network
<http://www.bf.rmit.edu.au/Aben/>
Centre for Applied Philosophy and Public Ethics (Australia)
<http://www.csu.edu.au/faculty/arts/cappe/public.htm>
St. James Ethics Centre (Australia)
<http://www.ethics.org.au/>
BusinessEthics.ca (Canada)
<http://www.businessethics.ca/>
Canadian Centre for Ethics and Corporate Policy
<http://www.ethicscentre.ca/html/resources.html>
Canadian Society for the Study of Practical Ethics
<http://www.carleton.ca/csspe-sceea/>

Clarkson Centre for Business Ethics and Board Effectiveness, University of Toronto
<http://www.mgmt.utoronto.ca/ccbe/>
Ethics Practitioners' Association of Canada
<http://epac-apec.hypermart.net/>
W. Maurice Young Centre for Applied Ethics, University of British Columbia
<http://www.ethics.ubc.ca/>; for links to applied ethics resources, see <http://www.ethics.ubc.ca/resources/>

# References

Abramson, Neil R., and Janet X. Ai. 1997. "Using Guanxi-Style Buyer-Seller Relationships in China: Reducing Uncertainty and Improving Performance Outcomes." *International Executive* 39 (6, November–December): 765–804.

Backman, Michael. 1999. *The Asian Eclipse: Exposing the Dark Side of Business in Asia.* Singapore and New York: J. Wiley.

Balfour, Frederick, and Bruce Einhorn. 2002. "The End of Guanxi Capitalism?" *BusinessWeek Online* (February 4). Available at <www.businessweek.com>.

Batra, Geeta, Daniel Kaufmann, and Andrew H. W. Stone. 2003. *Investment Climate around the World: Voices of the Firms from the World Business Environment Survey.* Directions in Development series. Washington, D.C.: World Bank.

Berenbeim, Ronald E. 1999. "Global Corporate Ethics Practices: A Developing Consensus." Research Report R-1243-99-RR. The Conference Board, New York.

———. 2000. "Company Programs for Resisting Corrupt Practices: A Global Study." Research Report R-1279-00-RR. The Conference Board, New York.

———. 2002. "ENRON Syllabus of Errors." Address delivered to a Conference Board India members' briefing, February 2002. Published in *Vital Speeches*, March 1, 2002. Available at <http://www.vtod.com>.

Berenbeim, Ronald E., and Sophia Muirhead. 2002. "Business Conduct Codes: Why Companies Hesitate." Executive Action 13. January. The Conference Board, New York.

Black, Bernard. 2001. "Does Corporate Governance Matter? A Crude Test Using Russian Data." *University of Pennsylvania Law Review* 149: 2131–50.

Bubnova, Nina. 2000. *Governance Impact on Private Investment: Evidence from the International Patterns of Infrastructure Bond Risk Premiums.* World Bank Technical Paper 488. Washington, D.C.

Campos, J. Edgardo, ed. 2002. *Corruption: The Boom and Bust of East Asia.* Ateneo de Manila University Press.

Clarke, George, and Lixin Colin Xu . 2002. "Ownership, Competition, and Corruption: Bribe Takers versus Bribe Payers." Policy Research Working Paper 2783. World Bank, Washington, D.C.

*Economist.* 2002. "The Short Arm of the Law." March 2, pp. 63–65.

Essrig, C. Lee. 2001. "An International Management System Standard for Business Conduct." *Ethikos* 15 (3, November–December).

Fan, Xiucheng, and Tim Ambler. 1998. "Relationship Marketing: Guanxi and Its Role in Marketing in China." Nankai University Working Paper. Tianjin, China.

Graham, John L. 1984. "The Foreign Corrupt Practices Act: A New Perspective." *Journal of International Business Studies* 15 (winter): 107–21.

Gray, Cheryl W., and Daniel Kaufmann. 1998. "Corruption and Development." *Finance and Development* 35 (March): 7–10.

Greene, William H. 2000. *Econometric Analysis.* 4th ed. Englewood Cliffs, N.J.: Prentice-Hall.

Heidenheimer, Arnold, and Michael Johnston, eds. 2001. *Political Corruption: Concepts and Contexts.* 3d ed. New Brunswick, N.J.: Transaction Publishers.

Hellman, Joel, Geraint Jones, and Daniel Kaufmann. 2000. "Seize the State, Seize the Day: State Capture, Corruption, and Influence in Transition." Policy Research Working Paper 2444. World Bank, Washington, D.C.

Hines, James R., Jr. 1995. "Forbidden Payment: Foreign Bribery and American Business after 1977." NBER Working Paper 5266. National Bureau of Economic Research, Cambridge, Mass.

Kaufmann, Daniel, and Shang-Jin Wei. 2000. "Does Grease Money Speed up the Wheels of Commerce?" IMF Working Paper WP/00/64. International Monetary Fund, Washington, D.C.

Kaufmann, Daniel, Aart Kraay, and Pablo Zoido-Lobatón. 2002. "Governance Matters II: Updated Indicators for 2000–01." Policy Research Working Paper 2772. World Bank, Washington, D.C.

Klitgaard, Robert. 1991. *Controlling Corruption.* Berkeley: University of California Press.

KPMG. 2002. "KPMG International Survey of Corporate Sustainability Reporting 2002." June.

Lambsdorff, Johann, Graf. 1998. "An Empirical Investigation of Bribery in International Trade." *European Journal of Development Research* 10 (June): 40–59.

Leff, Nathaniel. 2001. "Economic Development through Bureaucratic Corruption." In Arnold Heidenheimer and Michael Johnston, eds.,

*Political Corruption: Concepts and Contexts*, ch. 18. 3d ed. New Brunswick, N.J.: Transaction Publishers.

Leung, T. K. P., Y. H. Wong, and Syson Wong. 1996. "A Study of Hong Kong Businessmen's Perceptions of the Role of 'Guanxi' in the PRC." *Journal of Business Ethics* 15: 749–58.

Luo, Yadong. 1997. "Guanxi and Performance of Foreign-Invested Enterprises in China." *Management International Review* 37 (1): 51–70.

———. 2002. *Multinational Enterprises in Emerging Markets*. Copenhagen Business School Press.

Mauro, Paolo. 1998. "Corruption: Causes, Consequences, and Agenda for Further Research." *Finance and Development* 35 (March): 11–14.

Nabi, Ijaz, and Behdad Nowroozi. 2002. "Corporate Governance, Corporate Performance, and Investor Confidence in East Asia." In Ijaz Nabi and Manjula Luthria, eds., *Building Competitive Firms: Incentives and Capabilities*, ch. 3. Directions in Development series. Washington, D.C.: World Bank.

Netherlands, Ministry of Economic Affairs. 2001: "Foreign Corruption Can Now Be Prosecuted in the Netherlands: Implications for Small and Medium-Sized Enterprises." May. The Hague.

OECD (Organisation for Economic Co-operation and Development). 2001. *Corporate Responsibility: Private Initiatives and Public Goals*. Paris.

Partnership for Governance Reform in Indonesia. 2001. "A Diagnostic Survey of Corruption in Indonesia." October. Jakarta.

Rose-Ackerman, Susan. 1996. "The Political Economy of Corruption: Causes and Consequences." *Private Sector Viewpoint* 76. World Bank, Washington, D.C.

Shaw, Stephen A. 1999. "Suspension and Debarment: The First Line of Defense against Contractor Fraud and Abuse." *The Reporter* 26 (1).

Shimada, Haruo. 1988. *Hyu-man Wea No Keizaigaku: Amerika No Naka No Nihon Kigyo* (The economics of humanware). Tokyo: Iwanami Shoten.

Shleifer, Andrei, and Robert Vishny. 1993. "Corruption." *Quarterly Journal of Economics* 107 (August): 599–617.

Smarzynska, Beata, and S. J. Wei. 2001. "Corruption and Foreign Direct Investment: Firm-Level Evidence." CEPR Discussion Paper 2967. Centre for Economic Policy Research, London.

Sporkin, Stanley. 1998. "The Worldwide Banning of Schmiergeld: A Look at the Foreign Corrupt Practices Act on Its Twentieth Birthday." *Northwestern Journal of International Law and Business* 18: 269.

Sullivan, John D. 2001. "Democracy, Governance and the Market." Feature Service Article. Center for International Private Enterprise, Washington, D.C. Available at <http://www.cipe.org/publications/fs/articles/article3162.htm>.

Taka, Iwao. 2002. "Start SRI Funds for Reviving Japan!" *Nihon Keizai Shimbun* (July **).

Tanzi, Vito. 1998. "Corruption around the World: Causes, Consequences, Scope, and Cures." *IMF Staff Papers* 45 (December): 599–617.

Thomas, Vinod, Mansoor Dailami, Ashok Dhareshwar, Daniel Kaufmann, Nalim Kishor, Ramón Lopez, and Yan Wang. 2000. *The Quality of Growth*. New York: Oxford University Press.

Transparency International. 2001. "TI Annual Report 2001: The Coalition against Corruption." Berlin. Available at <http://www.transparency.org/publications/index.html#report2001>.

———. 2002a. "Bribe Payers Index." Available at <http://www.transparency.org/surveys/index.html#bpi>.

———. 2002b. "Corruption Perceptions Index." Available at <http://www.transparency.org/surveys/index.html#bpi>.

Wang, N. T. 2001. *My Nine Lives*. Writers Club Press.

Wei Shang-Jin. 1997. "How Taxing Is Corruption on International Investors?" NBER Working Paper 6030. National Bureau of Economic Research, Cambridge, Mass.

———. 2000a. "How Taxing Is Corruption on International Investors?" *Review of Economics and Statistics* 82 (1, February): 1–11.

———. 2000b. "Local Corruption and Global Capital Flows." *Brookings Papers on Economic Activity* (2): 303–54.

Wei, Shang-Jin, and Yi Wu. 2001. "Negative Alchemy? Corruption, Composition of Capital Flows, and Currency Crises." NBER Working Paper 8187. National Bureau of Economic Research, Cambridge, Mass.

Yeung, Irene Y. M., and Rosalie Tung. 1996. "Achieving Business Success in Confucian Societies: The Importance of Guanxi (Connections)." *Organizational Dynamics* 25 (2, autumn): 54–65.

POINT LOMA NAZARENE UNIVERSITY
RYAN LIBRARY